THE
RED LIONESS

ONE WOMAN. FOUR YEARS.
90,000 MILES. 650 PLUS PUBS.

CATHY PRICE

Matador
9 Priory Business Park,
Wistow Road, Kibworth Beauchamp,
Leicestershire. LE8 0RX
Tel: 0116 279 2299
Email: books@troubador.co.uk
Web: www.troubador.co.uk/matador
Twitter: @matadorbooks

ISBN 978 1785890 369

British Library Cataloguing in Publication Data.
A catalogue record for this book is available from the British Library.

Printed and bound by CPI Group (UK) Ltd, Croydon, CR0 4YY
Typeset in 11pt Aldine401 BT by Troubador Publishing Ltd, Leicester, UK

Matador is an imprint of Troubador Publishing Ltd

To My Dad, Tony.

INTRODUCTION

As you begin my journey, I have inevitably finished. It will be of no surprise to you that my mission is complete. Maybe that is what intrigued you to read the book.

What is clear is that I am the only constant in this story. When I began, life looked a whole lot more different personally, globally and of course, in the pub trade.

Some who began the adventure with me were not there at its conclusion – such is life's rocky course, and that doesn't just apply to people.

I picked the worst possible time to visit every Red Lion pub in the UK – right at the heart of the recession. In days gone by, the pub stood tall as the pillar of the community; in recent years it has often been the first thing to go as the economy bit the dust.

Lifestyle has changed, too – let's not forget the rise of the binge drinker at home as supermarkets lure you in with their BOGOFs, their 10% discounts, and their loyalty cards.

Plus, we're certainly more antisocial than we were when I started out on my trip. The pub – that beating heart of the community and social magnet – also falls foul of the digital era. Socialising is no longer a pint at the end of the day, it's more 'U ok, hun?' on Facebook, or a Snapchat message, or a Twitter war as you walk into someone's trolling, and even those who go to the pub sit there doing the very same on their phones.

The social networks have made us more unsociable.

However, this is not an anthropological analysis. I am not here to condemn and judge. I am just setting out the parameters that changed before me as I went from pub to pub. From Red Lion to Red Lion.

As you read on, you'll see me skip past some establishments and perhaps wonder why. Simply, out of 600+ Red Lions, some were just too tame. They did what they said on the tin – served beer and little more.

That's fine. But then there are the others with real stories to tell. It is no surprise given a pub's historical role in the community that I should open the door on some incredible pasts – from murders to tunnels, from Enid Blyton's local to Ian Fleming's. I have stayed overnight, drunk, lunched and dined in Red Lions; I have met the eccentric landlords, been in the cellars, and played games in them.

I'll not rate the food and drink in this book unless it truly is exceptional. It is not that kind of book. Instead, I will unearth an untold culture that taps into that whole British psyche.

It goes without saying that I only visited most of these pubs on one occasion. That means the narrative reflects thoughts I had in the moment coupled with observations and research I have done since.

So let the journey begin… And as you will see, I had not got a clue what I was walking into.

THE RED LION FAMILY

Mum – Jean – aged 82 – did 3 in UK (2 abroad)
Brother Andy – lives in Bristol – 2
Sister-in-law Jess – lives with Andy, Bristol – 4
Sister Debbie – 2
Brother David – 14
Nephew Matt – son of Dave – 1
Niece Milly – Longton – 1
Ex-partner Alan – 114 Red Lions
Robbie (girl) Charlie (boy), Shane, Livi – Alan's children
Friend Paula – 133 – my number one Red Lioner
Mate Fred – 33
Lodger Robert – 61
Mate Braz – 40
Friend Sharon – 19
Friend Sammy – 6
Daughter Hayley – 19
Grandson Cooper (Hayley's son) – around 15
Bradley – Sammy's (from Australia) son who lived with me for a year – 5
Friend Kim – (with her son Sam and Bran) – 1
Amanda – 17
Friend Helena – 49
Fireman Stephen (FMS) – 79
Friend Andrée (female) – 1
Friend Denise – 29
Friend Joanne – 22
Stephen Carey, follower – 6

Additional thanks go to Annabelle Smith and Ros Shiel and all the Dea Latis ladies for getting in touch initially and then making me an honorary member of the group.

A special thanks to Laura Seymour at Red Lion Gatwick Airport for making my 600th such a special one, not forgetting everyone else involved behind the scenes.

Ray Potter and Harlow Red Lion, thank you.

Also my friends at Hook Norton Brewery for going beyond the call of duty, from the brewery tour to their involvement in my final Red Lion.

A big thank you goes to Lisa at my last Red Lion, Northmoor, for being so enthusiastic and welcoming.

I must not forget Paul and Lynn at Hawkshead Red Lion who suggested a revisit, making my journey come full circle.

To all the media on my travels – thank you for your continued interest and support, especially John Gilmore and the team at BBC Radio Lancashire.

I would also like to express my gratitude to Matador for their wise counsel in the whole process of getting my story into print, and my editor Tony Horne at www.tonyhornebooks.com.

Finally…

The last word goes to Alan, who put into motion my crazy idea, and of course to you… If I met you on my travels.

HORSES AT HAWKSHEAD

9 APRIL 2011 - GRAND NATIONAL DAY

My partner Alan and I were staying at the King's Head but were out and about trying to find somewhere to watch the race. We had 12 bets riding on it.

No greater reason than that. The story starts here. We wanted to watch the world's most famous steeplechase. The Red Lion Hotel just happened to be our port of call.

As Ballabriggs romped home at 14-1, we didn't even get a place. My horses had fallen within minutes, as is often the case at Aintree. My interest in the race was gone in 60 seconds.

My mind began to wander. And then I caught sight of it out of the corner of my eye. The plaque.

'The Red Lion is the most common name for a pub in the UK'.

I wonder how many times the plentiful American and Japanese tourists had taken that as a picture.

I had heard this before, but not thought much of it. Only now, having the space to daydream given the disappointment at the race, did I start to wonder.

'Has anyone ever been to all of them?' I asked myself. 'They must be everywhere,' I mumbled. 'Which is the furthest? How much history lies within?'

My mind was racing.

'Do you think anyone is trying to visit all the British Red Lions?' I asked Alan.

The seed was planted.

'Don't be so stupid,' he replied.

I was already way ahead of him, and once I get an idea into my head and commit to it, there's no stopping me.

For Alan, that was the end of the conversation. I was consumed by it. And so, without knowing or intending, I had already visited my first Red Lion.

The Quest had begun.

WHEELTON TO BOOTLE

It was all I could think about. Google took over the next day. I was both relieved and surprised to know that nobody *had* visited them all. It just seemed like something somebody would have done, given that some of these pubs go back to the 12th century.

Good news, too – it really did seem as though it was the most popular pub name, beating off stiff competition from The White Hart and The Rose and Crown. It would have been daft to have overlooked the accuracy of 'Red Lion' being the most common name for a pub. Let's get it right from the off.

Whimsically staring into space during the Grand National had landed me here. I was on a mission. I had now never been more focussed.

I didn't know how many miles this would take, or how many days, months or years. All I could establish was that the previous year of 2010 showed there were 724 Red Lion licensees in the UK. One down, then, 723 to go!

And yet, my only Lion to date was when I hadn't even been counting. I made a mental note to return to the beautiful 15th-century inn at Hawkshead (LA22 0NS) at some point in the future. It *is* the town's oldest pub, with traditional, locally sourced British food and real ales. It is a perfect stop-off for Windermere and Ambleside, and could play the Beatrix Potter card anytime it liked.

'Helen' Beatrix Potter bought Hill Top nearby and married the Hawkshead solicitor William Heelis. Much of her work was written in this tranquillity of the British Lake District.

I hadn't known this when I was in the pub just a day before, but now I did it changed everything.

I knew that the idea of going into a pub to meet friends or to eat and drink was no more. The Grand National had shown me the way.

It would be impossible from this point to wander in and head straight for the bar. Pushing through those entrance doors meant one thing now.

I would stop and take a look around at ornaments, wells, plaques, and lions! Each time, I would ask questions, breathe in history and take it all in.

It occurred to me that if I was to embark upon this Quest I needed rules. There had to be some element of challenge to myself and there needed to be some sort of verification. I didn't want to find myself at Red Lion Number 300 only to be stopped by someone saying 'Prove it'.

Social media and my own photography would help, but in the end I settled for 'must have a drink in every Lion', principally to get chatting to the staff to educate myself and for them to remember. I also decided that if a Lion were closed, I would attempt to conquer it another day.

I pencilled champagne for the 100th and vowed to make that by Christmas. Beyond that, I had no plans. Except to start.

Just two days after Hawkshead, Alan and I went for dinner at the brilliantly named The Clog and Billycock, not too far from home. On the way home, he suddenly blurted out with a nod of the head that there was a Red Lion in that village, Wheelton. You can see from this alone that I had sucked him in despite his initial scepticism, and that beyond my rules I had no sense of organisation about my plan. I hadn't thought it through.

Wheelton (PR6 8EU) was about 20 minutes away, and despite the landlady Sharon's best attempts to get the pub up to scratch after the previous incumbent left it in a shabby mess, you may think I was slightly underwhelmed by my first Lion.

Of course, it wasn't that at all – this was Number 2 after Hawkshead and that was a tremendous place to start, if only I realised I had!

As I stood chatting to an old chap at the bar listening to his woes of having to walk home back up the hill because of his drink-driving ban, I really didn't know how this experience would be similar to or different from the journey ahead. But three things rang true.

I had met my first 'local at the bar', the pub trade was not in a good place and landlords and landladies were hoarders!

Sharon must have been asked this question a thousand times since – why did she have a triangular snooker table clock on the wall? There is no answer but I do know that wherever she would go from here, the clock was going with her.

Two days later we went for dinner at the Red Lion in Mawdesley (L40 2QP). Another Red Lion and a new train of thought – and this one, so simple. Dining from a fantastic menu in their beautiful conservatory and setting my mind upon a return for one of the sell-out speciality seafood evenings, I cannot explain why I had never been to this pub before, apart from the fact that we tend to stay with what we know in life.

Therein lies a clue. It was the second-closest to where I was living. I would be searching high and low across the country, getting more organised to the point that I had a UK map with pins going in it left, right and centre, but Red Lion Number 3 was virtually on my doorstep.

Good Friday followed and all roads led to Liverpool. Essentially, this was a shopping day but with just three lions behind me and so many more to go, you can see how the most routine aspects of life were being marginalised by the mission. Already it had become impossible to get in a car without eyes and mind wandering, and that's what made us stumble across the Red Lion at Burscough (L40 5TX).

This time we did lunch at the Lion. I was learning fast and on the go! It was a good, all-round pub but presented a dilemma. It was no longer a Red Lion. This was not in the rules!

I hadn't considered that some Lions may have shed their colour. It was simply The Lion. It had been a Red in the past but had now dropped it. I could only draw two conclusions – that perhaps locally that is the name that customers referred to it as, or it had a bad reputation previously and had wanted to disassociate itself from that whilst offering a nod and a wink to its legitimate history.

Either way, I decided it was in. My first Lion without the Red became Red Lion Number 4.

By that afternoon, it looked like we wouldn't even make Liverpool ONE Alan spotted another Red Lion on Bridge Road. Besides, much as I love to shop, shouldn't you really spend Good Friday in a Red Lion and not in a mall?!

Either he had caught the bug or knew me well enough to know that I was obsessed and even now, with so few visited, there was no turning back. He could have pretended not to spot our next pub and just driven on: something had got to him, too.

This time, though, we experienced our first genuine fear. It's all very well having this fairy tale in your head of Beatrix Potter penning children's books in idyllic locations, but for some the reality is that your Red Lion pub is just a good, old-fashioned drinking hole.

Welcome to Bootle (L21 2PB) and Bridge Road then… Everything about it looked dodgy. Succumbing to type, Alan feared the worst for his car in Scouse heartland.

I took my preconceptions of the area inside to the pool table where I could envisage the number of times the cue may have been used as a weapon in a Friday night scuffle.

'What are you two doing here?' The inevitable question finally came. It was that scene from *An American Werewolf in London*, except there were no moors out there to be careful on!

Already, with five Lions down, I had got used to entering and observing. This was the first time all eyes were on me.

'What is a nice car doing in a place like this?' I was asked as we were leaving.

I had no choice but to tell them about the Quest.

I had mentioned it casually in other pubs up to this point, but this was the first time I felt I had to. Looking back, how stupid must I have sounded to say they were only Number 5 – not even 1% into the adventure. The locals were right. That wasn't the kind of pub I would be in.

I hadn't even considered there would be dodgy ones.

It tested the water, though. I had put it out there. I was visiting every Red Lion pub in the UK and now they knew they were part of it.

To the locals, this was just their hang-out. To me, and to their disbelief, it had to be part of the story.

They gave me a friendly word of warning.

'Come back at 9 pm and see what really goes on,' I was advised.

I didn't need to. I had already got the picture.

Wheels intact outside, it left me thinking. Had I bitten off more than I could chew?

NEWBURGH VILLAGE TO ASPULL

Even at this early stage, I knew it was important to find the next good Lion. Too many Bootles could be disheartening. Even though I was only setting out to visit all the pubs and not really critique, it stands to reason that the nicer the pub, the better the ride was going to be.

A week later we called in at The Red Lion Hotel in Newburgh village (WN8 7NF). It's a short distance from Wigan and is now the only pub left in this beautiful place. You can see its roots straightaway as a stop-off point of yesteryear, sitting pretty on the old Leeds and Liverpool Canal.

A village like this probably *should* have just the one pub – ticking that heart of the community box. In days gone by, it wouldn't have been uncommon for there to have been several. It didn't occur to me that perhaps in the past, people drank more than they do today!!

And as quaint as Newburgh Village is, the Red Lion endorses that sleepy village mentality. Two things of note happened here.

Firstly, and not for the last time, a regular told us of another Red Lion nearby that we hadn't been aware of. Clearly, I couldn't rely solely on the internet to make sure I had discovered all the Red Lions. Mental note made: there is no better source than the local knowledge for information and anecdotes.

Secondly, village pubs have their own way of doing things! I ordered a bottle of Cava. Instead, I received a bottle of Veuve Clicquot.

It would have been easy to say nothing. Honesty got the better of me and we brought it to the attention of the bar staff. Suddenly the bar expert was summoned. It was swapped for the correct bottle.

'We have no champagne flutes,' he said. 'They break too easily.'

Wow – I thought – imagine paying £39 for that and having to sip it out of a wine glass!

I suspect the call for champers was rare, given their unprepared state. Wine, though, was flowing by the glass. On a Thursday there was a free bottle with every two main meals ordered. Today was Thursday!

Perhaps Newburgh hadn't made the transition from the old-style pub. I was brought up in an age where you could go into any pub and, beyond the usual beer or stout, you would always find bottles of everything that had often stood there for years and were rarely touched – from a Dubonnet to Babycham which they may have sold on an occasion like Christmas. Everybody always had everything in, regardless of demand.

24 hours later we approached Red Lion Number 7 at Bispham (FY2 0AR).

It sits at the end of Devonshire Road. It seemed like the world's longest road – that is until I went looking for the Red Lion in Miami recently, which was building number 19,051 Collins Avenue, but that is another story – it seemed to go on and on forever. You would hope to find sunshine at the end of the rainbow when you finally pull up.

It was OK, food was OK and service OK. Just OK. Alan's son Charlie is disabled and he returned from the Gents, which took him a good while to reach, shaking his head. There were only urinals in there at the time. The Gents with 'toilets' were at the other end of the pub. Charlie patiently made his way across the pub, tutting and muttering about this Red Lion thing.

Just over a week later, May had arrived and it was time to head to Yorkshire. Pub Number 8! So many more lay ahead, but already certain traits had become standard. We set off thinking 'What are we going to get this time?' I began to feel the anticipation as we neared each Red Lion looking for any giveaway signs!

It was clear already there was no brand template for The Red Lion. Back in the day, these *were* just pubs. There was no concept of chain or uniform standard. Coachmen went from town to town and locals went to the end of the street. The only common factor was alcohol.

As the years rolled by and Wetherspoons and pub chains have risen to prominence, the Red Lions have remained, but without conforming to any obvious traits.

That was becoming the beauty of the challenge. We simply didn't know what we *would* get next, and nothing could have prepared us for Burnsall (BD23 6BU) in Yorkshire.

This is the first Red Lion I fell in love with.

The beautiful drive lures you in, like a magnet pulling you towards the pub. Over picturesque countryside and an old, stone bridge with a stream running along, your brain trains you to look up for a church steeple. It had all the hallmarks of serene, becalming village life. It was picture postcard.

Once a 16th-century ferrymen's inn, always a 16th-century ferrymen's inn – its Victorian beams and brass preserved amidst modern touches, too. Excellent food, and with a superb choice of accommodation at the pub or The Manor House just 150 metres down the road, who wouldn't want to wake up to this, surrounded by fields and sheep? It was everything Yorkshire. It's perfect for the weekend rambler or cyclist. You can even stay in the Old Police House Holiday Cottage down the road. Imagine what secrets passed through those walls.

My gut feeling told me that if the police building had been turned into accommodation, then perhaps there was no need for it anymore – a rarity in modern Britain and a very good sign.

Later I was to learn that many Lions started out as police stations, morgues or blacksmiths!

For the first time on the Quest, I had stepped into somebody else's world and could happily stay there forever. I was always eavesdropping of course, but this time I wanted to belong and stay.

I knew I would be back for pleasure outside of my mission.

After Burnsall, it would be a long 19 days before we would hit the road again to find that pub in Aspull which the locals at Newburgh Village had mentioned.

It was time to take stock of where we were up to. The best way to do this, of course, was through the eyes of the people I was roping in along the way. Alan's Shane just blurted it out one day.

'Is this Red Lion thing ever going to end?'

Yes – for sure – but no time soon!

Aspull (WN2 1YA) was a reminder once again as to the declining fortunes of the pub trade. My Spanish prawns were excellent but nothing else was.

I can't fault the proprietor, but even he must have known that sage green velour chairs were of another era. And when I tried to order wine, the 'wine' menu said Red, White, Rosé. No name, grape type or country – a waste of a list, really.

At 8.10 pm, the chef emerged from the restaurant, announcing that 'if that's the lot, then I will close down the kitchen'. Of course, five minutes later, a newly arrived couple had to be turned away. They had the common dilemma in these hard times of trying to cut back on staff wages at the risk of turning away business: I have seen it since so many times.

Already at Red Lion Number 9, I was watching demise before my very eyes. It came as no surprise to learn later that this Lion has since closed down and become an Indian restaurant.

I wondered how many times this would repeat itself in the next few years.

THE CHESTERFIELD CHASE

29 MAY 2011

May Bank Holiday weekend could only mean one thing – a Red Lion fest. Destination Derbyshire. AND a new first: we were going to stay overnight in a Red Lion.

We planned on cycling the Monsal Trail through its newly opened tunnels, so with a trailer carrying our four bikes we headed first to Litton at Buxton. Yet, passing Hazel Grove on the A6 we noticed the lack of a Red Lion: it had been demolished. It had stood tall since the 1800s but was knocked down in 2008. This was the danger with tough times in the trade. Sell the land and say goodbye to years of history and community.

Disillusionment turns to delight when minutes later you find a Red Lion you didn't know existed like High Lane, Cheshire (SK6 8ED), though the tired-looking sign outside creates the wrong impression. Inside, it is newly refurbished, large and serves great food, but one thing will definitely catch your eye. For no obvious reason that any local could explain, on the wall hang a skull and antlers from a baby deer dated June 1922. It's clearly not the only dead baby deer ever, but I can't find out what links it to this Red Lion. Perhaps it was just a random decoration.

On we went towards Buxton itself. The journey alone is worth its weight in gold. Passing through Tideswell with its 'Cathedral of the Peak', stone cottages and bendy, narrow roads, you finally arrive at Litton (SK17 8QU).

I had barely been acquainted with Derbyshire, but this is a terrific spot to launch a walk in the Dales or retire to afterwards. The pub dates back to 1787 when it was converted from three farm cottages. It's a proper local pub with log fires, but you'll find a real mix of walkers and villagers. The low beams will have taken out many passing heads over the years. Instantly welcoming, it's one of those Lions where you walk through the door and know you are sampling history. Out the front, a sign of the past that goes hand-in-hand with the pub – the stocks still remain. I put Shane and Charlie in them just to check they worked!

Next came the bizarre, twisted church spire of Chesterfield, shining like a beacon drawing us in, and our third Red Lion of the day at Darley Dale, Chesterfield (S45 0LW) – a new boutique hotel, again originally dating back to the 17th century and plonked in the midst of dales, streams and windy stone-edged roads! Shane and Charlie lounged in the spacious family room while Alan and I wandered to the bistro to reserve a table for dinner. It is professional and friendly, and represented perfectly the old and the new. Dinner, especially my lobster thermidor, was excellent.

Top 5 Red Lion Overnight Stays:

Darley Dale
Lacock
Chipping Campden
Babcary
Stodmarsh

Next day we took the boys to the swimming baths, then on to the Lion on Chatsworth Road (S40 2BL), which looked a bit basic on the outside but did the business on the inside.

Remember how Mr. Sceptical had been a more than willing contributor to the Quest of the Lions? Well here is where Alan's agenda kicks in. He was a railway nut and we had to pass Brimington (S43 1JG) to reach Barrow Hill railway shed, Britain's last operating roundhouse and a former Depot of the Year. It had closed in 1991 and had been vandalised since, but was now refurbished and home to many classic locomotives. This is me politely saying it was a trainspotters' dream, and I must admit I found it interesting.

And of course, the railways and the pubs have been key comrades over the years. You will always find a station near a pub and, when the station goes, sometimes you have to fear for the pub, too. It was a surprise to notice here that the old British Rail logo was a Red Lion!

The trains had more to offer than this pub with just two elderly men in and a hyperactive dog. Alan had a quick half of not so merry 'Merry Monks'.

Next stop, The Square in Bakewell (DE45 1BT) right on the A619. Bakewell is famous for its tarts and also the start of the 8-mile-long Monsal Trail. These are the old railway lines which closed in 1968 and have been gradually reopened as recreational tracks and consist of several tunnels dug through limestone. We cycled four miles then turned to come back over the Monsal Viaduct running over the River Wye, taking in the fantastic views and wildlife.

This is obviously a reward pub! Though bustling with locals, it was clear that many visitors emerged from the tunnels for refreshment. You could easily have the perfect Sunday several times a year here.

Derbyshire was on a roll. We had Googled our next Lion looking for food, and that took us to Main Street, Birchover (DE4 2BN). Red Lion Number 17.

This is an unusual but beautiful pub. Dating back to 1600, the first thing you will notice when you walk in is the 30-foot well in the entrance! What stories the well has witnessed over the years... How many customers it has outlived...

Today it is covered with glass – Health and Safety, plus they couldn't be losing customers down there – but it's a striking feature that tells you you are somewhere special. The old flagged floor and low ceilings confirmed the age of the pub.

Matteo and Alyson bought the pub in 2006 and promise a Sardinian flavour. On our visit, every time we decided on a dish, the waitress came and rubbed it off the board: settling on good old fish and chips we were not disappointed. At least that tells you they were making the dishes fresh. They had simply sold out due to popularity. We pulled away as the sun was going down, a field of llamas to our right and a perfectly formed rainbow to the left. Bliss.

The next morning we woke to more perfect views and gorgeous sunlight. Of course, I can't guarantee the weather if you follow in my footsteps to any of these Red Lions, but Derbyshire will not let you down for early morning beauty, and, in hunting down Hognaston (DE6 1PR) on the edge of the Peak District National Park, you encapsulate everything this area has to offer. Hognaston is a sleepy, dead-end village – you leave and arrive from the same direction! That is the way it has always been. On the first road map of Britain in 1675, Derbyshire's only road goes through here, though then it was more of a cart track. Yet, getting there today is the epitome of everything around here, winding your way through places that time forgot and the modern era ignored. It's a must if you want to get away from it all.

It's so sleepy that it wasn't even open when we arrived at 11 am. We had to wait until midday. I am ashamed to say that I broke my own rules so early in the Quest. We decided to head off without stopping for a drink. Such decisions are made by fools in a hurry. It was only later that I learned that John F Kennedy Jnr had stayed here in 1977 with his wife Carolyn Bessette whilst attending a local wedding.

Can you imagine being here on that night and the resulting palaver? I am sure that if there is not a plaque inside, then it's the kind of story a barman tells any stranger within minutes of ordering at the bar! I paid the price for breaking my rules.

Despite the fact that our next Lion near Carsington Water at Kniveton (DE6 1JH) was also closed, Derbyshire was thriving. I was astounded, in fact, that so many Lions were so close together. I am sure the rural setting added to their charms, but also their staying power. Many had a regular clientele and a passing trade and all seemed to be in locations of another era.

Next, we would head to Wirksworth near Matlock (DE4 4ET). As we entered this lovely old market town, the Red Lion dominated. You couldn't *not* spot it. However, lightning struck a third time. It was closed!

That made three in an hour that were shut. Not to worry, this historic market town made interesting browsing until it opened. Compared to the traditional stone buildings of the town, the Lion looked nothing special. However, this was not the first time my initial impressions deceived me. When it opened, I began to be reeled in by the history.

It started out as a medieval inn and in 1770 became the Red Lion. Outside stands an archway leading into today's car park. In days gone by it was a death trap, as horsemen would arrive late in the day from their travels, tired and thirsty, and fail to duck at the arch whilst travelling at speed against the light. This Red Lion was haunted by one of those unfortunate horsemen. I learned that on average 100 horsemen a year died from not seeing arches such as this one. It was the traffic accident of years gone by – a hundred deaths a year amounted to two per week. This was serious business.

Two other points are of note at this pub. In the new era of the smoking ban, this Lion provided church pews to light up on outside, quite a stylish little den.

Also at Lion Number 20, the Quest came of age. Alan spotted a big old Red Lion sign ready for a bonfire. You can imagine, given our level of obsession, that this was sacrilege. When we explained what we were doing, they were more than happy to hand it over.

Into the trailer it went. I had my first 'trophy', so to speak. It made it all very real.

Down the road Alan diverted us to the Peak railway before reaching Matlock (DE4 3BT) on the Green. Immediately we were quizzed about the sign in the trailer – we had to assure the bar staff that we were not touring the country stealing Red Lion signs! At Matlock we cycled the other half of the Monsal Trail before notching up our 12th and final Red Lion of the long weekend – High Street, Bollington (SK10 5PF).

Across the Peak National Park and its delicate deer and through the tiny village of Kerridge we arrived at the Red Lion on the corner. So many Lions had found that corner spot in their communities – towns and villages had been built around them.

Here we were, still in beautiful surroundings, yet this Lion looked tired and drab even in the sunshine. Still, it had been a fantastic trip to Derbyshire. I couldn't have wished for more and this trip brought a new dimension to the Quest, the discovery of new towns and villages.

LEIGH TO NESTON

Grim and grey meant a Red Lion day, but grim and grey were all we found at Lion Number 23 (WN7 5JR). Old and run-down, Leigh's Lion had seen better times. Jock at the bar was reading the paper and horse racing ruled. What a contrast from Lion Number 1 where the very same had seduced me into this. The 'For Sale' signs outside told you the full story.

Next stop, just up the road at Hindley (WN2 2QA), things picked up. 'Good Food… Good Company… Good Times', the sign announced, instantly more welcoming. Child-friendly with a toy and game corner, and with friendly staff serving 'Bubbles' (my beloved Prosecco), it catered for everyone.

You could smell the recent repaint. It was a job in progress. The Gents were next for a refurb on June 16 – I was reliably informed – as if that would reel me back into visiting again!

The following weekend Alan, the four kids and I headed up to Skipton and ran into Parade Day. I wondered how many more times it would happen that my Quest would stumble into existing events. The real reason for heading this way was so that Alan could go to the Truck Exhibition at Harrogate.

I had to slip in a Lion. And it was thriving at the heart of this market town (BD23 IDT) and bearing its own little secret. I had never seen it elsewhere or heard of it since – in the fridge stood champagne beer. At 5.5% it was light and not as sweet as champagne. Trying it was unavoidable!

On the road out we stopped on Ripon Road, South Stainley (HG3 3ND) – but not for long. Told that we couldn't sit on the benches in the corner with under 14s (the twins Charlie and Shane were 13 and a half), we didn't linger. It was 2011, for Heaven's sake. Unwelcoming and ridiculous, you will not be surprised to learn it was also empty. This didn't impress Livi, Alan's eldest, who until today had not been on the Lion trail. She had a bet with me that I wouldn't reach 100 by Christmas! Game on.

By the following weekend we had our annual visitors. For the fourth year, we were hosting children (Natasha and Vitalic) from Belarus for the Medicine and Chernobyl charity. During their month with us, the radiation caused by the 1986 disaster is dispersed naturally which can add two years to a child's life. It was hugely important to me.

What must they have thought when we drove all the way to Sedbergh in Cumbria (LA10 5BZ) for chicken and chips? Due to the language barrier, I had pointed to my map full of pins and some Red Lion photos in the hope that they sort of understood!

A couple of years after our visit, the pub was named CAMRA Pub of the Season and it was easy to see why. A great village atmosphere and local produce from the butcher next door (though only between 6 and 8 pm). I was intrigued by its history. Even Carole the landlady didn't know how old it was. Licensing records actually began in the 1740s. My guess was this Lion came along in the early 1800s and had kept every ounce of its charm.

Less than a week later with the kids on their activity programme, Parkgate, Neston (CH64 6SB), became Lion Number 28 and is an absolute must for so many reasons. We were soon engaged in conversation, and they had wares for me to spread their word.

You can tell there's spirit in a pub outside of the 'spirit' in the pub when a charity calendar emerges! – January through to December, one side full of women and the flip of men. All naked. Terry, the manager, along with regulars had stripped off, raising over £6000 for Help for Heroes. I wanted one!

I was taken to a special area named Rhino Corner for photos and signings. Rhino Corner was where debates began and spread throughout the pub. Outside, up a few steps hid the 'secret garden', a beautifully enclosed area brimming with flowers, shrubs and benches.

From Rhino Corner another seed was planted. It hadn't even occurred to me. I learned that there was a Red Lion in Hong Kong and another in Madeira. I knew of Miami. Then one of the girls from the calendar piped up to add Turkey. This was how chat started in Rhino Corner with everyone piling in.

Alan described this as a 'belting little pub' and that's without us tasting any of the exotically names pies – 'Deerstalker', 'Moo and blue', 'Matador', 'Shamrock' or 'Kate and Sidney'.

To top it all, it had a sense of history and mystery. Nelson used to dock just along from the estuary for his rendezvous with Lady Hamilton.

She was born in Neston and was mistress to several older men, one of whom took her to his home town of Naples as a 'hostess'. She met Nelson when welcoming him around 1798 as a naval hero. Overlooking his loss of an arm and teeth, she flung herself his way.

In 1805 Nelson died at the Battle of Trafalgar and, for Lady Hamilton, debt, illegitimacy and liver disease followed. This was their pub.

DARWEN TO WARRINGTON

More of the Price clan were coming to the party. It was now 26 June and nine of us were heading to Darwen (BB3 3PN). This time, my daughter Hayley and her son Cooper were in tow. These were their first Lions.

There were still hundreds to go, but such was my obsession that others were asking why. I couldn't have let them down more as we pulled up on the high part of Blacksnape Road overlooking the valley. Car park – deserted. Pub – closed. Sign – saying 'To Let'.

This was a first.

In 2013, it sadly went for good, sold on to a business developer. Under the 2011 Localism Act a place at the heart of a community can be saved if 21 signatures make the petition. 21 they had but alas, this Lion was no more. We still had nine hungry people, so it was on to The Clog and Billycock once more.

Four days later at Earby (BB18 6RD), it was the same again. I had indoctrinated my friend Alex both into my chosen world of personal fitness and my personal world of chosen pubs.

Despite a friendly welcome when a local came out to take a photo with us – and us entering with full-on enthusiasm – we entered a dull, musty-smelling bar crammed with bric-à-brac such as a glass jelly mould, brass plates, and dogs… lots and lots of pot dogs. The bar lady was not only abrupt and miserable-looking, but also made it clear she did not want to be there. It always felt wrong when you abandoned a Lion and dined elsewhere as we did at The Craven Heifer down the road. No clutter, no smells, just the whiff of the indifference in our thoughts of the pub before, confirmed by the waitress as we dined well. How many people had therefore ended up at the next pub?

After a 'dead' and a 'dull' Lion, July came and Lion Number 31 was almost as close to home as you could get.

18

Just six miles away sat my closest Red Lion, and three months into the project, I had never been to Longton (PR4 5AU).

It was the live band which drew us in on a Friday night. I had been saving it until a free Friday surfaced: tonight was the night and my niece Milly was inaugurated – the one-man band did a variety of rock covers including my beloved The Killers. Loud and proud, within 20 minutes the place was full, my glass was full, and we had good old night of rock.

Just over a year later it was taken on by Ian and Bill. I have met them several times and they have doubled the turnover. The live bands are still a weekly event, but the beautifully kept beer garden and newly built mini-golf putting course are a big draw, the two pool teams are thriving, and poker nights and quiz nights keep the community together.

A week later life threw itself before the Lions... Shane had been called to Rochdale for the day to appear in the BBC's school drama *Waterloo Road*. That meant lots of hanging around and time to kill. Well, what do you know...? There was a Lion just four miles away. It was Shane's first time as an extra and my 32nd Red Lion, and through the cobbled square and a burst of hailstones, we discovered an old haunt of Archibald Campbell Tait's, or as he is better known to you and me, the Archbishop of Canterbury.

Once a tutor to Lewis Carroll, he stayed at the pub in 1819 – principally for medical treatment – proof again that pubs of old were a focal point for their society and served it in many ways. Today this Lion serves as an excellent start and finish point for many walks across the rambling countryside.

A lifetime of history – Shane's minute on-screen. Such were the parameters of modern life.

With a spare afternoon I took a drive to the Lake District for an amble round, and to pop into Grasmere (LA22 9SS). In fact, Alan and I stayed overnight here in 2009 long before the seed of the Quest was planted and I hadn't even realised it was called the Red Lion: it just shows how little notice I used to pay to mere names... though not 'mere' at all, names often steeped in history. This is an ideal base for a weekend in the Lakes at the Best Western Red Lion.

A day later, it was almost time for the Russian children to return to Belarus until next year. What would they say in time of their visit to England? En masse we headed to Winwick Road, Warrington (WA2 7DH).

Today equalled bad planning. I had jotted down four Lions from Google. Then I forgot the map. So we drove around Warrington on the off chance and, as the off chance would have it, we found one I hadn't looked up. Probably because it was closed.

'So, this is a dead Lion,' Charlie blurted out.

And, even though we had visited a few that had bitten the dust before, this was where the phrase was born.

We were now also on the lookout for 'dead Lions', though they will not be counted from this point on! DEAD NOT COUNTED.

Down the road as we headed to Newton Road (WA3 1HE) it was obvious this would become a story of negative and positive. The great Reds that had survived for whatever erstwhile reasons would dominate, only for those in decline or permanent demise to cast a shadow.

At Newton, there was a christening on, so they weren't doing food. Oh dear, the kids were hungry! We had a very quick drink and looked forward to a friend's barbeque, knowing we would be fed.

BLACKBURN TO CHEADLE

Warrington simply represented two ticked off rather than two getting ticks of praise.

A couple of knock-backs like those didn't deter and my friend Sammy was over from Melbourne. She knew of the Quest and was keen to jump on-board, but fingers crossed we found a Red and not a dead Lion and we were mindful that the last time we took Alan's little Super 7 sports car out it packed up on us! The omens were not good.

To find O'Marley's Red Lion (BB1 3HY) just off the services at Junction 6 of the M65 didn't fill me with confidence. You can write the next line yourself: locations can be deceptive. I'll be using that several times more!

Many of the tables outside are under a wooden gazebo, under which stands a huge Red Lion statue next to the menu board. It was the first I had seen. The list was inventing itself.

An engraved stone above the door told us this was the oldest pub in Blackburn – now that was an oft-repeated claim to fame amongst my Red Lions. Who could really argue, though, with anything dating at 1735?

I gathered my evidence in photographic form only to be challenged as to why I was taking them. Was it really that odd to take a picture of a nice pub? A gentleman named Conga offered to get one of me with Sammy whilst casually informing me that there was no Red Lion in his town. Many would tell me of Lions I didn't know. He was the first to almost bemoan the absence of the lair.

At Burnley ten days later (and only because Alan was off to an auction!) was a curious renaming of the Red Lion. On Manchester Road stood 'Decadence at Old Red Lion'. Decadence in Burnley? An unusual and inappropriate choice of name!

This was interesting – the pub had undergone a makeover and the interior become all grey. There was nothing red about it. That was not a rule per se – but clearly somebody had made the decision to move on but cautiously, hence the retaining of the Red Lion in the pub's name.

It's a good pub to watch the world go by outside on Main Street – large and pleasant – but there are also seven pubs within two minutes' walk. Only time would tell if the Burnley people wanted decadence or a back-from-hibernation Red Lion.

Three days later, Dalton-in-Furness came calling (LA15 8AE). The school holidays were in and that meant only one thing – into the Lions' den.

Off the M6 at Junction 36, we bypassed Cartmel, arriving at an estuary called Arrad Foot with a great view of a lighthouse on the hill. Beware if you have kids in tow needing to run off energy – quicksand alert!!

It was like standing on blubber. Lighthouses are always a talking point and this is a great place to linger en route with a picnic. In Dalton itself we parked up in front of a terrace dating back to 1683 in the shadow of the castle at the steep end of Market Street. I hope that description paints the picture.

Sadly, this Lion and the other two pubs across the street were all up for rent. In run-down areas I could understand if the economy hit the locals, but here it didn't seem right. Was the hill too steep after beer?!

Inside, it smelled damp and felt dark and dated – not in a charming way. We headed off in search of our next Lion.

The problem was – as we discovered after calling ahead – it hadn't been a pub for 11 years and was now a guest house with another name. The jigsaw of the internet sometimes had a few pieces missing. As life moves along, the internet doesn't always catch up.

On we went to Ulverston where it was better news with brilliant views. At Lowick Bridge (LA12 8EF) we found an old stone farm and a small but cosy beer garden, nor far from the Slate Quarry Caravan Park where a couple at the bar were staying! Small, tiny and dark with low ceilings inside, the toilets looked like they last had a makeover 15 years ago. At the front stood a sign proclaiming 'Robinsons'. At the back, another announced it was 'Red Lion Hartleys' – breweries, owners and landlords could come and go but signs might outlive them.

Soon we were to say goodbye to Sammy who had been sucked into the Quest. A couple more Red Lions with Georgia and Holly (the daughter of a friend who hadn't yet jumped on-board) was clearly the send-off required!

At Withington (M20 4BT) we found a 17th-century inn at the heart of affluent, leafy South Manchester. Many of the tables overlook the bowling green at the rear. The two are clearly linked – difficult to know what came first: the love of bowls or the love of beer?

Just after, we headed to Cheadle (SK8 2AJ) to an excellent Lion, welcoming for all ages. The owner John Egan offered us a Robinsons beer towel to add to my 'trophies'. He had spotted true potential here at a time when there were at least 50 pub closures a week in the UK and had knocked back other pubs to put the time in here. It was starting to pay off. The old pictures of a 1914 Cheadle and the football teams of the time adorned the walls. Even nearly a century on, it was impossible not to think of those who went to war and gave us the freedom to drink in their honour.

We made off in search of the Lion at Swinton (M27 9UW). The motorway would not allow us to exit! I had reached 40 Lions and this would wait another day.

BOLTON TO COLNE

Next day we were heading for Selby to see punk tribute band The Sex Pistols Experience (another of Alan's passions) – well, why not?!

Stops needed to be made and first was The Red Lion Hotel on Salford Road, Bolton (BL5 1BJ), with Sharon, her daughter Georgia and Sammy in tow (Sharon's first). This massive pub had been a coach house since the 1870s, was rebuilt in 1905, and was now a Fayre & Square pub with a Wacky Warehouse. How we loved to tear up history in the name of commerce.

After knocking over every drink going, we bid farewell to the girls and continued on to Wakefield (WF2 0EE).

At first sight, the pub looked rough. Inside, it resembled something out of the 60s – more like a social club with tables set out like a bingo hall. It seemed to reflect the area but at least it was still open – many shops and businesses around were boarded up.

We left without our T-shirts. That's not to say clothes were coming off. Alan received a card with a stamp for ordering a pint of Theakston. Eight of them meant a free T-shirt. We didn't see anyone wearing one!

Wakefield spoke volumes about the recession.

Next stop was Pontefract (WF8 1AX). It seemed that the entire town was out on a session, as market traders were packing up and karaoke was blasting out of The Elephant. The Red Lion is on the market square between the church and the museum. It's the oldest building in the town (and according to one drinker, the most expensive pub) and right next door the bustling Liquorice Bush was thriving, selling its liquor. It seemed a greater draw than the Lion's 'Reading Room'. It's a shame it wasn't busier. It *does* have a terrific history going back to the 1400s *and* it's haunted.

Many owners over the years became plagued by strange occurrences. One was so afraid that he screwed every door on the second floor shut.

A new owner came along and reopened them in 2006 only to discover the same! Some had put it down to black magic, others illegal medical practices. Or maybe it was down to the case of the defrocked Catholic priest?

It bore all the usual ghostly hallmarks from unknown footsteps to objects being thrown, to strange lights and dark shadows. There remain 25 abandoned rooms in the building including the attic, the ballroom (once a courtroom) and the medieval cellar. The third floor had been used for abortion – one visit in recent times by a medium suggested that one of the rooms cherished the soul of a lost child.

A pub with spirits??!

As we woke the next day in search of Hambleton, Selby (YO8 9JL), once our hearing had been restored after the 'Pistols' gig the night before, the local radio mentioned that tomorrow was 'Yorkshire Day' – 1 August. We would miss it by 24 hours, for better or for worse! Indeed, at the Red Lion locals were advised by way of a small blackboard 'Don't miss it'!

I could see this spreading throughout the country. Days like this were good for the pub trade even if the owner wasn't quite sure what he was doing for the day, not having heard of it before, despite living in the village all his life. He wasn't going to miss an opportunity, though: Yorkshire Day was hot on the heels of his Hot Dog Day earlier in the week!

On to Bradford (BD5 8LT) and the heart of the Asian community. This Lion stood out for that reason alone. A piece of traditional Britain had gradually been crept up upon on all sides as the flavours of multicultural Britain and its business, sounds and smells and buildings like the mosque formed a new city around it.

I am amazed the pub is still there, but still there it is and remains a working-class British pub where non-Asians drink. It literally was like a little piece of England in a foreign city.

Not far away is the Red on Manchester Road (BD8 9RA), which first opened its doors in 1842. Now, with original large stone flags, it consists of three tiny, cosy rooms and serves these unknown brands simply referred to as 'Cola'. This was very unusual and very cheap.

On the way out, we passed a pub on the same road called The Blue Boar. I said to Alan that it wouldn't take long to visit all the Boars! Sadly, too, we spotted another dead Lion at Little Horton, prompting me to Google just how many had gone to the wall.

What I found was a site named 'The Closed Pub Project' – was this me in reverse? I much preferred *my* Quest, visiting those which were open.

Our last port of call, reached through the bleak Dales, a reservoir, and villages dotted with stone factory chimneys, was Colne, the final one of the weekend and Number 47, first stopping at Oxenhope train station, just a dozen or so miles from Colne. We refuelled on soup and coffee at the fixed buffet car, watching an old steamer coming in here to the end of the line then turn around. There is no rush to leave a place like this. Alan was drawn like a magnet to anything trainy. Red Lions and trains work hand-in-hand.

Across the moors through Pendle, we spotted Colne (BB8 0LJ) Red Lion at the heart of the town, with a stone red lion sitting on top of the porch and a very worn Red Lion written into the floor of the entrance. A pub says a lot about its town. Wakefield, as we saw, had its bingo look and was suffering. Colne, at least, had kept its character and left me thinking that, if I had a Red Lion, I would want a statue outside.

We went directly for farewell drinks with Sammy, who had researched a Red Lion in Melbourne!! I will be there before long, I am sure.

LITTLEBOROUGH TO LONDON

With Charlie and Robbie on holiday, Alan and I took Shane to Eureka! in Halifax, adding on a couple of Red Lions afterwards. The A58 through Ripponden is a lovely Sunday afternoon run. We passed a large dam and noticeably a few more closed pubs along the way.

A small, handwritten note on the door of this Wilsons pub (brewers since 1834) told us children were not allowed. Not even in the corner, not allowed at all. Rare these days, surely this was shooting yourself in the foot, or putting your head in the Lion's cage?

It's a strange place – four rooms, each like somebody's front room! We sat in one with an exposed dark stone wall on one side. Up a step, it looked like the weekly turn would perform. The background music was very 70s. The barmaid knew everyone by name. It was very much a locals' pub from 30 years ago. We were out of place.

We headed to Austerlands (0L4 3QB) straight after a very quick drink. With its limited décor, only a few locals playing dominoes seemed to – dare I say it? – dominate. I really felt we were intruding.

There is nothing much to tell except that, in February 2012, Barbara Kinder pulled her last pint here. Retiring, but with the business failing to attract a buyer over a 15-month period, it looked like flats were its future.

One hundred pubs had been lost in Oldham in the last 20 years – Barbara hadn't had one person interested in taking over this Red Lion. At least we hadn't driven a million miles to tick these two off.

Four days later on 11 August, Alan and I headed to Askern, Doncaster (DN6 0AB). The internet describes it as one of the worst places in the UK to live. My mission was simply to take in a few Red Lions whilst visiting Valerie, an old friend from Marbella, where we were neighbours. She is now in a residential home in Lincolnshire.

We cut across the A1 to the A19 through Campsall, passing a lovely church, and found the pub facing a picturesque lake swamped with geese and ducks. The pub, though, was in a sorry state, only dating back to the 70s with a few sorry hanging baskets at the front and one lonely bench. All it offered was an unusual mosaic of a Red Lion next to the door on the outside front wall.

The pub was a mess – the toilet seat was on the floor yet the pub had the biggest screen I had ever seen. Within a year of my visit, the landlord Liam Evans was savagely beaten after standing up to troublemakers trying to peddle drugs around the property. I was saddened but not surprised.

In Doncaster centre, the Lion at the marketplace (DN1 1NH) is now a Wetherspoons! This 260-year-old pub sits opposite the market. It seems like on a Thursday the market is replaced by early revellers.

It was a proper drinkers' pub, and we sat by the window looking out to the empty market stalls, while at the next table a really drunk father was trying to give his even more drunk son a talk about women!

It had won CAMRA's Award for Real Ales and it gets busy at weekends. It has since had a big makeover in May 2015. From here, we were directly on to Folkingham via Bawtry, where we spent a lovely hour with Valerie.

The return journey and more Red Lions. On to Newton, Sleaford (NG34 0EE), in Lincolnshire. Just five minutes down the road from Folkingham and pointed out by a little blackboard on the A52, this was an odd one. The dark wood door of the stone building was engraved with a lion, and the original coach house had been extended to make a roomy pub. The new landlord had made some changes, but oddly the bar had been moved to the first room you entered which, due to a small, quirky law, meant he no longer had a licence to serve booze! You wouldn't really expect a quirky law like this to still exist.

Lion Number 53 is Thurgarton, Newark (NG14 7GP). We were hoping to eat so I rang to find out when they stopped serving food as it was getting late, though we were making good time. Then a country lane and two slow-moving lorries plus our own wrong turning meant we missed the cut-off point for dinner. The bar girl said we would get food at the Magna Carta down the road, though it was a shame because it smelled lovely and would have been a perfect setting to eat in, and delving deeper it seems to die in.

Warm and cosy and reportedly dating back to the 16th century as a favourite of the local monks, it's the little incident of 1936 that puts it on the map. Landlady Sarah Ellen Clarke was mysteriously murdered in her bedroom with fatal neck wounds. For her niece, the horse trough did it for her – this time they had gone for her throat.

It's odd: something as notorious and gruesome as this would have surely cast a shadow on the place, but today that old newspaper article is on the wall for all to see. The passing of the generations instead turns it into merry folklore. I will revisit sometime on one of my trips to see Valerie.

Top 5 Murders:

Thurgarton
Alvechurch
Polesworth
Llangadog
Hatfield

LONDON LIONS

Fancy a summer holiday in the Black Forest? Yes, but only if sandwiched by London Red Lions! The Quest was now second nature.

We got the train from Preston the day before and train man Alan could not resist a night in the £200 million refurbished St Pancras Station Renaissance so that we were literally in the station to catch the 6 am Eurostar to Brussels the next day (which we missed). Round the corner is the Red Lion Kingly Street, Soho (W1B 5PR). One review I found of the pub described it as having a 'European feel'. With a big Red Lion on the wall of the tiny front room, the brewery was the same as Bradford's Red Lion two weeks before. The oak panels make it quite dark inside. It was a sunny Sunday so we were soon outside continuing our walk about.

Just off Pall Mall is the Red Lion Crown Passage (SW1Y 6PP). Slightly tricky to find, this bills itself as the '2nd Oldest Licensed Premises in the West End' and 'London's Last Village Inn, open 11 am to 11 pm, Monday to Saturday'.

I was not expecting the mouthful of abuse when finding the passage empty and the door closed. I knocked on the door, puzzled: it was only 4 pm. No answer, so we took a few photos then I saw a man through the thick green glass. I tapped on the window. 'Do we look like we are open? Now f**k off.'

Stupid me – I forgot today was Sunday. But even so!

The Black Forest was amazing. We enjoyed four days of glorious weather hiking, boating and even horse-carting, then we were back into St Pancras, and I was always going to get back on Lion duty before the train journey to Preston the next day. A quick check-in at the Ibis near Euston and then we wandered into the busy evening. Nowhere to be seen was the Red Lion at Angel Islington (EC1V 4NJ), possibly because the sign outside was a picture of a dog! No wonder we had walked straight past.

This is a bustling multinational Lion mainly due to the fact that it is the theatre pub. Oozing character with its huge paintings and curved staircase leading to the theatre, a sign announces: 'the earliest local historical source in 1826 identifies the old Red Lion as the place where Thomas Paine wrote part one of *Rights of Man* in 1791'.

I hadn't heard of it, but then I don't read much on the French Revolution! And as for the dog, Rolo had been a favourite pet with theatregoers and actors for years, staring out of the window of the pub most mornings, before being retired to the countryside. My first Lion with a dog on the sign! At this point I was unaware that further down the line there would be a Red Lion kangaroo sign. The place is unique. We sat amongst the hive of activity for a while, then went back to the hotel.

The next day – a landmark Lion, underneath the steps of power!

Red Lion Parliament Street (SW1A 2NH) is the nearest to Downing Street. You didn't need a plaque to tell you that big players in history had made big decisions here. Indeed, the pub dates back as far as 1434, though it was rebuilt in 1900.

It wasn't just the politicians who drank here: the frames on the walls confirmed it was the inspiration for many of Charles Dickens's adventures around Westminster. Today, always heaving with tourists, Londoners and politicians, this is a true establishment. On telling the bar girl about my Quest she said Fuller's had another Red Lion close by – more good information – and she went to ask her boss for the address. She returned promptly and said the manager Peter was having a bad day, but my Quest had put a smile on his face and insisted on buying us a drink. It had to be a pint of London Pride and that put a smile on our faces!

A hop on the Tube and jump in a taxi dropped us at the other Fuller's at Mayfair on Duke of York Street, the exact opposite of Parliament Street. Busy but quiet, with space-saving, spiral staircase, this immaculate Lion was our smallest yet. Mint and ale pie and sausage on a stick was offered in this almost elite, club-style den.

There was still the matter of the Crown Passage to address. I wondered whether they even deserved my custom, but technically I needed to go in there. I wondered if we would spot the same – possibly Polish – accent which had sent us packing first time around!

It was the right choice to return. The landlord of eight years was mortified when I reminded him there had been a visitor knocking on his door last week: his face went red, and he remembered in an instant what he had said.

It was a great little pub, too, notable for its one regular who told me he didn't come here often, just once a day, every day, and if I saw his wife I would understand.

'We would have divorced years ago but none of us wanted custody of the kids,' he added.

I bet he's still there today telling anyone who will listen. And he's probably still married, too.

The landlord kept apologising and said things always come back to bite you on the bum. How true: we all have our 'off' days.

We crossed The Mall, rushed through St James's Park, and made it for our 3.30 train back home.

ILKLEY TO PICKMERE

Alan's auntie led us here – a much delayed visit. En route to Pickering, North Yorkshire, a Red Lion sign jumped out at us on the A6034, Silsden. I wasn't even aware it was there again. Partly, though, because it wasn't.

Dead lions were cropping up all over the place. As we headed to Ilkley (LS29 7BT) the post office was also gone. A sad sign of the times. We had visited 58 Red Lions and at least six more had been shut. 10% was not a good statistic.

Our approach was full of contrasts – the Tetley sign outside look faded, the ivy at one end of the stone pub inviting. The pub looked like it dated back a long way, but it looked dated, too.

Inside, plenty of paintings hung on the wall – many for sale. It was 1.50 pm so we managed to get a lunch order in before the 2 pm deadline: thoroughly tasty and satisfying. We continued on through Blubberhouses (I've always loved that name), enjoying travelling through the heather-covered moors on such a sunny day.

Three days later we were off to Swinton (M27 9UW) with Robbie and Charlie along for the ride. This very big corner pub, a Crown Carvery, is a proper eatery, even offering Sunday 'king-size portions'. No, Britain wasn't heading towards an obesity crisis at all. I find all that very off-putting but it was extremely busy. There was a massive 'Grab a Teddy' machine right in the middle of the main room which caused endless stress and strops from all the children and parents who were pretending they had no money.

Having forgotten our map – again – we tried to locate Walkden (M27 9UW). I had to ring ahead and it sounded rowdy. When we got to this 17th-century pub, I realised why: Manchester United were beating Arsenal 8-2. Dave, the landlord, was thrilled when I handed him the card telling him he was Number 61. At my 50th RL I had cards printed, and my mission was confirmed – I was past the point of no return. My

Twitter and Facebook were gaining followers as I put photos of each Red Lion up there.

Heading home to Preston, I spotted another surprise Lion. I didn't even know about Atherton (DL5 1BJ). Originally two houses dating back to 1862, Chris has been here for ten years: this is a real pub with real people telling real stories. It needs a lick of paint, but at £1.50 a pint nobody is complaining. The local Lions were steadily being ticked off in a random manner.

By the time I returned from a week's holiday in Crete, the Quest had gone mental. In my absence, the *Lancashire Evening Post* had run a feature. The next thing I knew, *Granada Reports* arranged filming me at the Red Lion in Cheadle which I chose because on my original visit they were all so friendly and I had chatted with John, the owner, and his manager. I took Hayley and Cooper for support and, once filming was over, I took a call from BBC Radio Gloucestershire who offered me a list of their seven Red Lions. After a lovely lunch at the invitation of John Egen all roads led to Northwich (CW8 1QL). I say all roads. What I meant was the one-way street on approach and us driving down it the wrong way.

The jinx of my daughter struck again. As with her Lion at Darwen, Northwich wasn't open: I must check beforehand in future, as this only opens at 6 pm. Invigorated by the day, we backtracked to Pickmere (WA16 0JX), determined to get in one new Red Lion today.

Pickmere is a beautiful village but I found this one strange. A small note announced 'sorry no food today', as the manager was doing relief at another pub. The slug trails on the carpet did it no favours, but the staff were pleasant and I needed to relax after the stress of my first filming experience. More effort was needed to stop this being a closed Lion. In fact, four years on I did a photo shoot with *Waitrose Weekend* magazine and the photographer took me back here. It is a whole new story, fully redecorated, clean and extremely busy. I was happy to see things had changed for the better.

By the time Alex and I arrived at Shadwell near Leeds *five* days later (LS17 8HH) it seemed that word had spread within the trade about my Quest. I met Annabel from the group Dea Latis, formed by smart women all working in the industry. This was an organisation particularly addressing the notion of women and beer, although real ales are becoming more popular, and so are shots and alcopops. A lower percentage of British women drink beer than in European countries! It wouldn't be the first time it came up in conversation that you would really expect visiting every Red Lion in the UK to be man's work! Either way, I had crossed a new line: my journey could be very good news for all.

We had been due to meet at Jackson Bridge, Holmfirth, but it was closed, and by the time we got to Shadwell, Richard the landlord knew we were coming – partly because I kept ringing him for directions but he, too, had been sent the article from the *LEP*.

Richard had run the pub for six years, but bought it only 12 months previously; now every August he hosts his own festival. He bought our drinks and we lunched with Annabel who is a sommelier for Cask Marque.

Annabel, meanwhile, invited me to the Beer Writers Awards in London later that year where they would make me an honorary member of Dea Latis. Whilst some Red Lions were closing their doors, other doors were opening for me.

LEISURELY LINCOLNSHIRE

Essentially this trip was to revisit my friend Valerie now living in Folkingham. Any old excuse for a Red Lion weekend with Hayley and Cooper starting with Lion Number 66 at Crowle (DN17 4NE). Newly redecorated with lots of oak and a log-burner, the barmaid led me into the restaurant to reveal their fantastic Lion mural. It was a quiet time of day so not too much was going on, but it was the next Lion at Epworth (DN9 1EU) which stole the show. When I tell you that this beautiful market town hosts 'The Festival of the Plough' and 'The Epworth Show' every year, you'll get a sense of the endless fields of tractors and crops which surround it.

It's the Battle of Epworth, though, that puts this 400-year-old pub on the map. It was fought directly in front of the Red Lion in 1852, as the local Tories on horseback fought opposition supporters from nearby Gainsborough. With a host of famous former residents, including Sir Ian Botham, Lesley Garrett and Sheridan Smith, it is John Wesley who gave the town its fame.

This is the birthplace of Methodism – Wesley used to stay here when preaching. In the pub's 'Tartan Room' hangs a portrait of the man himself, saved from the big fire in The Old Rectory in 1709.

The interior displays many of the building's original features – we sat on some church pews – Epworth features in the Domesday Book and ghost tours are regular in the town: does this paint the picture?

Next, a few miles down the road, is the Red Lion Redbourn (DN21 4QR). It's easy to see why I was unable to book accommodation here. It is popular, set facing a green and a pond with ducks scattered all over the verge. On a summer's day it is perfect for an early evening drink, just like today! The sun was getting lower, and the drive on towards Horncastle is a lovely, relaxing one with little company on the roads except for a few tractors and wagons.

I was not expecting a Red Lion at Market Rasen. Again this one had fallen by the wayside and only time will tell as to whether it gets rescued.

Further down the A158, it was the same again. This time the village of Baumber had lost its Red Lion. This was alarming. If these statistics (13%) continued to the end of my journey, we will have lost about 90 Red Lions in four years, assuming my estimate of timescale to complete the Quest is on target.

As we pulled into Horncastle (LB9 5BL) the mid-September sun had disappeared, a man was standing in the doorway directing us to the car park, telling me to park behind the little theatre. Another one! This wasn't just the Red Lion pub, this was The Red Lion Theatre Number 2, though more of a village stage than London's Angel Islington. We entered a warm, friendly, very old town centre pub to find hundreds of keyrings hanging from the ceiling above the bar and a collection of lions on the fireplace. Around the pub there were plenty of pictures of times gone by. In the 1820s there used to be a horse fair at the Bull Ring here. The pictures showed nothing but field after field. Today houses stood on the land.

Tim was fully briefed on me, having heard me mentioned on Chris Evans's show on Radio 2. (Yes, it had gone that far now.) Now, I learned from him and his wife Judy that his father Eric Benson had started the theatre in 1984, and that every six weeks a performance is put on and funded by the local community. I love that community life.

By the summer of 2014, word reached me that the pub was boarded up and for sale, and the theatre group just about hanging on, fearing a search for new premises.

It had resonated as that community pub when I was there. Now it seemed, for whatever reason, once again that the heart was about to be ripped out of the community.

My 70th Lion was an overnight at Partney (PE23 4PG). We were excited to settle down here for the night. In a beautiful village location at the foot of the Lincolnshire Wolds, this pub couldn't move for awards from accommodation to food to hygiene. It was very well thought of.

And it didn't disappoint – opting for traditional Grimsby fish and chips, it was simply the best catch I have ever tasted. The inn is a survivor, too, seemingly unaffected by the recession. The village had been famous for sheep farmers until the Foot and Mouth Crisis from 2001 onwards decimated the industry.

Before that, Partney had already taken its place in history. The Red Lion was the local of Matthew Flinders. It was he who discovered the passage to Australia. Indeed, he was such a significant Royal Navy ships officer that, whilst returning from one trip, he incurred the wrath of the French and was duly imprisoned. Only the intervention of Napoleon set him free. Many places down under are named after him. In turn, he had christened several Australian islands in memory of surrounding towns and villages here.

This was what the Quest was about – sitting in a seat that inevitably had been graced by such an influential figure as him. The village had been virtually wiped out by the Plague: only the cottage next door survived as they had their own well. Who would know that so much history lies behind this tranquil agricultural area?

Next morning's Red Lion in Skegness (PE25 2RU) was a different kettle of fish. The secrets of the past at Partney ran headlong into the epitome of the modern era. By 11 am the latter was already open, bustling with a mixture of holidaymakers, locals and men on a session becoming rowdy. We relaxed on a comfy sofa with coffee and had a drive along the prom before backtracking along the A158, as there were no other Red Lions close by. Or so I thought!

Almost back at Partney, just a couple of miles away is the beautiful village of Spilsby (PE23 5JT). It's a small, friendly local pub brimming with knick-knacks, mirrors, trophies and family photos. You felt that personal touch. Strangely, they only did food on a Sunday or Monday. I hadn't considered Monday as an eat-out day! At the front is a tiny door leading to the cellar which runs under the lounge. At the bar, an ever-helpful Red Lion anorak told me there were four in Birmingham, but not to go in three of them! I reminded him that I was visiting EVERY Red Lion in Britain.

We had two more Lions to visit on this leg, and Raithby (PE23 4DS) was also just a few moments away – that made three in just a few miles and the closest trio to each other I had encountered so far.

This Lion was so quaint, dating back to 1600 – beautiful pink roses climb the outside. As you enter it feels like you are walking into a little cottage. You don't see many so unspoiled. We still had to reach a few Red Lions and visit Valerie, so we were on our way in no time.

We had planned next on East Kirkby (PE23 4BZ) where every Wednesday the Lancaster Bombers make a fly-past. Just near the aviation centre lies this Lion. Outside, two blackboards announced 'Under New

Management' and 'Happy Hour 5-7', but it was CLOSED! I think the pub was shut during the day due to lack of villagers. We continued our drive towards Folkingham without ever going in.

A little further along the A155 is a beautiful 1800s estate house, Revesby Red Lion (PE22 7NU). On the original brewery site, it really does look like someone's mansion house from the outside. Inside is a large restaurant to the left but we chose to have lunch in the sunny, comfy lounge, and from here the journey onwards is laid-back and delightful over the river, with Tattershall Castle as a backdrop. It is a beautiful area to explore.

On to Ruskington (NG34 9GZ) past its narrow river and idyllic ducks, only to find this Lion was closed between lunch and evening. Recent Lion trips had served as a reminder for those who live in towns and cities that in the sticks they don't always open all day.

I rang but nobody answered. The only presence we felt was a fearsome unchained Alsatian on the roof looking down at us. We got in the car and made for home as darkness fell and accidentally found ourselves in Jackson Bridge (HD9 7HB). Hayley was navigating and this highlighted the twists and turns of the Quest. Only two days earlier, I deliberately came to meet Annabel and it was closed and now by accident I arrive to find it open!

We were in the heart of *Last of the Summer Wine* territory. Between 1973 and 2010, 295 episodes of this sitcom about a trio of old men and their youthful antics were made here – in Holmfirth. And of course The Red Lion itself and the cottages out the back can dine out on this forever – it was here that many scenes were filmed.

I had been in many Red Lions were I had run into similar trios at the bar who thought it highly entertaining to dub themselves as 'Last of the Summer Winers' and here I was on the doorstep of its origin.

It is therefore a must to visit because of its place in British culture alone.

Top 5 Quirky:

Jackson Bridge
Dittisham
Dayhills Farm
Truck Stop
Snargate

SHROPSHIRE

Two days later at 6 pm, Alan and I set off with a vague plan to head south, as Shropshire still had no pins in my map of conquered Lions. Holmes Chapel (CW4 7AQ) is a good pub and excellent value – two meals cost just £7.95. You can't beat that. It was very popular and bustling. Massive, too, with five big rooms, it contains the curious feature of large statues of hands and faces all around.

We continued further down the M6, booking a hotel en route. Next stop Market Drayton (TF9 1JP). We found this Red had a big, glass-fronted Joule's Brewery attached to it which had only just been built. It stood directly above Market Drayton's aquifer which is good news, as the best ale starts with a pure water source.

The original pub is very old but has been added to and decorated. The food was hearty and local. Adjacent to us, six Scousers were dining under a picture of John Joule himself. The family had always brewed, but their fame is largely down to the famous physicist James Prescott Joule who gave his name to the standard measure of energy – the joule. Brilliantly, James had been born on Christmas Eve 1818… in the brewery itself. There aren't many people who have a story like that to tell!

I mentioned my project to the Liverpudlians. They had been in another Red Lion themselves that afternoon in Cheswardine after walking along the canal. Much to my frustration, I could not find that Lion on Google. What drew them to my Quest? I told them about Bootle.

Bootle again! They could not believe I had dared to enter, and that was the local knowledge talking. In reality, I had no choice on this Red Lion thing.

They had a merry old time under the portrait, and there were other portraits, too. Six Liverpudlians sounded like more, to be honest! Departing through the 'Mushroom Room', another picture was hanging.

The Joule's famous Red Cross trademark remains the sixth-oldest beer mark in the world, which is some feat.

And how did it start? It was those monks again back in the 12th century. They didn't half like to drink. They even blessed each barrel with a cross to identify its superior quality.

12 hours later, we drove the narrow lanes of rural Shropshire, passing endless bales of hay to Cheswardine (TF9 2RS). It's always lovely to park up by a canal and with some time to spare, an hour's walk took us from Bridge 53 to 55 and back.

The pub opened promptly at midday and we were soon joined by eight of the most gossipy men on earth! Of course, being the only female there and with that atmosphere, word spread immediately about what I was doing. One of the locals happened to be a freelance journalist and, before I knew it, I was becoming the next article in the *Shropshire Star*.

At the back of the pub is a micro-brewery called The Lion's Tale. Given my newfound fame, landlord John was keen to explain and show me around. They made three types of Lion-Bru (!) on the premises. At 66 degrees, sugar formed from the hops and they made 90 gallons per week, only selling it on-site. John bottled it, too, saluting my visit with one to take away. That was nothing compared to how far three bottles of his Lion-Bru had already travelled. They had made it as far as Everest as three of the locals (with a bottle in tow) had undertook an expedition there. That was some achievement – for both the beer and the locals.

Inside, it was crammed with pictures, quotes, awards and shields. Outside, a random tandem bike dominated the front wall. This was a terrific Red Lion, easily one of my favourites so far.

Just two miles down the road I greeted my 81st. I am not sure if being so close together is a good thing! I found Wistanswick (TF9 2BB) on the right-hand side of the road facing a field.

On the wall was a great caricature of the landlady and her husband; on the menu board an offer of 'jugged hare' – something I had never heard of.

I learned it was the whole animal cooked as one in a casserole in its own blood. I am not entirely sure about that!

On to Whitchurch (SY13 1BB) and a route lined with Tudor houses. This Lion is a 1670 coaching house, formerly with stables for 100 horses. It had been closed for a couple of years but now was reopened. Alas, only three people were in watching Spurs v Liverpool on the TV.

This was another pub with spirits – the ghosts ripped up the carpets and threw glasses around. But notably it's the first Red Lion where the 'i' had become 'y'. This was a Red Lyon.

With still two more to do today, we arrived in a downpour at Malpas (SY14 8NE). Located on a hill across from a stone monument which seemed to be a very Malpas thing, this Lion is dominated by what is underneath. Cellars, tunnels and more tunnels, leading across the road to The Crown and up to the church, though now bricked up. What was the function of all this underground activity? Curiosity got the better of me and Wikipedia explains that in 1679 the tunnels were excavated for the canal under the hill d'Ensérune, 165 metres long! In today's world, they came to the fore again in 2014 when the Frack Free Malpas group met at the Red Lion as the government explored the possibility of going underground with fracking. And life goes on!!

Inside the pub, everybody there would tell you about the fish tank – three fish 25 years old had it as their home. Can you imagine living in a tank for a quarter of a century?

Our final visit of the day was at Little Budworth, Tarporley (CW6 9BY). En route at Eaton, I spotted another 'dead' Lion abandoned. The figure was mounting fast. Through Tarporley, taking a sharp right to Little Budworth, we passed many large, neat houses, Holmston Hall Fishery and Oulton Park Racing before arriving at Robinsons Red Lion in the bright sunshine, as if the downpour never existed. This is one I remember for the people, and who knows if you were to visit tomorrow whether you would find it the same, or I did I just arrive on an odd day?

The barman had been there just two weeks but was very forthright on his opinion of Tony Blair, whether we wanted to hear it or not (we didn't). Alongside us, a very drunk student was ordering a triple vodka while telling us about his French degree. He then spoke mumbly jumbly on the phone to his girlfriend from… Ukraine. Bizarre. Being the only pub in the village, it probably attracts a variety of clients. Who knows what I would walk into on another day?

CHESHIRE!

Now six months in and no sign of stopping, my Red Lion Number 85 was coming up on the hottest 1 October on record. After sitting in Booths supermarket selling raffle tickets for the Chernobyl charity with Charlie, we set off for Warrington (WA5 2LZ) where the landlady recognised me from *Granada Reports*. The pub has a Fuzzy Ed's Funhouse at the end where Shane and Charlie burnt off some energy – no ghosts or tunnels here! It is very reasonably priced with lots of 2-for-1 offers, and if you wanted to get the bus somewhere after visiting the pub there is a Red Lion bus stop!

Just a stone's throw away is the Red on London Road, Stockton Heath (WA4 6HN), which looked lovely on such a beautiful day. What a shame as a country we don't have more days like this because when the sun is out the Lion smiles, and at Stockton Heath overlooking the canal as barges come and go, you are just a short stroll on foot to a bustling town centre with fantastic restaurants.

This is also my second Lion facing a bowling green – there must be more to this than meets the eye!

Only three days later, Alex and I decided on a midweek lunch jaunt. Dicklow Cob in Withington (SK11 9EA) has to be worth visiting for the name itself! Leaving the M6 at Junction 18 and up the A535, you see a long viaduct with the big, white image of Jodrell Bank – a must for the space dreamers and night sky obsessives. This Red is a hidden gem. Clean, modern and classy, we sat on church pews (again) enjoying a succulent prawn platter. Steve, the landlord, informed us of a new cask ale Robinsons were launching called... Elbow.

Elbow are the pop group who are known for the hit 'One Day Like This', much used as a backing track for many TV shows, including the Olympic coverage on the BBC. Apparently they had helped design the ale with Robinsons beer makers at their brewery in Stockport. The release of the beer coincided with the release of their album *Build a Rocket Boys!* and the pump clip is the same design as the album cover. It was very popular and ran for a couple of years only to be replaced by Iron Maiden's 'Trooper', who were involved in the crafting of this ale which ended up being their most popular worldwide export beer. What a tale!

With some trepidation we left for Goostrey (CW4 8PJ). I had just read a long, ranting review about the Red Lion there. On arrival, I couldn't move for Lions. Two large Lion heads carved in wood at the side, and in the entrance there were four more made out of sandstone. The inside of the pub was dated with a worn carpet and lots of bandits and game machines, as I had been warned!

Outside the sign said, 'Bikers welcome, different pubs suit different people'.

That about summed it up.

Two days later, with a drastic switch in weather to winds and hail, I picked up Hayley and Cooper, and went off the beaten track to Hawkshaw, Bury (BL4 4JS). This is a great pub with eight rooms for an overnight retreat; we sampled delicious food on a £10 for two-course menu while sitting underneath a portrait of J.W. Lees himself.

The brewery now owns around 170 pubs. Lees himself was a retired cotton manufacturer who bought some land in the 1820s and went to brew! The company is still family-owned. I tried half a 'Governor' – beer created with the chef Marco Pierre White. Portraits were slowly but surely working their way into the Quest and helping me unravel the whole Red Lion experience, putting faces to names.

A WANDER AROUND WILTSHIRE

BBC Radio Wiltshire had called on learning about my imminent visit. I was to do two interviews before heading that way the next day. It was now 8 October and something subtle had changed. People were interviewing me before I set off. Local radio stations were now in on the Quest.

I had pencilled in six of their Red Lions, but first came Bromsgrove (B61 8AQ). Two things leapt out about this pub. The area behind the bar was very small and could only accommodate one person at a time, so the landlord was constantly pulling pints. Furthermore, I learned that it had formerly been a surgery. How many pubs can say that? Bromsgrove was a stop-off on the way to Wiltshire and the perfect place to fuel up on one of their super fresh sandwiches on thick-cut bread.

Cricklade (SN6 6DD) is a beautiful Saxon town with stone houses, pubs, churches and a Red Lion dating back to 1610. A winner of numerous awards, it merges the modern and the historical whilst championing nine real ales and guest beers! I immediately said I would like to return and stay overnight. Three years later, I tried to book accommodation but it was full: I will make it back here one day.

Just five minutes down the road is Castle Eaton backing onto the river (SN6 6JZ). For no obvious reason, there is a large Turkish camel water carrier at the front painted red with the words 'Welcome to the Red Lion'. This was a first. I had yet to be made aware of the Turkish role in the Red Lion story!

That was not the only odd element at play. The pub bears a certificate from the former Swindon North MP Michael Wills which states that the 'Red Lion at Castle Eaton is recommended for serving great beer and food' (fair enough). It is signed by the former Member of Parliament whose title is recorded as a 'Member of the All-Party Parliamentary Beer Group'. These things really existed.

On to East Chisenbury at Pewsey (SN9 6AQ) on the most scenic of routes and the most unusual set of directions yet to find a Red Lion. Passing through beautiful Marlborough and all its thatched cottages, we passed a tank crossing and a sign saying 'Red Lion 1 mile'. It was as though people had come from far and wide to find it. It goes down as my first thatched Red Lion. Michelin-starred and AA-rosetted, it oozes class. A must visit.

With the sun slowly disappearing we made our way back towards Marlborough in search of Avebury (SN8 1RF), a Stonehenge-type village whose myth is built on a circle of ancient stones. In fact, the Avebury Ring predates Stonehenge. It's the oldest stone ring ever known. The pub was first licensed in 1802 and is famous for its 86-foot well which dates back to the 1600s. In other words, the pub was built around the well and the Well Room is now named after Alexander Keiller who excavated the stone circle around the pub. What's odd about that is that Keiller was from Dundee and heir to his family's marmalade business, but somehow got caught up in a ring of ancient stones in Wiltshire!

We spent that night at Lacock (SN15 2LQ). Here is the land that time forgot. Step into the 13th century and a beautifully untouched village. The Red Lion itself exudes quality. From its flagstone floors to Georgian interior, its candlelit tables and open fireplaces, it really is one of the great overnight stays. And the food will leave you wishing you could try everything on the menu. Home-baked Camembert or wild boar sausage with mustard mash: it really hit the spot for excellence.

But there is more to this Lion. We had wandered into a TV producer's dream. Jane Austen's *Emma* and *Pride and Prejudice* were set in Lacock, and the BBC's *The Cranford Chronicles* saw the pub transformed into a shop!

And then there is Harry Potter. Lacock Abbey was used as a backdrop for many of the scenes in the first two films – *Harry Potter and the Philosopher's Stone* and *Harry Potter and the Chamber of Secrets*. The Abbey cloisters and side rooms were transformed into the classrooms at Hogwarts School.

If there was a Red Lion to tick all the boxes so far, this was it.

Next morning Graham Rogers from the radio called for a five-minute live chat. I seemed to tick the BBC Local box.

As we set off on the A350 I glanced at a local paper which was running a story about the Quest. The headline read 'Grandma's Pride'. Alan laughed; I was mortified. Not 'Cathy's Crazy Pub Crawl' or anything like that. Now I was a pensioner on the loose. I knew what I was doing was slightly eccentric, but was there any need to portray me like that? *Note: be more careful when speaking to the media.*

En route, Wiltshire was full of all its rural charms and challenges, too. Three baby pheasants were trotting down the lane with no sense of direction, and on the B3095, just past the magnificent White Horse carved out in the countryside, we swerved at the last minute to avoid a dead badger in the road. You didn't get that in Preston.

We proceeded on to Kilmington (BA12 6AP) and Number 97.

Arriving seven minutes before its midday opening and waiting in the car, one car after another pulled in. The pub is tiny but popular, perched alone at the side of the road. Once inside, drinks were poured and the men got into a big rugby discussion. For them it was the beginning of a good old Sunday banter; for us, we needed to move on.

Driving through glamorously named hamlets like Longbridge Deverill and Sutton Veny, we ended up at Heytesbury (BA12 0EA).

Mike, from Adelaide, was running the show and was three weeks into his new career – one he had never had before! Struggling to get the head right on the beers, he recommended me a 'Half an Arty Farty' – how do they think up these crazy names for ale?!

The pub had been closed but now was bustling and really was a community local. I felt Mike would do well here because of his attitude, but I wondered what his clientele had done when there had been no pub open. Alcohol can bring social problems, but not being social can also be a problem.

Top 5 Thatched:

Brightwell-cum-Sotwell
East Chisenbury
Cropredy
Babcary
Mawnan Smith

THE GLOUCESTERSHIRE GALLOP

BBC Radio Gloucestershire came calling. We both knew that a landmark was looming this weekend. It was now 15 October 2011, a glorious autumn day to celebrate the first big milestone.

But which would bring up the century? It wasn't Newent (GK18 1AH) – a sparse pub with no pictures and barely any seats, next door to the old Tudor village hall… on stilts! The village's sole claim to fame being an onion fair every September featuring competitions for growing and eating onions.

Today the barman was stressed and barely acknowledged us. The rugby team had failed to pick up their kit for that afternoon's match – proof again that so much sport begins and ends back in the local.

Number 99 was Huntley (GL19 3DU). Andrew from the BBC was meeting me here and recorded a pre-100 RL interview. Already, I really was one-sixth of the way through. I knew it was an achievement, and yes, before anyone asks, I was too far in to stop.

When I told the crowd inside what I was doing and which pub I had just come from they laughed, saying there were always fights at Newent, hence no throwable objects like chairs and pictures, all fuelled of course by the cheap ale. As was happening more and more, when locals learned of the Quest, they wanted to add to it.

And so on to the 100th. Andrew from the BBC led the way in his little red car along the A40 and onto the A48, pulling up 15 minutes later.

I was unbelievably excited. At various stages of this journey, I had seen new little pointers and quirky little features which I couldn't have imagined beforehand, but 100 was a big thing to tick off. You can say you've seen the haunted, a well, a micro-brewery or a theatre Red Lion, but to reach the Big 100 made it all real.

Westbury-on-Severn (GL14 1PA) honoured the occasion appropriately. Imagine if it had been dead or closed? Instead we entered a beautiful, 16th-century inn just opposite the graveyard. I imagined how many times that had been staggered through after a late night at the Lion.

Passing round glasses and toasting with Cuperly Verzy champagne, I celebrated with the locals who loved the idea. I had, of course, become wise enough to call ahead and check they did have champagne. That was one thing I learned so far that not all did. Patrick, the landlord, runs a good pub, too, based on decent food and a friendly atmosphere. Regular Tarry filled me in on the graveyard. Cattle had grazed where man was now buried, and the church predated the pub by a good few hundred years.

It was the perfect village to acknowledge the first hundred and, feeling as high as a kite at the achievement, with a warm, giddy sensation we left.

But also I knew we had to march on. One hundred soon became 101 and I was keen to visit another five today alone!

Next was Wainlode Hill, Norton (GL2 9LW). We were still following the BBC man, which meant a break from navigating so I could really take in the beautiful countryside and English gems en route, such as the big boat made out of hay!

The Red Lion faces the river where we wound down and reflected at a table facing the banks – as locations to dream away a sunny day go, this would top the list. And certain days witness the mini-tidal wave that is the Bore of the River Severn which crashes down the river about six times a year and reaches speeds of up to 30 miles per hour – a magnet for the surfers and a spectacular event. A handy campsite is situated behind the pub. I made a mental note to return sometime when the Bore was in town!

After a stroll around Cheltenham we headed to the Red Lion in the marketplace at Northleach (GL54 3AJ). Just next to the church (again!) stands this 16th-century coaching house. An archway leads you through to the courtyard – always a nice way to enter. This pub, though, goes in the file marked 'Landlords'. Inside, next to the door, sits a motorbike.

In the lounge the bar lady showed us a picture of Kev and Carol who run the place. It was from 2010 and their wedding picture. There they were, next to the bike.

Then I noticed Kev wobbling at the end of the bar, unbelievably wearing the same clothes today as on his wedding day, even down to the hat where he had a deck of playing cards tucked in the side. I wondered if this was his regular attire.

They sold lighters, too – with 'Kev and Carol welcome you to Red Lion Northleach' on! I don't smoke but I bought one anyway to add to my varied collection of souvenirs.

This section of the Quest is a good tour. You will find nothing but beautiful villages with wonderful names if you take the A429 from here. Upper Slaughter becomes Lower Slaughter, Stow-on-the-Wold or Moreton-in-Marsh… Take your pick right across the Cotswolds. A brown Red Lion sign pointed us to my 103rd.

At Little Compton (GL6 5RT) Alan gave a thumbs-up to the excellent Stow-on-the-Wold traditional Cotswold ale. It is not open all day so we wondered up Pill Lane and took a few photos until the door opened at 6 pm. It fills quickly, ticking all the boxes of any preconception you would have for a pub in this area, from the stone to the beams to the inglenook fireplaces. I wasn't surprised at how tastefully decorated it was.

As ever the landlord, in his third year, flagged up an unknown Lion. From Little Compton, all roads led to Long Compton, continuing the Red Lion hunt. Just a couple of miles along, but in a different county sits this Grade II listed building. This pub is up there with the best when it comes to the 'Delicious smells coming from the kitchen' category.

We would have stayed if we hadn't booked dinner at our final Red Lion for today where we also had a room reserved, and what treats we missed in doing so. From a crayfish sandwich to cod and chips served in the Red Lion *Times* newspaper, attention to detail is king. Like Little Compton, Long Compton deserves all its accolades.

Nearby are the Rollright Stones, a Neolithic monument to a late king who fell foul of witchcraft. These stones are the king's remains. This was not an isolated incident. In 1875, a 79-year-old woman named Anne Tennant was on the way to the bakers when stabbed by pitchfork in cold daylight by one James Heywood, who proceeded to carve crucifixes in her bloodied face. Back in the day, this was the standard local way of identifying a witch.

Heywood, who had known the victim for 30 years, was found not guilty at court despite admitting to the murder!

Arriving in the dark at the end of a long but celebratory day, we checked in at Chipping Campden (GL5 6AS).

I say Red Lions are like a box of chocolates: you never know what you will get and today's little surprise was a four-poster bed. What a cute room with low-beamed ceilings, fireplace and small cottage windows at a very decent £70 per night. Highly recommended, and, proving again that you could really take your pick in these parts without the quality of food ever letting you down, we shared a mushroom, leek and stilton brochette and simply the best Thai cakes I have ever had. Efficient staff working between the restaurant and the 'stable bar' ensured a perfect end to a brilliant day.

The next day, just 12 miles away we found the Red Lion at Stratford-upon-Avon (CV37 6YW). Might I breathe the same air as the man who put this place on the map – William Shakespeare? Stratford was always busy. The Japanese loved it in particular. Some of the buildings were the oldest I had ever seen, dating back to 1169.

It's a great place to people-watch and the Red Lion is the place to do so by the canal. You couldn't help but wonder if the great Bard himself had done the same. It's something you would like to know – that you were sitting in the great William's pew. Although I can't find evidence, I have a sneaky feeling that the original sight of the Red Lion was not here on the canal but in the town where now there is a Red Lion shopping arcade!

It had a murky past, though.

One autumn evening, a Mr Edward Mullis was drinking at the Lion. So, too, were Francis and Bartholomew Begley. The latter were sweeps who travelled the country and had agreed to sleep the night in the stable at the pub. At closing time, they got into a heated conversation on politics. One of the Begleys was felled by Mullis. Bartholomew Begley died due to bleeding on the brain.

Begley pleaded guilty to manslaughter and was bound over to keep the peace and fined £10. Begley's father was blamed for encouraging his son to fight. I am sure the fine was hefty in those days. Clearly the justice system was less complicated.

From Stratford, we were drawn to Solihull (B93 0LY) and a 1672 Ember Red Lion opposite the village church, just in time to see the bride arrive to tie the knot. It occurred to me that this might happen more and more – that every time we walked into a Lion, we were walking to other people's histories in the making, regardless of what secrets the pubs already held. From couples arguing to those starting on new journeys, there was still that idea that life revolved around the pub.

Outside, the pub had an unusual ironwork sign jutting out high above the street. I had a light bulb moment, which showed that my silly idea was taking on business proportions. I decided to use it on my Red Lion business cards.

But it was the wedding that fascinated me. The bride pulled up in a beige and cream-coloured retro VW camper van in tip-top condition! The seed was sown.

I nipped across the road and asked the driver about the cost. At £500 a week, it would be the ideal way to amble round Devon and Cornwall's Red Lions next summer!

Making tracks, I rang the Red at Earlswood (B94 6AQ) but there was no answer. That paved the way for Hopwas, Tamworth (B78 3AF), and another canal setting! That was two in a day, this time overlooking the Coventry Canal.

It was a good place to end an exhilarating weekend of 11 Lions. I was flying now and didn't want it to stop, randomly ringing towns and pubs all the way home, mentally planning where we would go next.

Top 5 Canals:

Stratford-upon-Avon
Hopwas
Fenny Stratford
Kings Langley
Newburgh

MOORE RED LIONS!

Four days later, I was back on the road with Cooper and Hayley. Moore is a tiny little village on the banks of the Bridgewater Canal – that's three canal pubs now. There's not much here but it is perfect, if you have mooring rights!

The pub is a couple of hundred years old with a recently added snug part. It's friendly and villagey but I remember it for a small moment of doubt.

The blackboard.

'Did you know there were 900 Red Lions in Britain?'

Mmm. I needed an exact figure. There *may* have been 900 at one point. As I have seen, many have closed. I believed there were now between 600 and 700, but certainly no more.

I didn't believe the 900 figure but it was proof that people (especially in pubs!) passed off knowledge as fact. I did, though, need a definitive answer but was only to get that within my last week of the challenge. I couldn't claim to have finished the Quest, only for someone to tell me I had missed one.

From Moore, I had to wait a whole nine days before setting out again. Wales was calling.

It was a pleasant October day and we were on the road early as Alan had to take some car parts to a site in Anglesey. Passing the dragon etched out on the grass embankment, we entered Wales seeing a tribe of wind turbines in the sea for the first time.

Through Colwyn Bay and onto the A548 at Abergele, we descended the valleys towards Llansannan (LL16 5HG).

This J.W. Lees is the only pub in the village and one of just 54 in the *Britain's Best Real Heritage Pubs*. This is an extraordinary pub.

It has the only remaining bull pen on the right as you walk through the door. At around 500 years old, the buildings out the back are the original pub. Chris, the landlord, had been there seven years when we called in. He opens until 3 am on a Saturday night, with live bands in a marquee out the back. On a Tuesday they offer computer lessons, followed by Welsh lessons on a Wednesday.

The pool team win everything and Chris and his wife even look after the public toilets in the village, constantly topping them up with flowers and pictures! You can sleep next door to the pub in accommodation for five at just £25 a night each.

It was heart-warming because it still had all those values that drew people to pubs in the first place, whilst surviving in a contemporary way. Can there be another pub where you can rock your socks off and learn Welsh? Indeed, uniquely the Red Lion hanging sign outside has one side of the board in the native tongue, Llew Coch. I would be seeing many more of these as Wales has almost 60 Red Lions.

There's more. It is a regular location for TV shoots. S4C often use it for their Sunday night show 'Hwb', not that I was familiar with that programme.

And if there were any other boxes left to tick, it obviously is haunted, too! The story goes… As many pub tales tend to begin, that when the big fire goes out at night, the apparition of a 17th-century political Roundhead appears. A friendly ghost by all accounts!

The Lion at Cyffylliog (LL15 2DN) was tricky to get to. The tiny B5435 was closed so, once Alan had unsuccessfully tried to squeeze the Land Cruiser past the bollards and barriers, we diverted through Groes, along a narrow mountain pass where we played second fiddle to pheasants wandering the road.

Above the very low door of the pub, it stated that our licensee was Nirmal Singh. This was another first. I had not yet met a Punjabi landlord.

In between busily dressing the pub for a Halloween party and displaying Hobgoblins Halloween promotion, he explained to me that he had been looking for somewhere to live in this area, and with the pub up for sale, he rented it for a year then bought it.

It didn't look like he had betrayed the original pub layout. I loved the fact that the pub told the story of the countryside. The old stained glass windows in the side lounge were of individual river and landscape scenes across Wales; the gents' toilets (I was invited to see!) were floor-to-ceiling brightly coloured unmatching tiles originally from the local church.

Inevitably it led to the question of other Asian Red Lions. Nirmal pointed us in the direction of the Red at West Bromwich which was all Asian and that we must eat there. I loved that people we met were chipping into the Quest as well.

The Red Lion at Mold (CH7 1ET) was a flying visit – an old-fashioned market town pub with two halves, one side for food and the other for locals. Between Mold and Flint at Junction 33 of the A55 at Northop (CH7 6BQ) is a big Red Lion, with restaurant space for 70 and a lounge bar accommodating the same and with further facilities for functions, all beautifully decorated.

The stonework above the doors gives you the clues. From the front it looks like it is closed, but the side entrance displays confirmation that the building was added to majorly in 1989.

It is impressive but its size, ironically, reduces its warmth. Lacking atmosphere, we got back in the car towards Holywell (CH8 7TD).

'Holywell, The Lourdes of Wales', announced the sign! The pub gave off no air of healing qualities, looking drab from the inside, as though the air was filled with the choking smell of smoke. This Lion was odd.

The small bar was like the front room of a terraced house, and for no obvious reason hosted a shelf dedicated to Laurel and Hardy. Well, I Googled it and couldn't find a link! That one must go down in the category of 'Landlord's own personal interest'!

I enquired whether smoking was permitted here and was adamantly told no. It was long after the ban but someone had clearly sneaked one in. As I walked to the Ladies through a throwback-type, old, smoky room, the pool players were all rolling up from their tins.

They were friendly enough, but believe me not holy.

And so to West Bromwich (B71 1RH) for the all-Asian Lion... It was now 21 October 2011 and it had been the longest gap between Lions at 23 days!

I had not lost interest, desire or resolve. Life just happened. It had been a hectic few weeks. When Alan said he had some parts to fetch from the area, I jumped at the chance to get back on the road... but no! The Red Lion that had been so recommended to us was not open. We spotted the large brick Red Lion on the left, but the much-revered Red Lion Tandoori BBQs and Balti House was having naan of it.

I called them. They opened at 4 pm and served food from 6 pm, but it was only 3.30 when we turned up. We would have to return. Refusing to go home empty-handed, Stone beckoned (ST15 8AJ) and was already busy by 4 pm. Friendly but rough around the edges, I noticed a map on the wall of the Stone Real Ale Trail and with that a Red Lion I was unaware of at nearby Dayhills: that was one for another day.

By late-November the Christmas markets were up and running, and that meant Chester! What a beautiful city and ample excuse to shop with Red Lion refreshment breaks along the way! I wanted my friend Alex to help me choose a dress for the 'Beer Writers Awards Dinner' to which I had been invited in December.

At Northgate (CH1 2HT) Jay the barman recommended calamari, so I duly obliged with a glass of mulled wine. As he and some locals learned about my mission he took off his Red Lion apron there and then and gave it to me, adding that it will need a wash, whilst pointing me in the direction of Handbridge (CH4 7HL) a couple of miles away.

The list of souvenirs was stacking up. It was odd and endearing what spontaneous gifts people would leave me to ensure their Lion was remembered!

We were racing the clock now, fighting to get home before the school bell, so Handbridge was only ever going to be a flying visit. The swiftest way was to jump in a cab. He would know the way. We asked our driver to turn off the meter and wait: he quizzed us as to whether we were buying the pub.

I hadn't actually considered such a thing until this point. Again I made a mental note. I have no desire to buy one but I do have a spacious garage!

I tried to turn the door handle but it was closed. I then went to a side door and the Belfast-born landlord Andy popped his head out of the window to explain they were only open in the evenings.

Individual Red Lions have their individual opening times!

He knew who I was, though. His friend had brought in a cutting of me and had kept asking 'Has she been in yet?' Well, today was that day.

The Quest could often get those doors open and Andy posed for photos whilst offering us a shandy, explaining that he had been here two years and it *wasn't* a Red Lion when he arrived. The previous people had lost the Red Lion name and called it something else, but when he got the local sign man down to make him a new Red Lion sign the guy said no need, the original one is still underneath. So this had been a smothered Lion and now is revived!!

This was an interesting thought – were there other Lions out there who were in between identities that I might not track down?

LUTON TO BRISTOL

In theory we were heading to London to see Alan's brother Adrian who works as a technician at Sky. In practice, we nipped off the M1 at Junction 18, along the A428, passing two massive wind turbines and found the Red Lion.

Hillmorton (CV21 4EG): this pub was a first! I had never seen a wooden skittle table before. Nor had I entered a pub with a large, wooden model car hanging from the ceiling.

The owner also had our next Red Lion at Kilsby (CV23 8XP), which is a warm, cosy pub with a fire at one end and, again, skittles! The manager explained that 'cheese', as skittles was sometimes known as, was huge in the area with 45 teams in the league! Who knew?!

Another first, though – the nearest two Red Lions with the same owner.

At the Sky studios we did an interesting tour and tried out the Channel 5 sofa! Adrian was still working so we headed off to Greenford (UB6 9BE) about four miles away, arranging to call at Adrian's in the morning.

According to a Scotsman at the bar – there is often a Scotsman at the bar! – this *wasn't* the original Red Lion. That was up the road. This was only built in the 1930s. Either way, it was as close to a 'typical' London pub as you could get.

Despite my new friend from north of the border pointing out some other Reds I didn't know about, we had to get to Luton Red Lion (LU1 3AA) by evening.

Lion Number 122 is in a handy location for the airport or for London. Essentially we just needed a bed for the night. It was busy when we arrived, smack bang in the middle of Luton's heaving nightlife with a very loud DJ; people-watching from the window was entertaining, and eventually we made it up the eerily creaky stairs to bed.

The next morning, a sense of good grief at the night before. Empty bottles and shattered glass, Luton was slowly waking up. What a contrast to the serenity of some of those trips through Gloucestershire!

The Red Lion at Welwyn Garden City (AL6 9AJ) got us back on track, passing a pub called The Crooked Chimney which surprisingly had a crooked chimney. This is a popular, busy pub with quality food.

Just on the edge of Sherrardspark Wood, close to the town but out in the country, it has lazy Sunday lunch written all over. A quality pub with an amazing selection of wines.

On the way to Adrian's we called in at Hatfield (AL9 5EU). This stands on the Great North Road but was tricky to find. Well, tricky if you don't know Old Hatfield and New Hatfield!

You've got to love the log fire inside. It's fake! Hence the note saying 'Please do not put logs on the fire, it's gas!'

However, that is not the tale that everybody tells here. Keith Moon, of the legendary rock group The Who, puts this Lion on the map.

The pub opened on 4 January 1970. Keith Moon was there. The clientele were largely working-class skinheads who took offence at Moon's rockstar wealth. The story goes that they hated his choice of expensive brandy and despised his car.

It's the car which holds the key to the story. By closing time, the scene had become ugly. As Moon left in his Bentley, the locals pelted it with coins and begun rocking the vehicle.

Normally Moon didn't drive – even when sober. His bodyguard and chauffeur Neil Boland got out of the vehicle to confront the thugs. Moon tried to drive away to safety. Tragically, Boland ended up underneath the car and was dragged down the road, later pronounced dead at the hospital.

Moon was cleared of the accident, though he did plead guilty to the driving charges. The tragedy haunted him until his own death in September 1978. So many Lions with so many tales!

By 2 December 2011, I was back in London. Just eight months into the Quest and I was special guest of Annabel from Cask Marque and Dea Latis at the Beer Writers Awards – not that I had actually written anything about a single beer, though I think we knew that day was coming.

I was really looking forward to the event, despite my bag being stolen while having dinner the evening before. Its not the obvious money and cards which are the problem, but the reading glasses, camera and worst of all the train ticket home! The whole of the next day was spent getting some money and buying the essentials like handbag and purse for a start. The evening was fabulous, with a different speciality beer to accompany each course, and it was great to mingle with the trade. I suppose I was now strangely involved in their world and, although visiting every Red Lion pub, not attached to anything in particular. I was possibly in a unique position.

The next morning I found The *Old* Red Lion at Holborn (WC1V 6LS) and yes, that does count. At the heart of Covent Garden, this is a smart stop for one after a hard day in the city-type pub.

Any sign I might be winding down for Christmas? No! You can count that out. In fact my Christmas Eve had been planned meticulously. Everything was organised and the kids were with their mum. And the landlady at Frodsham (WA6 7AH) was expecting us! Frodsham is a very cute historic market town, birthplace of Daniel Craig and Gary Barlow from Take That. Carolyn, who had trebled the turnover, dubbed this Lion a 'boozers' pub', though that doesn't really do it justice in terms of the Quest.

It met many criteria that had established themselves by now. It was my tenth on the High Street, my third with a bowling green, and certainly not the first next door to a police station.

The town, too, looked every inch Christmassy with all its lights up and down the street. Merry Christmas, everyone!

Frodsham was a safe bet for Christmas Eve, just half an hour away, but for New Year we pushed the boat out setting out for Mangotsfield, Bristol (BS16 9HD). As part of a complex plan, we dropped the kids, picked up a friend Mark, went to Deepdale to watch Preston North End for a 1 pm kick-off against Sheffield Wednesday, only to leave at half-time (they were losing) then hitting the M6, M5, M4 and M32 to make Bristol by 5 pm.

I had a few Lions on my list, but settled on Mangotsfield where they were setting up for the FNB New Year's disco.

'What is the FNB?' I asked the landlady.

'The DJ calls himself Fat Northern Bastard,' she replied!

She must have been asked that question a thousand times, though we left before getting to meet the fellow Northerner. It broke the ice, though, and they asked if we had tried Staple Hill (BS16 5NL) which both 118118 and Google had led me to believe was closed. The barman's magic book of local pubs confirmed otherwise, and so we were there in the flesh. A bonus Lion.

Shut!

They were opening at 7 pm for a New Year party. However, good news. I phoned them from outside… They knew of the Quest and Tracey said 'Shaun, open the door it's that Red Lion lady', so they opened up for me! If I could keep this up long after I had completed the lot, this could come in very handy.

Shaun and Tracey had only been in a year and were building the business up well. They showed me the skittle alley out the back. I had never given a second thought to skittles in my entire life until recent weeks when they had suddenly become part of the Red Lion furniture. In fact, the pub was the base for the league.

Shaun filled me on the history of the building. There had been a pub here since 1810 but it wasn't a Red Lion until 1826.

With tickets to see The Sex Pistols Experience at The Fleece in Bristol to 'ring in' the New Year, we made our way off into the night, bringing down the curtain on the first 128 Lions.

I told myself I would make 200 by the next May. Only time would tell.

Remember my bet with Livi that I wouldn't reach 100 by Christmas.

2012 MEANS ELLESMERE PORT!

It had been a whole fortnight before we got going again, and our first stop of 2012 began on Friday the 13th! And there were to be three of those this year, all 13 weeks apart. Good luck!

We planned on driving the 50 minutes, having a drink then getting back to have dinner locally. Fortune was smiling on us at Ellesmere Port (CH66 1QQ), though that wasn't the same for everybody. This was the only pub I have ever been in with a list of banned drinkers on the wall. It wasn't a short list either, with one culprit sent packing until 2016. There were no clues as to their offences, but this Red Lion was playing judge and jury!

Next to it was another list of all the bands playing. Tonight's was warming up as we arrived. They convinced us they were worth hanging around for so, nipping out to eat in a nearby restaurant and booking ourselves into a local hotel, we returned for the live music. The same band had transformed themselves with pink wigs and shiny, tight, flared trouser suits to become Wizzard or Sweet lookalikes! Though they were actually called Kookachoo!

From the first note, they owned that pub. Kindly, in between their songs they welcomed me to Little Sutton and mentioned Cathy and her Quest. We left at midnight with a souvenir CD of theirs to check into the hotel, which we hadn't even seen, with not so much as a toothbrush. What a great night!

Two days later, we were in Rawtenstall (BB4 7TG), an old mill town with its sloping terraces. The pub was more like a small house with a front and back room. Locals had obviously been coming here for years. On the window ledge sat an old model of the Red Lion.

Rawtenstall is a stop on the old East Lancashire Railway line which still runs. We picked it up at Ramsbottom just in time to see a great steam engine pulling in through the puffs of cloud. A real throwback Lion in a real throwback town.

Towards the end of January, a last-minute change of plan meant we were heading to Staines (TW18 4PB).

The plan had been Staffordshire and just an overnight on the Friday because we were scheduled to marshal the Chernobyl 10K on the Sunday, but Alan called to say he had to pick up a van from Surrey. I found the cost of a single ticket to Staines was £174! Of course, a return was cheaper at £85. Why is that?!

When we got to Staines we took a cab across town to the Red Lion which had stood there since 1610. It is a warm, cosy pub packed with paraphernalia, including a price list converting pounds, shillings and pence into decimal! That happened in 1971. I remember all the new shiny currency!

The next morning I planned on six Red Lions after picking up the van. It was not a van at all but a yellow Convertible Saab which I had been trying to track down for some time and, unbeknown to me, Alan had located.

Disaster! Just five minutes after the surprise of my life, the paperwork hadn't come through and we couldn't take the car until Monday. I would need those return tickets after all, or... we could hang around until Monday morning and Red Lion away! A quick Google took us to Waterloo and Westminster Bridge (SE1 7RW). This was odd. The Red Lion had become The Walrus!

I couldn't count it.

So, Lion Number 132 was Iver in Buckinghamshire (SL0 0JZ) which is now a Chef & Brewer pub within the Grade II listed building. It has a cute, little history in that it was originally built by the local parish council to raise funds for the church. Of all the excuses!

It hasn't always been a Lion, though. It became The Gurkha for a while and only reverted back in 2001.

At Langley (SL3 7EN) and so many Lions in, I finally discovered the origin of the pub.

Amongst some old pictures on the walls was a quote stating that the most popular pub name in Britain was due to John of Gaunt, the most powerful man in England in the 14th century. When James I came to the throne, he diplomatically ordered that the heraldic Red Lion be displayed in public places. The crest of the Red Lion belonged to the badge of John of Gaunt. I had been in 133 Red Lions. This was the only one to tell its tale.

When the locals realised what I was doing, one of them chirped up that he wished his wife would take him on a pub crawl round Britain!

I thought about this a lot on the way to Stoke Poges (SL2 4HN). That man had identified something with that comment. The Quest would not have the same impact if done by a man.

Also, social media had begun to join in. I had met Alex at a previous Lion, and he begun following me on Twitter: not only was I welcomed by the manager here who also had an article on me, but also the public were now recommending tips to me. On the strength of this, Alan chose the Piccante Pizza whilst I took fish cake with mango hollandaise. Alex from Twitter had got it spot on.

I realised that whilst the first 50 or so Lions had just been something I did, now people were catching up in real time. Articles were being sent ahead of me as though each publican was wondering when they would get a visit. This all had enormous potential and this Red Lion at Stoke Poges remains one of my favourites. Attention all bubbles lovers. On Sparkling Thursday, Prosecco is £15 and champagne £20. We went on to have a fun night finding a great place to stay on LateRooms.com.

Further evidence that I was on to something came at Burnham (SL1 7JZ). It was also common now that when I told people what I was doing, they automatically chipped in with the Red Lion they knew.

One couple here flagged up the Isle of Wight Red Lion which would be one of my furthest away in England when I got there. Another couple discussed other pub names they could visit. Alan piped up with The Railway, as he loves those trains and there would be no driving! I wouldn't want to take on a lesser challenge! They settled on The Railway, which was not a bad idea since they would be right next to transport and this weekend with no car we had run up a few taxi bills. I wouldn't like to guess what all this had cost *me* so far.

HORSELL TO HOPE

Today, Horsell's (GU21 4SS) website states 'casual enough to be comfortable, smart enough to feel special'. That is exactly what it is. Modern, but with traditional features preserved, and an unusual menu. I was happy to be guided by the waitresses towards a salad of broccoli, feta and fresh soya beans, an unusual combination.

All around were pictures of 'Brooklands'. We hadn't realised we were sitting on a little piece of history. Mercedes-Benz had opened up a museum/experience just down the road from Horsell on the site of the ancient Brooklands racetrack.

It sounded like a fantastic day out with a kids' play area, too, but also, of course, exhibits of cars from yesteryear. They also now have a Concorde experience. If you are at all interested in vintage machinery, then plan your day here. Don't just stumble on it as we did!

My next Lion remains uncounted. For now. The Red Lion in Dubai – my first overseas is for another book. This could never end!

Once home I picked up Georgia and Holly for a half-term lunch and made for Cheshire and Dodleston (CH4 9NG). Red Lion withdrawal symptoms had been setting in. About an hour from home this Red is set in a beautiful rural village. A regular award-winner at the Chester Food and Drink Festival, it is perfectly located as a start and end point for countryside walks.

It pulled its first pint around 1737 under the name of The Red Lyon. It was odd how spellings had been tampered with over the years. In 1845 it took centre stage as the scene of a battle between Irish and English farm labourers. As well as the amount of time these pubs have stood tall, they clearly, too, are the map to local history and that sometimes means conflict.

From here we set off to Wales and Marford Hill (LL12 8SN). Wales isn't too far from Cheshire, but anywhere is a long way to go when the pub is shut. Inviting blackboards outside and a phone message saying food was served between 11.30 am and 9 pm didn't tell the whole story.

I rang but nobody picked up, leaving us with the odd spectacle of a photo session at a pub we couldn't get into. Passers-by must have wondered what was so amazing about their pub. We will dub this a Sleeping Lion.

I was also curious about the Red Lion at Hyde (SK14 2BD). It keeps cropping up on websites but without a phone number. Determined to solve this, I drove up and down Manchester Road but to no avail. Frederic Robinson sent me a list of their Red Lions and, sure enough, it *was* on there but lo and behold, I couldn't find it.

I did manage to track down a chap called Graham who runs a venue nearby who told me it *had* closed down a few years ago and was now a company called Plastic Fantastic. I am not sure how the brewery was unaware but I, at least, had solved my puzzle.

Unsurprisingly, this is not the only mystery unresolved. When I had been on BBC Radio Lancashire the previous September, a caller rang in to ask if I had been to the Blackrod Red Lion (BL6 5EF).

Again, for the last few months I had been calling the number on and off and… nothing!

I couldn't dismiss it unless I knew definitely. I phoned the Indian restaurant on the same street who believed that someone had just taken it on. Full of curiosity we set off to discover.

Bingo! It was open and serving what Alan described as the best beer so far, which is a pretty big deal after 139 Lions.

Mike, the manager, explained that he had reopened in June 2011 and, although he had lived down the road in Adlington where they liked a drink, he had never known such hardened drinkers as in the Blackrod! This was a new category in itself!

Even more extraordinary is the fact that when there is a football match on, Mike sells the beer at £2 a pint until the first goal is scored. A nil-nil is bad news for him!

As I told him my story and vice versa, a couple of locals chipped in with further Lion updates. The Lion at Haigh which we had visited last May was now an Indian with a different name. Again, the rate at which the Lions were closing was alarming.

Oh – and why had Mike never picked up any of my calls? Blackrod doesn't have a phone.

A lot can change within a week, and literally seven days later I moved house. I moved out of Alan's house and back to my own. Some things just don't work completely. We are still friends, I see his kids and… that wasn't quite his final Red Lion.

The 3rd Annual Beer and Chocolate Event by Dea Latis was on in London on 27 March 2011. Once again I was invited. All this from just reading a sign at a pub in the Lake District on Grand National Day!

You might think chocolate and beer do not mix, but try it! I sampled the 9.5% Jacobsen Pale Ale with Barley Wine matched with the Thorntons Continental Alpini!

Of course, I made time for the Quest and took Hayley with me so that we could catch up with a couple of her friends from Spain, now living in London. Despite this being my fourth Red Lion trip to London, I had not yet visited Eldon Street (EC2M 7LS) in Moorgate. We met Eli, Hayley's Spanish friend now living in London and headed on to Moorgate: naturally bustling, this Lion boldly states 'No 1 Eldon Street Red Lion' engraved in stone outside.

It also appears to have been a magnet for the arts, with the immediate area featuring in Samuel Pepys's famous diary, the movies *Mission: Impossible* and *Run Fatboy Run*, plus a commercial for BBC Radio 2.

I was not expecting much from The Red Lion, Hoxton Street (N1 6NH). I had been told it looked run-down. This couldn't be further from the truth. We met Laura, Hayley's English school friend from Spain at Old Street tube station. As we approached it does look like a typical East End pub, but inside it has gone bohemian with beaded lamps, large mirrors, comfy sofas and tulips on every table!

The bar is very small but I noticed a sign saying 'Roof Top Terrace'. This place is full of surprises. Hayley and I wondered up the stairs to find the toilets, then up another level to more seating and the kitchen, then finally the sunny roof terrace on the fourth floor all set up for that night's BBQ with heaters and tables and a great place to capture the view of the area and all its chimneys. Unpretentious, I thoroughly recommend this pub.

One week later, it was 6 April and I had completed almost a full year on the Quest. 'Was it wise to hit the M6 on Good Friday in search of more Lions?' wondered Hayley.

Small things like that were not going to get in the way of Lion Number 142 at Tarvin (CH3 8EB), just a few miles from Chester. After ordering a beer, we discovered that the pub didn't do food, forcing us to pop over the road to the George and Dragon before they stopped serving whilst the bar lady kept our beers for us!

From here, a quick stop at Penyffordd (CH4 0JR) in Wales, about halfway between Chester and Wrexham, revealed an unheard of Red Lion at Hope, minutes away (LL12 9NG). A couple of the lads at Penyffordd offered to 'take' us in *our* car if we gave them a lift back. Why not?

I had almost universally been received with goodwill on my mission, even at places like Bootle, where I was warned off. These two partners in crime had no idea that we would find a 'Run This Business' sign when we got there. The pub had only closed down the previous Friday.

Next door stood a White Lion. The lads said we shouldn't be racist about our Lions and we weren't, so we joined them for a quick one! Local humour!

I couldn't include this dead Lion or the White Lion on the list. For the Red Lion, however, there is still hope.

A DIP INTO DURHAM

Next day it was time to indoctrinate a new member into the tour. My friend Paula had nothing better to do on Easter Saturday.

Imagine the look on her face when we pulled into the car park at Trimdon (TS29 6PG) in County Durham to see its grim exterior, washing on the line, paint falling off all over, and not a hanging basket in sight. Tony Blair's old patch.

'Please, no! Where have you brought me?' Her face dropped.

However, that was not the complete picture. Inside was much more pleasant, though pretty deserted with just four people in.

John, the barman, more than made up for it with his patter. He had travelled a lot and took an interest in the Quest. In minutes, I knew everything. He had recently lost four stone, one of his friends was a shooter for the county, and the other two people in the pub were a ballerina and a footballer. John was determined to be a millionaire by the age of 28. I didn't doubt him for a second.

Then, in swayed Gary, who had always wanted to be called George, had consumed his first pint at 9.30 am, and wanted to come to our next pub with us.

We turned him down!

'Is it always like this?' Paula asked.

The answer was never.

Without George or Gary or whoever he was, we found The Greene King Red Lion in Darlington (DL1 1NG), one of the oldest pubs in the town centre and a Grade II listed building. We then ventured to the edge of Durham and Plawsworth (DH2 3NL).

Not knowing the area at all, we realised on the A1 that we could have shaped our route somewhat better.

That said, you can't miss the Red Lion here just off the A167 (known locally as the old A1). Its creeping ivy up the walls stands out a long way back from the road. It seemed a popular eating place with such pleasures as Cow and Cork Night, but we couldn't stay as we had a table booked at our next Red Lion!

Just a couple of minutes away is the Red Lion on Front Street (DH3 3BE) in Chester-le-Street. The sat nav really didn't like this place but we made it in the nick of time to eat: kitchen closes at 7 pm.

Every time I think of this pub I cry with laughter. I popped to the toilets while Paula ordered drinks. When I returned, she had gone. Looking around the large, almost empty pub with the DJ setting up in the bar to the right, and a massive screen showing football on a raised area to the left, my eyes finally focussed on a small table with a crisp, white tablecloth on its own under the football screen... with Paula seated with her head behind a menu.

It was like a sketch out of *Monty Python*.

A man watching the football never batted an eyelid. I was unable to restrain myself as I approached the table.

'We have to order quickly as the kitchen is closing.' Paula popped her head up from behind the menu.

Tears of laughter rolled down our cheeks. No other tables or diners in sight.

Whilst Paula's bacon and Caesar salad was very good with baby lettuce, my wrap was the worst I had ever tasted, so hard I had to prise it open to find a couple of shrivelled mushrooms, a few pepper slices and absolutely no sauce. They forgot the cutlery, but to be fair it did only cost £2.99 for the wrap! I didn't have the heart to say anything to the staff who were very attentive. Plus, for entertainment value it exceeded 10 out of 10. The DJ came over asking what brought us to Durham. I said I was on a Red Lion tour, and he immediately started looking around and asked where were the rest of them.

'Oh it's only me!' I replied.

He thought I was some sort of coach trip!

Often I get asked which are my favourite Red Lions and, whereas some have fantastic foods and rooms and are on my favourites list, so are experiences like that, which you couldn't make up.

Our fifth Lion of the day was close by, too, in Ouston (DH2 1JH), which is technically still Chester-le-Street. Number 149 was a brightly lit working men's club, very busy with the anticipation of a rocking Saturday night ahead as The Hairy Beavers began setting up!

They had been doing the circuit since the 1970s.

At the bar, a reminder that people had their own ways of letting me know they had clocked me. Without even looking up whilst pouring a pint, the barman said he knew about the Quest – well, the tour, as he referred to it. He added that there was another Red in Birtley, only minutes away (DH3 1LS) that I didn't know about. We grabbed a cab outside to check it out and clock it up. Opening the doors in excitement, the lights were dimmed and the dance floor was rocking. I looked at Paula.

'*Phoenix Nights*,' she blurted.

Edging towards the bar, I asked one of the locals, Davy, if the singing was a turn or karaoke, it was that dark and crowded.

'What do you think? It's f★★★★★g crap,' came the dismayed response.

As Paula waited to be served I nipped over to the karaoke man.

'Can Paula sing *Coward of the County*?' I asked.

He showed me the long queue of those waiting to sing.

I whipped out my Red Lion business card and said we couldn't stay long but 'It will be worth it'.

When Paula is in the mood, by golly she *can* entertain.

I had accidentally, of course, forgotten to tell Paula who was surprised to hear her name called out. Like a true pro, she delivered, slapping her thigh and doing the country strut: who wouldn't know that Dolly Parton had turned up?

It was a riot with the crowd calling for me, and an icebreaker, too, as it accepted us into the community and that seemed to be the calling card of the North-East Red Lions – a little dated but with warm, quirky characters as long as you were open to it yourself.

Davy, alone at the bar after a wedding, asked if he could join us back to Ouston. On this occasion, why not? We had stayed so long at Birtley that the band were on their last song on our return, though we did spend another hour chatting to them and our new friend Davy.

Back at the hotel, we laughed and laughed some more. It had been bizarre and random. It really was the people who made it.

The next morning we left 'Durham County of Prince Bishops' and headed out to one of its most remote towns. Welcome to Crook (DL15 8AL), literally on the road to nowhere.

This is a cute pub and we took loads of photos before entering what had been a farm. The landlord had taken over nine years previously and begun work on repairing the 300-year-old pub.

'You know you are getting older when Happy Hour is a nap,' he was fond of saying. He also loved his cars – with model vehicles dominating the décor.

I can highly recommend this pub on many levels – location, interior, exterior, cleanliness and friendliness.

It was also better than Happy Hour for us. The owner refused our request to pay for anything.

This was Lion Number 150.

YORKSHIRE LIONS

Friend fireman Stephen (FMS) had now joined the Quest. It was attracting all sorts of people on the way. He had 16 days' leave, so asked me if I fancied a Red Lion day out.

He had no say, of course, where we were going and had probably never heard of Upper Poppleton (YO26 6PR) until now, but he was intrigued as to what a Red Lion day entailed.

Mapping it out, Upper Poppleton is a great location for York – for the city itself and its Viking museum, for the Dales or for the races.

It was May Day and I remembered I had told myself at New Year that I would have done 200 Lions by May. I was 50 short.

I wasn't the only one with a focus on an obsession. The bar lady, too, had her own passion – making doll's houses to the finest detail. After hearing all about the electrics, the kit, her clients, the costings and curtains, we made our excuses and left for Knapton (YO26 6QG) on the A59.

FMS was loving it, and here was an early introduction to the random characters we would meet. Knapton was picture postcard and run by the chef Annie Prescott who has worked in some of London's finest like Le Gavroche and with names such as Michel Roux. The lunch here was brilliant and we laughed over some of my Red Lion experiences.

From here, we got lost on the 4.5 miles to Haxby (YO32 2HQ). I was eagerly looking out for the pub, passing another called The Tiger before Google indicated that we had missed it.

Turning around, we spotted it through the trees lining the street in their white blossom. Set back from the road, it looked like a village shop.

Perhaps I caught this pub on an odd day or maybe it was always like this, but on the Tuesday afternoon we turned up, it was busy and busy with eccentricity.

One man showed us a picture of his new granddaughter whilst telling us several times how ugly his son was. The latter responded by muttering that his dad was a 'f★★★★★g nutmeg'. FMS knocked his Carling everywhere and the girl behind the bar was hiding chocolate from the cook.

All very odd.

These Lions were close together. York (YO1 9TU) was a mere five miles away.

Alex, the barman, invited me behind to pull a Guinness for a customer while FMS was taking photos, which has to be done! Some of the locals thought I was filming *Undercover Boss* – that was interesting. I hadn't heard that one before.

There is a lot of history in the pub. A recent refurbishment confirmed its age, with the discovery of a baking oven placing it somewhere in the 13th century.

However, it is the highwayman Dick Turpin who places it on the map.

On the run from the authorities, he hid inside a priest hole in the pub's chimneys. He didn't escape for long, though. He is buried just a short distance away, executed in 1739!

En route to our next one I checked the photos to discover that FMS had actually videoed me pouring the Guinness. It was hysterical. He will have to learn how to use my camera properly if he is joining the Quest!

The Red Lion at Wetherby (LS22 6LR) is a warm, local pub smelling good from home-cooked food. It is also a Racing Pub of the Year. I am not sure if that's a title given to pubs near races or who regularly show them. It was a new category on me. A quick game of pool turned into three as FMS unsuccessfully tried to win a game, thinking each of my wins was a fluke. It was rare to be in a pub and behave like you were in a pub since the Quest began.

At Bramham (LS23 6QU) look out for the empty egg boxes behind the bar! The bar staff took orders from the locals who paid, then the egg men came and filled up the boxes. It was good that community life still existed. Six very different Reds conquered made a great day: I didn't think that would be fireman's last!

ISLE OF WIGHT

Paula was back for more Red Lions and it was a 9 am start to get all the way down to Southampton. Would the Isle of Wight entertain her as much County Durham? It is that long old trek from Preston to the bottom of Britain. That meant plenty of stops. It was road trip time. Abingdon (OX14 4JB) in Oxfordshire was open early. The landlord of just six weeks introduced himself as Fudge. I didn't ask why.

'Have you ever been in a Red Lion where there is a league of the game Aunt Sally?' I was asked.

I didn't know even know what it was. Obviously I was excited at any new distinguishing features 13 months into the Quest!

It seems unique to this part of the world. We certainly didn't get it up north. A wooden head sits on a post and each person throws six sticks from a distance to knock the head or the doll off. We tried spectacularly, scoring one out of six. They didn't invite us into the league with that score.

The fact that there was a league was quite mad. This was a good start, though, with Paula seeming to be an omen for extracting the crazy in the Quest.

At Brightwell-cum-Sotwell (OX10 0RT) she summed it up beautifully. We had just driven into 'Midsomer Murders'.

Situated between Didcot and Wallingford, it is a regular in its regional category for Pub of the Year and endorsed by CAMRA, too. But it is the thatched roofs, pillar box and village store that anticipate John Nettles investigating a murder on your approach!

In 2001, 500 years of history went up in smoke when one of the chimneys caught fire, but they have done an amazing job restoring it to close to its original look – 60 firemen saving the timber at the time.

It is a great little pub popular with royals down the years, too.

George III dined there during a stag hunt in 1781. Later, the then Prince of Wales, the uncrowned Edward VIII, also visited when beagling during his student days at Oxford in 1914.

You can tell that this is hunting country.

Passing bright yellow fields of rapeseed, we pulled in at Cholsey (OX10 9LG) just a few miles on.

It looked clinical and long with its great lion statues outside. Inside it comprises four rooms all very quiet at the time. I have since learned that it had a refurbishment in 2014.

Having explained that we had just come from Brightwell-cum-Sotwell, we got chatting about *Midsomer Murders* again. What were the chances of this? Two of the men at the bar had been extras in the programme – one had got told off for looking bored.

We also learned that Agatha Christie was buried just down the lane. She died in 1976. We took a moment to visit her grave. When you think how widely read and watched she was and still is, it was amazing to be sitting in her local.

Lion Number 160 was Blewbury (OX11 9PG). Paula, the good luck charm, spotted this. I hadn't plotted this but the little brown sign pointed us down the lane towards it.

What a discovery – perhaps they like the anonymity. Again another thatched roof, and a big open fire. We were definitely in thatched roof territory.

This was also the second time the Quest has lit up the eyes of the male population – one asking me to repeat that I was visiting hundreds of Red Lion pubs, describing me as his dream woman.

Another said he would contact me on Facebook and I would know who he was! Puzzled, we headed for the Isle of Wight ferry out of Southampton.

Sitting in car lane 8 we had an hour before sail time so rushed up to 55 High Street (SO14 2NS) which was not an easy task for Paula in those heels! It's one of the few Red Lions with its own Wikipedia page and it is understandable why.

Dating back to the 11th century, it claims to have 21 ghosts! All around the pub are armoured coats and weapons and a massive cage housing a parrot called Molly.

This Red has featured on a BBC4 documentary and every Saturday runs ghost tours. The cellar has a bricked-up doorway with 27 miles of tunnels under the city. Wow! Pirates' territory.

Amongst the ghosts, locals will tell you that a barmaid visible from the knees upwards drifts through the bar areas; others will pinpoint the Southampton Plot – a dastardly plan to replace King Henry V with Edmund Mortimer, 5th Earl of March.

The site once housed the courtroom which sent these men down.

What a spine-tingling place but an excellent stop just before crossing the Solent on the Red Funnel ferry named the Red Osprey.

Our next Red Lion was Freshwater (PO40 9BP) the following morning. I had booked a table for 1 pm and that time was enough to drive the 26-mile width of the island, taking in The Needles and Newport.

Located next to All Saints church (mentioned in the Domesday Survey of 1086), it has wisteria running up the walls and a Red Lion on its chimney.

An article about the Quest was on the corkboard already! One gentleman mentioned to me that his son ran a Red in Barton-under-Needwood. I made a note!

The pub serves outstanding food – I had a crab and avocado salad. It was understandable why it was decorated with Egon Ronay awards.

Mike, the landlord of 20 years, refused payment and sent me on my way with a bottle of Red Lion Pale Ale, warning me not to drink it which, by his own admission, had been on his shelf for some time. I had collected another souvenir from this truly wonderful Red Lion.

The next day we returned to the mainland to Bedford Place (SO15 2DB) in Southampton.

Our strategy was to leave the car parked up at the port and take a cab. The driver was under the impression that the pub was no longer a Red Lion, so we went to check anyway. Along the way he pointed out some of the terrific Titanic-related monuments. Some 660 members of the crew were from Southampton.

The taxi driver was mistaken, however. This Lion *did* exist and I learned from the landlord that the Tottenham Red Lion had burnt down. In fact, I later learned how. That was one I would not be visiting.

We hopped back in our taxi and just a ten-minute drive away was Bitterne (SO18 5RT). Raised higher than the street level, this red and cream pub looks fantastic on a sunny day.

We had the meter running so it wasn't our intention to linger – especially when one drunkard at the bar talked me through each of the three names of women tattooed on his arm in between chatting to his imaginary friend, Charles!

We had come a long way on the trip. So why not cram in one more Red Lion on the way home? Cropredy (OX17 1PB) in Oxfordshire was perfect.

Step back in time! Turning into the narrowest street ever, if it wasn't for the few cars in the street it could have been a hundred years ago!

It had seen some interesting times. Originally in 1497, it was the church mortuary. It then became the village gaol. In World War II, it became an overflow hospital. Every four years, villagers re-enact the Battle of Cropredy Bridge from 1644, and every 12 months the folk band Fairport Convention organise The Cropredy Festival. The pub also houses its own Red Lion Music Store where you can buy a pint and play some instruments. What a little gem.

Top 5 Haunted:

Southampton
Whitchurch
Atherstone
Egham
Avebury

BARNES TO BATH

My friend Andrée and her husband Kevin, who is an MP, invited me to the famous Ronnie Scott's jazz club in London. They live only a mile from a Red Lion so before meeting Kevin in the City, Andrée and I first called at Barnes (SW13 9RU), who were already following me on Twitter. Word continued to spread about the Quest.

Those Lions I hadn't yet visited must have wondered when I would. They would soon know as I would always introduce myself once I had bought my drink. There was no element of me going undercover.

The barman asked if I had been to Skipton – how could I forget? That was the pub with the champagne beer! The legend of that pub had clearly travelled.

But this Lion has its own story to tell. Jimi Hendrix wrote 'Purple Haze' here… so the story goes. I don't know if he was a regular or just passing by, but if the former, then surely he penned much more here, too.

Since I visited I also learned that every year they now have a Sausage Roll Off – sort of a live *MasterChef* evening for sausage rolls with former *Celebrity MasterChef* winner Lisa Faulkner actually judging one year! Some entrants came from as far as Devon.

How much variety can there be in a sausage roll? Lots, I would imagine now.

Sitting in its lovely, sunny garden with bubbles on ice was the perfect apéritif leading on to an amazing evening at the jazz club. I stayed over at their house.

Andrée had work early next morning so, with time to kill before meeting up with her at another friend's house, I drove to Wokingham (RG40 1AP) about 30 minutes away.

Authentic and traditional, this pub found its own unusual category to which no other belonged. It was principally a Thai restaurant, though blending into a relaxing place to read the paper in the morning.

FLAMING JUNE

It was June, it was raining – what to do but track down my remaining 'local' Red Lions? I should say at this point that it had been nine days since my previous Lion.

The reason? I had slipped one in in New York. That overseas Red Lion tour was growing roots!!

FMS was keen to try and catch Paula up on her Red Lion visits, and I have to say he almost does at one point. We called in at Denton (M34 6DB). It was a Saturday afternoon and, with no one in or much going on, it was a quickie prior to heading off to Joseph Holt's Manchester Brewery Red Lion at Prestwich (M25 5XX). This pub was filling for the England v Belgium kick-off at 5.15; we had a drink then got home in time for the second half.

Now I was having to go further afield to enter my untamed Red Lions and planning became trickier.

Still, it was time to get back to Yorkshire.

Destination: Heckmondwike (WF16 0HX). FMS was hoping to get into double figures. Parking just underneath the war memorial, I realised I had come unarmed myself. I couldn't be on tour without my camera. We might not be coming back this way so a quick purchase from a second-hand shop and we managed to charge up the battery in here!

The landlord Mark had only been here a few months, and when I asked him about 'The Wike Horse' across the road, he said that pub had been 'The Commercial' the previous week.

I have since learned that there is another new owner at this Red Lion. After a brief closure, it was now in the hands of Nick Kershaw. No – not *that* Nik Kershaw.

At Guiseley (LS20 9BB) I was amused by the hanging baskets with *plastic* flowers in them! The best hanging baskets are those with fresh, fully blooming, colourful flowers in, those with plastic flowers (depending how faded they are) come next, no hanging baskets next, empty hanging baskets next and LAST, worse than anything are hanging baskets with dead plants in. But that's just my opinion. It is first impressions and doesn't cost a fortune or too much time.

The owner pointed me in the direction of Otley (LS21 3HJ) of which I had been unaware nearby. Once again, more plastic flowers in the hanging baskets. It must be a Yorkshire thing.

At Crossgates Lane, Leeds (LS15 7PH), I felt emotions I hadn't had since Bootle. We were genuinely in fear.

The pub had a rough-looking brick exterior. At the entrance a couple of men with tattoos and their Rottweiler dog were smoking as we shuffled past them. It was one of those moments when you knew everyone was watching you. It was late afternoon, very noisy and big, we didn't linger or take photos. Fear meant this was a quick in-and-out visit, although the friendly staff did direct us on to our next Red Lion.

Just five minutes away, we were able to relax at our fifth Lion of the day on York Road, Leeds (LS14 2AD), always able to look back and laugh over some of these characters, who I am not saying weren't friendly, but it just seemed like a place were non-locals wouldn't go.

This was actually an Old Red Lion. I am not sure how old you had to be to embrace that category. Many were very old indeed.

Our final Lion of the day was at Meadow Lane (LS11 5BJ), still in Leeds. Once we had checked into our hotel and had dinner, we flagged a taxi. Our Kashmiri driver was convinced it had closed. This was bad news – taxi drivers know everything.

Thankfully, we spotted it with its lovely Sam Smiths stained glass windows. Sadly, the taxi driver was nearly right. John and Christine, the landlords, had only been in four days, and they really had a job on their hands. A few at the bar recalled how it was once busy and full of character.

Unfortunately, at 10.30 on a Saturday night, it felt like a morgue. Some Reds had been just that. I felt enormous sympathy for the new tenants.

Fireman was happy that he had done 14 now.

THE WEST COUNTRY IN
THE CAMPER VAN

The girl whose wedding we watched over at Knowle will have now been married ten months, if only she knew her influence on the Quest.

It was time to load up the car, pushbikes and all, clock up some miles and some Lions on our way to collect the camper van in Okehampton. This was not ours, you understand, but after a naughty little Red Lion in Puerto Banús (not counted except to say that overseas Lions now totalled three!) we hired a split-screen VW and first stop was Wellsway (BA2 2UA) on a roundabout in Bath... A good place to sit in the beer garden and feel the excitement of the week to come. Then onto a cute, beer-award-winning Lion on the canal at Woolverton on the A36 towards Warminster, with a platter of dips and breadsticks. We had crept a bit closer to destination Devon and only 20 minutes from our hotel for the night. The next few days would be Red Lion mania!

Well, assuming we avoided any unwitting disasters...

Crack.

Half a mile from the Old Mill Hotel at Batheaston, we lost a bike. The bike rack snapped as we drove over a speed bump. My first thought was thank goodness we weren't on the motorway. Second thought was I didn't think it looked like a sturdy bike rack when FSM brought it round; third thought was I was glad I told him to put my bike on first.

A strange but helpful local came over. Fireman was bright red with fury, muttering it wasn't fit for purpose. I said I would wait with the bikes while he drove the car to the hotel, walked back down, and we would cycle up. Off went my car and FMS, then local boy insisted on riding one of the bikes back the 500 metres uphill to the hotel. I agreed, only to realise he was racing me. I changed gear. He was oblivious that he was taking out every car wing mirror en route as he kept glancing over to check he was winning!!! Crazy.

The next morning started badly. Halfords was obviously the first port of call to buy a sturdier bike rack. Our second was Paulton (BS39 7SW). Closed and not counted, but not all terrible, as the builders said it was to reopen soon. I genuinely cared that the Red Lion name lived on.

Next was North Brewham (BA10 0JL) at Bruton. The sign on the door said it should be open. The only sign of life was washing drying in the sun. It should have been open – it wasn't. I won't return. This is a sleeping Lion. FMS was learning what fun and games were to be had Red Lioning!

You can imagine our relief seven miles down the road when we finally found Wincanton (BA9 9LD) open.

I hoped in this part of the world to find character in some of the pubs. This didn't let me down. A local artist had designed the logo and painted it on the inside. Adorning the exterior, a painted milk urn and beer barrel sat on a porch above the door.

This is a very relaxed pub with a deli and café bar within. The owner sent us on our way with staff polo shirts, black with the gold logo on the back.

We had a lot of slow miles ahead of us, mostly on the backroads, and we had to collect the camper van before 5 pm. Slightly late, they were waiting for us. We loaded up, handed over my car keys, and took off in our home for the next five days, dropping in the small village of St Columb Major (TR9 6RH) and today's final Red Lion before camping outside of Newquay at Trebaron campsite.

By the next morning, reality hit. It was not all fun being squashed up in a camper van, but a welcoming burst of sun just told you to get on the bike to Newquay.

Only two obstacles to overcome – fireman's bike had developed an irritating and worrying click that was not there before the speed bump incident, and, of course, Cornwall with its cliffs, can be very hilly and tough cycling in this heat. By the time we reached the Red Lion at Newquay (TR7 1HE) we really were ready for a drink. It was only to open in an hour but for once, we had time on our side over the next few days. It was important to get all the Lions down here done in this one trip, but at least we didn't have to rush back on the M6.

So we decided to come back at midday, opting for a chill on the beach, sun, sea, sand and people-watching. Surfers tackled the waves and families on their summer holidays lapped up the glorious weather. On the slope off the beach and back to the Red Lion there were worrying developments on the bike front. Nuts and bolts were falling off left, right and centre! Things weren't going smoothly. FMS was getting redder. On the Red Lion front, this was what I had come for. It has to have one of the best natural views of any of the Lions. The canal ones were wonderfully therapeutic, but perched high up overlooking the harbour and eyeing miles of beautiful sandy beaches amidst that whole Newquay vibe make this is a special Lion. Inside I asked for two Diet Cokes and a hammer and got exactly that from the helpful staff. The hammer wasn't going to fix the bike, but I remembered passing a bike shop earlier. For £12 we got all fixed up with a new pedal bar!

From here we returned to the campsite and cooled off in the pool, then on to Redruth (TR15 2AE), this time in the VW. It is a busy pub on a quiet, sloping street with a mixture of characters drinking – really drinking. Then on to Penzance (TR18 5JP). We were literally at the end of the line. This Lion is the furthest south and the furthest west, a double Quest landmark.

At Helston (TR13 8TG) I invented a new category of Lion, or at least a variation on a theme. We pulled up just opposite the Humphry Millet Grylls Monument, a rather impressive structure, to see that the pub was shut. After calling up to a first-floor open window, a lady shouted down that we had another half an hour before they opened at 6 pm.

Great – we explored the quiet town until... 6 pm came and went. I knocked, called up but still nothing. And so half an hour later, I renamed this from a sleeping Lion to a lazy Lion.

I shan't be back – you either want business or you don't!

On the other hand, there's the Red Lion at The Square, Mawnan Smith (TR11 5EP). This is a beautiful, white-stoned thatched roof pub on the corner of the village. Its unusual name comes from its history of blacksmiths. Once, there were four in the village as it grew up into a staging post for shipping goods across the Helford River to the Lizard Peninsula.

With the roads so awkwardly connected, you can see the Red Lions here became obvious stop-off points on the long journey to the South-West.

Local photography also identifies the village as playing a key role in D-Day. Many American troops passed through here in 1943 for the dress rehearsal on the invasion at Trebah.

The Red Lion at Truro (TR4 8EU) is not actually the original pub. A lorry driver's brakes failed in 1967, crashing into the old building and leaving it virtually unrepairable, which is a shame because the previous Red Lion which had stood since 1769 was dubbed 'the finest property in Cornwall'. Some 200 years of beauty and history go up in smoke just because of dodgy brakes.

The next day we picked out the Red Lion at Bodmin (PL30 3DN) or is it a Red Lion? I have to smile at this one. The pub was run by an Australian. There was no lion on the outside hanging sign. He had got it changed to a kangaroo! In fact, as we sat out in the sun with coffee and sandwiches, the man at the next table introduced himself as the artist who did it.

If you want real Cornish character, I feel pretty confident recommending Liskeard (LP14 3JL). I can't guarantee you will run into the bunch we did but I would say it's a safe bet. It felt like the kind of pub where the same people had been turning up day after day and you could set your watches by it.

Liskeard is very sleepy. I felt like I was walking into a saloon as the six men at the bar all turned their heads like in some sort of western. This was no place for a Coke or a wine. I ordered a bottle of Bud! Any feeling of intimidation came and went in seconds and soon we were laughing and bantering with them, too – their hats ending up on my head.

One introduced himself as Stumpy. When I asked why, he jumped off his stool and came up to my shoulders.

I don't think any of them owned a comb!

If Plymouth hadn't been calling, I would have stayed all day. Just a great fun pub.

Stonehouse Street was easy enough to find but there *was* no Red. It had become Lord High Admiral. It had changed two years ago. I couldn't count it. It was an ex-Lion.

Skirting Dartmoor on the A38 as the sun beat down we came off before Newton Abbot to the small village at Ashburton, where the same happened. Well, there was a Red Lion but it was padlocked and, according to one local builder, had been ever since he had lived in the village. How long had that been? It was just standing there, asking to be restored and opened up. It looked forgotten.

Perhaps sensing that today was not our day, I rang ahead from Dartmouth before heading off to Dittisham (TQ6 0ES). It's quite a trek off the A3122 and down to the estuary. It's also typical Cornwall. Narrow lanes, only wide enough for one vehicle at a time, and not forgetting we are in a camper van. Second gear all the way, it felt like we were chugging to the end of the world.

Thank goodness it was open, and what a pub and village! Step back in time once again. This time to about 1750! Firstly, the views are stunning. A calm lake scattered with boats, nothing but thatched houses, Paignton twinkling in the distance, and a soundtrack of birds only! It couldn't get more perfect. And I think the community knows it is their little secret.

If you need a bank or hospital quickly, you are in the wrong place, but apart from that who would ever leave?

When we pulled up in the car park, one man approached to see if we were lost. I had got so used to people being aware of the Quest that it had genuinely been some time since anyone was incredulous at the lunacy of it.

The Red Lion is also the Post Office, a tourist shop, the grocer's and the B & B.

Obviously, this is a favourite Lion haven.

We had stopped for the night in Paignton, bringing back all sorts of memories. I had worked here as a waitress/chambermaid when I was 19! I couldn't resist a trip down memory lane. We cycled through the holiday town which seemed a lot bigger and busier than I remember. I tried to track down the hotel I had worked in but, like many of the Lions, it had moved on to a new persona. I was pretty sure I had located the building but alas, it was no longer the 'Harwin Hotel' of my youth!

On to Sidbury (EX10 0XD) and a tiny hamlet off the A380. It is opposite one of the oldest churches and graveyards I have seen, picturesque but closed! I tried the door and waited. Then a little head appeared!

I told Neil about my travels.

'You had better come in then,' he said.

I felt for him. He was quite down about trying to make a living in the trade. The Punch Taverns have a five-year plan to close down 2500 pubs, and are perceived as doing little to help the quiet ones. Plagued by a wet summer and many cancellations for the B & B, Neil was feeling the pinch.

It's a beautiful walking area, too, with stunning countryside. He confessed he did not expect to see out the remaining 18 months of his lease. I felt very sad walking back to the van.

That was July 2012. Two years later, I learned that the village had raised over £100,000 from 150+ investors and attempted to buy the pub from Punch Taverns citing (as I had learned early on in the Quest) the Localism Act which preserves its role in the community and blocks its sale. Unfortunately, they still could not meet the asking price, but a Tom Barrington, who has lived in or around Sidbury for some time, swooped instead to take the pub on.

I don't know what became of Neil.

From here, I thought it was best to keep ringing ahead. Devon seemed to be in its own time zone. Good news! Axminster (EX13 5AU) was open all day.

Lion Number 191 and Axminster, the home of fine carpets! I think they thought we were strange here. I took loads of photos outside. Inside, I noticed the barman looking at me constantly. Then I spotted the CCTV. I am not sure they had heard of the Quest. We cooled off, the temperatures were rising and the camper van was boiling!

The Red Lion at Broadclyst (EX5 3EL) reminded me how many Lions were opposite the church. Where there is a church, there is a pub, and vice versa. This, though, was the first time we had toured the graveyard whilst waiting for the pub to open. It is a popular, lively, traditional pub. It is busy, busy, busy, doing weddings, christenings and various other functions. Still the landlady took the time to chat as we sampled the Devonshire Yellow Hammer.

Very occasionally, there would be days when my Lion visits would, through the random nature of life, find me entangled in someone else's story. If you think about life, that was always going to happen. It was the wedding and the bride which inspired the camper van.

Next, that very same camper van got mistaken at Shobrooke (EX17 1AT). At around half-6, we chugged up to the lovely building to find a gathering of vintage vehicles! They all turned to watch us parking, thinking we were one of them. We weren't!

The landlords were new and working hard: I hope the industry doesn't disappoint them. We wandered around the vintage cars, and here I learned that if a car was older than 25 years no road tax was payable.

As we called briefly at Tedburn St Mary (EX6 6EQ) I was conscious that 200 Lions was on the horizon. I needed a good one to mark the occasion and it would be here in Devon, dead and sleeping Lions aside.

Chulmleigh (EX18 7DD) meant I was now five short. What a time to descend on it. Turning through the windy lanes of the A377, we didn't know we were about to get immersed in Chulmleigh Village Festival WEEK! Can you really make a village festival last a week? Seemingly so. It was bedlam. I expect it takes them longer than a week to recover!

Where do all village festivals end up? In the local. The locals tried to persuade us to stay another night as Friday was the best night! Good heavens – better than tonight? We explained that the camper van had to be returned the next day so had no choice but to decline.

Wonderful wooden décor and stone fireplaces met wobbling farmers with plastic glasses strewn everywhere. We were too late for food. It had been a long, hot day and we were glad of a room tonight!

The Red Lion at Exbourne (EX20 3RY) is a pub with principle. Since I visited it has been named North Devon CAMRA Pub of the Year. It really believes in local. It only serves beer from Devon, Cornwall or Somerset, and supports local suppliers.

Uniquely (well, almost so) it is one of only three pubs in Devon not to serve draught lager. It has no fruit machines or jukeboxes.

For cyclists and walkers, it's a perfectly located pub for the Tarka Trail, a figure of eight route of tunnels and paths around Barnstaple over 180 miles long taken by Tarka the Otter in the book of the same name.

The pubs were getting better and better. As locations go, few will top Clovelly (EX39 5TF). What an exceptional place in a private Devonshire village, so keen on preserving itself that you have to pay to enter the village and cars and bikes have to be parked outside before making the one-mile steep walk down the cobbled path to the harbour village.

And from the Red Lion, you are almost touching the boats in the harbour. Though it wasn't filmed here, it's sort of *Doc Martin* territory.

Apart from its beauty, it's the classic West Country Charles Kingsley novel *Westward Ho!* that puts the pub on the map. The writer spent his childhood in the village.

This Red is in a rare category – pubs you would spend more time outside than in. This wins hands down for its location. It was difficult to leave here tempted by the afternoon tea!

Working our way back, we called at Oakford, Tiverton (EX16 9ES).

All was quiet in this very small village. Then a couple of people came out of the Red Lion to have a smoke. I asked when they opened. It was 45 minutes from now. We were in no rush but I mentioned the Quest.

Then, once again, I walked into other people's dramas. They invited me in, apologising for the chaos. The landlady had given birth just five hours earlier. How unexpected was that? As I ticked off Red Lions and discovered all sorts of stories connected with them, *of course* I would walk into people's current real-life stories. Kindly they gave us a drink and then passed me the baby to hold. How things have changed since the days when it was a standard four days in hospital after giving birth.

Not wishing to outstay our welcome, we thanked them and moved on. What a very special little special moment.

Joy like that floats over you when you get back on the road. It's the beauty of the moment and the randomness of stumbling across it. Of course, the curse of the Lion can always upset the apple cart and lo and behold, it was by stumbling across a man trying to catch a runaway goat I learned that the next Red at Marston Magna was now a house! I couldn't count it, obviously.

This could upset the calculations. Now Babcary (TA11 7DZ) was Number 199. This is in a unique file marked 'Spontaneous'. The bar/restaurant looked so lovely, we decided to book a room there and then. On this Red Lion runabout, there are many spur-of-the-moment choices.

From its leafy exterior to its stone-flagged floors to its gorgeous six rooms, it just oozed quality. The next morning we got the bikes out and cruised the deserted country lanes. Just perfect.

It would have made a great 200th!

That now fell to Arlingham (GL2 7JH) as we began to head back north. Arlingham is a quiet village with the long, white-painted Red Lion set on the right. A ceramic plaque on the wall advertised 'West Country Ales, The Best in the West since 1760'. A cute porch welcomed us: it was empty inside.

It would have made a great 199th!

I since learned that a year after my visit, this was one village which had bought the pub, closing it briefly for refurbishment and reopening in November 2013.

That was interesting because it implies that a pub was on its knees, possibly shunned by the locals, but then deemed so important that the locals rallied together to save it.

It was a bit of a chicken and egg.

And so our West Country tour ended at Powick (WR2 4QT). Oddly, it advertised a bottle of wine and two steaks for £25... including being picked up from the other pub in the village and taken back afterwards. Bizarre. Local rules apply.

It had been a terrific tour in awesome weather, packed with fun and diversity. I had now visited 201 Red Lions.

Top 5 Coastal:

Clovelly
Cromer
St. Margaret's at Cliffe
Swanage
Southwold

NOTTINGHAM NIGHTS

I had waited all of five days after Devon and Cornwall before the bug bit again. From the English Riviera to the one-time crime capital of the UK. I had momentum now, and August 2012 presented the weather and a lot of opportunity to crack on and absorb more British places.

As always, plan for one thing and expect the other – my first at Sandiacre (NG10 5HW) was nearly not to be. The classic dumb blonde diesel/petrol moment had finally happened, and this time not to a dumb blonde.

With Paula in tow, with whom I had shared many of the crazy Lions so far, we got off to the worst possible start, waiting three hours and shelling out £260 for Fuel Fix to drain my car of petrol and set us on our way with the correct diesel. (No pun intended with the 'shelling'… It was a BP garage!)

I can't explain what happened, but it happens to many of us at some point in life, and yes, even men!

Thankfully, Sandiacre in Nottingham was just a mile from the M1 and by the canal, so we didn't add further frustration by getting lost in city centres, and we were able to take the steam off the journey by cooling with a Desperados and a red wine and chatting to Carlo, who you wouldn't know was the landlord and had been on-site only for two months.

I don't know why he felt the need, but he imported his two red lion statues from Portugal! With Red Lions regularly closing down in the UK I am sure he could have encountered some closer to home.

Portugal… my abroad portfolio! I must Google Red Lions on the Algarve.

Eight miles north is Hucknall (NG15 7AX), but first the pub we passed on the way made me think. I wondered just what the story is behind 'The Flying Bedstead'!

It seemed an odd name for a pub. That is another thing I find interesting on this Quest: the history behind the names.

This Lion was an amusing little place, noisy but funny with two sofas, a tiny dance floor and lots of reggae music. The most popular part of the pub was the 'new heated smoking area' out the back. Next to the DJ box were six sweet dispensers. It is not just anywhere you can lean over mid-dance and get 50 pence worth of Minstrels or Dolly Mixtures!

The smoking ban came in on 1 July 2007 in England. Lions were typically traditional working men's pubs. This 'new heated smoking area' obviously was a consequence of supply and demand. The ban is often blamed as a factor in the decline of our British pubs, but on my travels I have learned that many more factors contribute.

We spent the night just near the station at South Clifton (NG23 7AD) and woke to the sound of the trains! Yet our first Lion of the day was not right next door to the railways, as many were, but in the tiniest little village of red-brick barns and gorgeous houses. I didn't really expect this in Nottingham. I thought we were heading to gritty city pubs and expected the odd casualty of a dead Lion or two on the way.

I had always seen it as worrying if I couldn't get an answer when I rang ahead for opening times, but as I drove up to the Red Lion after three calls trying to locate the pub, I realised, too, that it can be a reflection of lifestyle and a pace of life which is largely forgotten.

That also meant you might just find three locals at the bar (more Last of the Summer Winers). Pubs like this have their regulars and their stories and, whilst loyal night after night, you do need more than three people to keep a place going, though, so it was still a worry.

Of course, the characters at the bar more than made up for a large crowd. One character from South Shields, in keeping with Paula's experiences when we went to Blewbury, proposed to me. This was not the first time my Quest had greatly appealed to unmarried men at the bar, branding me as the perfect woman, because my mission was going to pubs!

'My first two wives died of magic mushrooms,' he began seriously. 'The third died of a broken neck.'

Naturally, I worried about my fate of being next.

'What happened with the broken neck?' I asked, on the edge of my seat.

'She wouldn't eat the mushrooms,' he replied.

And we all fell off our stools laughing.

I realise his two friends would have heard this joke night after night but every pub had its entertainer, and it was always a bonus that the Quest broke the ice to find them.

Explaining my Red Lion journey, he went on to explain that the pub name 'The Duke of Cumberland' originates from the Duke giving everyone in his regiment on retirement sufficient funds to buy a public house, and they were told to name it after him. This was not the only time I had heard similar. You could summarise a lot of the origin of the Red Lion as 'an old coaching house, near a railway or a church or funded as a reward for fighting in the war'.

Those reasons alone would tell any historian (which is not me, by the way) that these were great places to unravel the growth of modern Britain, and of course that continues today as the working man can't afford the pub and the recession alerts us to the possible extinction of our pub, our history, our community.

As an example, on the wall hung a very simple book called *The Pig Club*. In 1935, those people in the village who had a pig could pay 6p into the insurance fund so that if it died, they would be fed meat from everyone else's pig. The community is a necessity. I hadn't heard of the pig club before today.

On the same wall was a photo from 1947 when heavy rain caused the water level to go as high as the front window of the pub. Imagine the lock-in!

These pubs really were narrators of our time, and a great place for the anecdotal. The Irish chap at the bar told me of a book called *Motorhome Stopovers*, which listed all the pubs you could stay with a caravan for free as long as you spent some change at the bar. I was enlightened once more and I guess so are many of you. What a little find.

Each Lion is an individual. The trail is never dull. The next at Walesby (NG22 9NU) was closed: when was it going to open? *Was* it going to open?

Not one to mope around wondering, I took action. Less than ten minutes down windy, quiet lanes we found Wellow (NG22 0EG), set back and raised on the edge of Sherwood Forest, but most importantly home to the most delicious home-made chips I have had in years.

I have deliberately avoided overcommenting on the food on the Quest, unless unique or exceptional. Other books do this but the fact that I rarely use the phrase 'home-made' is possibly an indicator as to the amount of pre-made food being served in pubs. When you smell it and it really tastes good, it is twice as good for that reason.

The pub is long with a small bar at the entrance, a middle room and a third for dining, and sells beer, locally made at Marple called Old Lion Ale. So much character has gone out of the trade and it can sometimes be hard to find pubs serving locally sourced produce but I always appreciate it when I do, again keeping the community strong.

When I arrive unannounced at a Red Lion to find they had already pinned up cuttings of me from the papers, it made me smile. It is not an ego thing. It just told me that people were spreading the word about my quirky mission, which is good for the industry and very encouraging for me. There I was. I had been on the board for the last six months in *The Sun* newspaper.

We went back to Walesby. The staff at Wellow had said it opens at 3.00, or maybe 4.00! I am glad we did. It was a friendly local with plenty more unknown Lions cropping up in conversation. A little game of darts was our entertainment here.

Next, a Red Lion dilemma. We travelled down the A616, turning into the village of Farnsfield (NG22 8EY) looking for Main Street and spotted The Lion.

'Was this the *Red* Lion?' I asked the chef.

'Until about a year ago,' he replied.

What to do? It was now simply The Lion. Do I include it and how many more times would I have to look at my own rules before rewriting new ones?!

Inside it was alive but it had lost its colour somewhat – perhaps this was the first I had called out loud as an 'Off Colour Lion'.

The front of the bar was quirky – a collection of half-doors painted red with knockers and numbers on, some upside down.

The landlord John Bob sat with us to explain quite simply that he had taken it on a year before and it was run-down with a bad reputation. He was now concentrating on top of the range and had lost the 'red' to rebrand it and shed its former image.

Perhaps out of compassion, or because it was still registered as a Red Lion, I decided to include it – but mostly because the bar lady was called Louise Cheese!

A couple we met in the car park had run one of only two Yellow Lions. So many Lions and so many colours!

Sometimes on the Quest we would look at each other as if to say, 'Shall we do one more tonight?' and Nottingham's one for the road became Underwood (NG16 5HD), some 20 minutes on from Farnsfield.

A hive of activity on the inside, a beautiful country pub on the outside with ivy overhanging The Red Lion sign, this is a perfect spot to end the day.

The next day was 5 August 2012 and after a quick run and checking out of The Jury which was now full of hung-over stag and hen parties, I discovered my first parking ticket. It had to happen!

Nottingham's Alfreton Road (NG7 3JE) Red Lion has been replaced with something called The Organ Grinder. An ex-Lion, though thankfully still a pub.

Unfazed, we went to Heanor (DE75 7QG). It was now a Wetherspoons. You always knew what you were going to get in a Wetherspoons – a few serious drinkers (even at 1 pm on a Sunday), some family and a scattering of older folk often sitting by themselves. It had reopened in 1998 after being closed for several years. At least it was back on its feet and hadn't lost its identity.

Ripley (DE5 3BR) was the same – another Wetherspoons. This was somewhat creepy. As usual we took our photos outside. But when we entered we were called over and asked to explain why. From time to time we had met this and there was normally a reason – it is not unheard-of for pub landlords to put the building on the market without even telling the licensee. After learning this I started taking my photos after we had been inside, unless the sun was disappearing, as twilight isn't great for the camera. This time it seemed to be the memory of the pub being burnt down that caused their concern.

Once a thatched building, it was now basic brick after the rebuild. I had seen this a few times – especially with thatched Reds. Sometimes they had been built identical to the original one, but there must be a cost issue.

There was no reason to assume that me taking a photo would mean arson would follow. Though I discovered later that was exactly what happened, as a lady in her twenties with learning difficulties had set fire to this Lion and a nearby cinema – in the case of the Lion causing 40 or so people to be evacuated after lighting a nappy dispenser in the Ladies.

Once we had cleared this up, on the advice of the bar staff, pointing out of the window and over the hill, our last Red Lion became Fritchley (DE56 2FT). Friendly staff were once again coming up trumps. It wasn't on my list for this weekend as it is Derbyshire.

Just off the A38, this turned out to be a special surprise, though it looked closed. The noise from the back told us otherwise, with everyone gathering on the patio.

Greene King had named it 'Best Pub in Britain' – and nobody was in it. They were all outside, and why not on a bright sunny day? The landlord, though, was rightly proud. It is some achievement, whether you disagree with the vote or not. Never mind 600 or so Lions, I believe there are around 50,000 pubs full stop, in the UK.

And with that glow of achievement, we were given the key to its little gem of a stable bar to let us have a look around. It was stunning, almost like a museum that you could live and breathe in real time. Real ale and cider are served next to the horse trough, with its cobbled floor and gulley for horse sewage to drain away. Its old, stone walls were covered with antiquated farming tools, and the wood-burner would warm the den in winter.

And the pride and sense of history were genuine – the landlord showing us the pictures on his phone of when he turned up one day on his carthorse.

What a find, and we were so close to not dropping into this special piece of old Derbyshire. Discovering secrets was a very special part of the Quest. And somehow my friend Paula had now clocked up 26 Red Lions!

RETURN TO DERBYSHIRE

Since moving out of Alan's we remained in contact. He must have missed being on the Red Lion trail, so he suggested a 'railway' visit taking in a few more Reds. We got the train to Wirksworth, Derbyshire, but we had already visited here earlier on. Some Lions that we had visited had had second chances; others I wanted to go back to for pleasure 'in my own time', post-Quest. It followed, I suppose, that if I hadn't quite finished a region and had to revisit that we might go back over old ground.

One of the benefits of this, of course, would be that early Lions might not have got to grips with the size of the job at the time, but a year on perhaps would be pleased to see us and offer us more anecdotes and experiences once they had seen retrospectively where this was all going.

Of course, anything could also happen in between visits from having caught the place on an off day first time around to the dreaded 'dead Lion' tag.

On that visit this was where we learned of the now legendary unfortunate low archway accidental beheadings.

Wirksworth was still very much alive and kicking.

So our first new territory became Hollington (DE6 3AG) in Ashbourne. Despite the distraction of a lost wallet – and believe me a minor personal disaster can really alter the path of the Quest – we blatantly defied the sat nav, taking all the tiny lanes here. It was barely a village, surrounded by combine harvesters and tractors!

Just 15 minutes outside of Derby, it is nice and cosy inside with a log fire and a blackboard menu. There's something nice and new about a blackboard menu over the printed laminate ones at the bar. Even if that blackboard menu never changes, you can believe that somebody wrote it up fresh every day and that removes the microwave pre-packed thought about pub food. More should do it!

Cutting across Belper, we arrived at Alfreton (DE55 6BB) – a grey stone Red Lion and perfect pit stop for… the pits.

This is old mining territory. These days it is a favourite with the ramblers. Essentially, 'The Five Pits Trail' runs for just over five miles and is a relatively new thing dating back to 1989, following the route of the former Great Central Railway which served the five main coal mines in the vicinity. Some of the trail has been named 'Tom Hulatt Mile' which commemorates local runner Tom Hulatt who took part in the first four-minute mile, even though most people only recall Sirs Roger Bannister and Chris Chataway.

The interesting little difference between Tom and his more famous peers is that he worked at Williamthorpe Colliery and used to run the five miles there and back each day. It's a real untold story and very much of another era. He also worked as a rat-catcher! I would never know detail like that without the Quest.

Next today I will remember the Red at Aston (S26 1DJ) at Todwick, partly for its extreme busyness, but mostly for advertising Christmas on 12 August.

En route to Catcliffe (S60 5SR) we passed the disused pit of Aughton where the main miners' strike took place in 1984. Grim times and the pub still looked it a bit. Communities were decimated back then. Not just employment but village spirit went, too. Some places had changed their identity and got back on their feet, others felt like it was just yesterday. Like this one.

At the heart of the Lion now where once many pitmen would have drunk their wages away was the Angling Club with 32 members – again a marker as to how much sport or social activity had been formed at the pub over the years. Alan had his Red Lion and railway fix, and my total was now 215 and about one-third of the way in.

★★★

A fortnight passed before my next outing. It was August Bank Holiday weekend and that feeling that the long nights had already begun to slip away meant I should push on.

I arrived at the Haven Campsite in Pwllheli near the Red Lion at Porthmadog (LL49 9ED) just five minutes before the 3 pm Wednesday afternoon wrestling match in the clubhouse!

I was to stay just one night with Amanda, Kim and their two boys, and after the wrestling experience I was ready for the half-hour drive with roof down to the Red Lion, though only nine miles in reality. I remember this pub for its quietness. Only the sound of pool balls dropping broke the silence. Just two men were sitting silently drinking their pints.

Typical August Bank Holiday weekend… I awoke the next morning to grim, rainy, chilly weather, having fallen out of a tiny, smaller than single, bed in the night.

I left them to enjoy the last day of the holiday and set off home via the small village of Llanrwst (LL26 0LL) and parked up across from a cream and blue-coloured Red Lion.

I rarely visit the Lions on my own, though I enjoy it when I do. It normally attracts the odd look or two. Not here, though, where the pub had already attracted the odd one or two itself – a loner at the bar reading his paper was fair enough, but the only other customer was playing pool by himself and singing every song on the jukebox at the top of his voice! He seemed happy in himself, but I question what kind of happiness?! I asked of Tyn-y-Groes (LL32 8TJ), saying I had rung several times and was too close not to visit, but alas, it had closed last year and was now up for sale.

I didn't need to go there, pushing on instead to St Asaph (LL17 0RY).

I had no phone number for this Lion but, at literally a minute from the A55, I had to investigate. Nobody had tipped me off that it was no more, so I took my chances.

Mmm. Driving around the town, I saw no pub or any evidence of one. This can't be right. How did I have it on my list? Not only did it exist – once or now – but there wasn't even evidence of this dead Lion anywhere so I stopped to ask a man walking down the road.

'You'll not get a drink in there,' he warned me. 'It was a great little pub and used to be my local with a large Lion at the front until some wallies [his term] took it over and ruined it.'

He said he would give me a drink at his house if I was thirsty!

He kindly pointed me in the direction of the site of this former Lion. There was barely a clue there, and I took photos to make the point.

It was now a private house.

KELLINGTON AND BEYOND

Red Lion Number 218 loomed at Kellington (DN14 0NX). The previous two counted for nothing.

This was a one-off Lion equidistant from Selby and Pontefract, and prompted by something other than the Quest – well, almost!

I had bought a mirror on Ebay for my very own Red Lion bar. Yes, the garage was taking shape and all the trophies I had picked up along the trail were going in. I had morphed into what I had been pursuing. This was never my intention, just a consequence of it.

It was almost incidental, though somewhat inevitable, that we called in at a Red Lion whilst collecting the mirror, but, having been this way before, there were few left to visit. It was the first time I had seen the Robin Hood cooling towers on the way.

The landlord was an ex-miner who had got back on his feet through the trade.

This, though, was a relatively new Red Lion.

Once six terraced cottages, it made a long pub. It only came on the scene in the 1940s. To be honest, this lands itself in a small category, most having a few hundred years' head start on it.

With the change of the seasons, the count had slowed. I had pencilled in the weekend of 21/22 September for ten more Lions. Good old Travelzoo and deal finder Paula, we would start at Ellesmere (SY12 0HD) in Shropshire.

I also had a couple of interviews lined up. Good news – when I rang Ellesmere, Mike the landlord knew of the Quest but also fell into a rare island of 'mutual acquaintances'. It turns out that he had run The Anderton Arms in Preston for six years where he and Paula shared a friend! Coincidence was a natural theme. People will always talk in pubs. It was only a matter of time before I, or we, ran into someone else from the past.

As colourful hanging baskets go, this ranks Number 1 out of the previous 219 pubs. Out the back, its lovely patio was also painted with a beach scene – summer all year round and a persona to reflect its owners.

At Oswestry (SY11 1PZ) we missed the reporter from the *Shropshire Star* by two minutes, having fallen foul of an evil little one-way system! The town is the largest market town in Shropshire and straddles the England-Wales border. The pub stands in the far corner of the square next to an indoor market and facing a beautiful old building which is now a playhouse.

It's a very pleasant pub but short of clientele. The reporter must have thought I wasn't coming so I called her and we rearranged to meet at the next RL.

Now, as we headed to Bomere Heath (SY4 3DP), she was already ahead of me. Faith had rung forward to check the pub was open but found it would be by 4.30 pm. Not many pubs opened at that hour these days, and equally it would be slightly embarrassing if the press were waiting for me yet there was no reason to do so.

No need for concern, when we arrived at 4.05, it was open and Faith was already sitting there with a drink. Sparky, the landlord of three years, had opened early for us. I think Faith may have had a word. It was her local!

It turns out Sparky was really named Tony. Although I had experienced this before, here cemented another new category… Landlords who go under a pseudonym.

I don't know if it was easier for the locals, if it suited the language of banter, or if publicans just had something they didn't want to put out there, which meant a nickname was always better.

One very nice touch was that, every Friday, Tony/Sparky would put out bread and cheese, presumably as reward for completing the week! What a good idea, I very much rated it. I felt it would make you more inclined to pop in for one at the end of a hard few days, and also there very few occasions when you got something for free. I can see continental pubs or restaurants offering you a plate of olives while you order, but at home the tab would always be up and running. It was simple but left a feeling of goodwill.

Faith was keen to get back and edit the interview as it was going straight onto the BBC's after 5 show. Just after she left I received a call from the *Shropshire Star* asking whether I could be at Battlefield in 20 minutes. Sparky said it wasn't too far, so the trail continued to Shrewsbury (SY1 4AB).

As we pulled into the car park, the photographer was eagerly waiting and in a hurry, ushering us in and getting Paula to help rearrange the blackboard at the front, stage-managing the raising of my half-bitter shandy in the air, taking umpteen photos, making sure my eyes were in the correct place, as Paula stood behind her also taking photos. It was all over in ten minutes. She rushed off, telling us it would be in the *Shropshire Star* tomorrow!

With the tight schedule finally over we sat listening to Faith's interview in the car park at Battlefield, cringing at our voices. I say the most stupid things on the spur of the moment (I guess you could liken this to when I said 'Do you think anyone is visiting all the Red Lions?') and Paula, after calling me 'bonkers', didn't stop for breath for a very long time. She had been roped in, too.

One-time onlooker and now clocking up the Lions like there was no tomorrow, she was doing media, too, and with that the acknowledgement that the Red at Battlefield becomes the place where I had not manipulated the story but where the story overtook my passion.

We needed a peaceful Red Lion to end the day and thank goodness for Longden (SY5 8AE).

I think it is important to say the sun was setting when we arrived. Of course, you could be reading this anywhere in the world or turn up at this pub in a gale or a heatwave, but I mention it because you can probably picture it through my words if I add the sun-setting comment.

We drove along country lanes alongside farmland and some beautiful, grand houses, some half an hour on arriving at the only pub in the village of Longden Common. It was one of those country meanders where you are leisurely chasing the sun, going nowhere fast but very conscious that it is about to go, hanging onto every view and last drip of warmth before it goes for the night and with it the illumination of the gorgeous countryside.

Of course, there is no point in such anticipation if there is no pay-off when you get there, so to walk into the back garden of hens, geese and ducks, plus the horses in the field, which the landlord said we could ride, just completed the scene.

How many pubs do you turn up at when the owner says 'Have a ride, then come for a drink?!'

When everything came together and this treasure is the last pub of the day, there is a huge feeling of satisfaction at the bar when you sip your celebratory drink, and also given that, for parts of today and previously, the Quest was sort of becoming a job, it's the last drink of the day where you remember, too, that it's at the pub where most people go to relax, wind down and share their day.

Inside Longden Common's Red Lion, you will find a welcoming crowd with their own little quirks.

Did we know Sparky put out bread and cheese every Friday? We did! But we were not aware that he got really annoyed that one couple only came in every Friday for the bread and cheese, bought a half each, filled up on the mini-feast and then left? Lots of question and invitations… Could we come back for next week's farmers' market?

The honest answer to that was that it looked like Paula would still be there, unable to be prised from her seat. But no, we couldn't: I still had a lot more Lions to do!

Awakening to a clear, sunny day we took in a stroll along the river watching boat racers in training before Lion time. And on we went.

Red Lion Number 224 was Wrockwardine Wood (TF2 6LA). It was as hard to find on the sat nav as it was to say or spell, circumnavigating the little town for ages before stumbling across it at the end of a cul-de-sac. Are there many pubs in a cul-de-sac?

At 1 pm it was empty, but a little buffet was set up for a first birthday party, and Sandra the landlord came down to say hello. Perhaps more interesting was her 17-year-old son who told us all his girl troubles. New category alert! Teenage sons starting to form a love life whilst still living in the pub…!

Then I spotted it at the bar. The Quest is fun. It has never stopped being that. Every pub – quiet or busy, historical or dead – I learn something, but what I hadn't budgeted for was the attention it had brought. I had got used to the interviews and photos, but I hadn't become accustomed to how cringeworthy I always felt reading or hearing them back. I picked up the *Shropshire Star* and found myself beaming back at me!

The next town was heaving with police for the big – ahem – match between Telford and Newport but, despite the obvious lure of fans to a pub, we couldn't find it. It was as though someone was hiding all the Red Lions in this area!

Equally, as some publicans lose faith with the trade, many don't give up on the connection with the people. So, when Julian at Wellington (TF1 2EW) directed me in on the phone, it really was no surprise to find him on the car park looking out for me. The Quest had this effect on people. It didn't matter if I was in the *Shropshire Star* or on the BBC, it had often felt that, when I turned up and they knew it was me, they felt special and proud to show off their Red Lion. It was *their* bit of media. It was an acknowledgement of worth to them on a very friendly, non-competitive basis. And you can judge this, too, in the amount of time the landlords had to give to you. It was never a sell or a job. It was always pride, history and honesty, with their own personal life story thrown in. For me, and perhaps for them, it was the best social network/ history lesson going. That is not to say that occasionally landlords aren't indifferent to my presence and even offhand and protective, as if I was there to put a curse on it or something.

Outside the pub there was a sign saying 'Table-Top Sale 11 am–1 pm'. It was over. I was gutted.

'I could have done with that for the garage bar I'm building,' I told Julian. He looked at me like I was mad.

'I have got the base of two tables,' I continued, 'and just need the tops.' Now Paula looked at me like I was mad.

'We don't sell table tops,' he confirmed. 'What did you think, that we were having the table leg sale next week!!!!!'

I know now that a table-top sale is a collection of items that people no longer want, displayed on a table!

Julian had two big Lions for his pub which he bought from another Red Lion which had closed down, much closer than Portugal, I may add.

Chatting so much, we had left it too late to make the Red Lion at Sutton, which for once I *knew* had a 3 pm closure and which meant we would have to return. No bad thing.

Instead, we hit the A41 and dropped in at the very nice Red at Marchwiel (LL13 0PH) for two waters, and without lingering we next tried to find Coedpoeth (LL11 3LP). The more I came to Wales, the more convinced I was that it was not ready for sat nav, even after the sat nav boom. In the end, we flagged a passer-by down who told us to follow him until Morrisons! It was decent that people were still happy to do this.

We pulled up alongside him at the lights and he pointed us in the way of the Red Lion where he had played darts for so many years.

What a contrast to our last Lion. Busy, definitely, but somewhat old-school with a family half and a man's half. You didn't see too much of this these days. Some locals advised us to hang around as there was a band on, but I sensed it would get rather messy and after the barman messaged another Red just literally two minutes away to find out whether she was open, we decided to make tracks.

Nowadays, you wouldn't find two pubs opening up with the same name within two minutes of each other. I can, though, understand that back in the day a pub was a pub and they probably didn't evaluate brand values like people do now, and if there were two Red Lions within two minutes of each other, it probably just seemed as though there were two pubs close by and no more. There wasn't a website to back them or identify them.

The barman also told us there hadn't been a darts team for four years. Time flies and it passes us all by. It clearly had been a long time since our friendly helper had been in the pub and, for some reason, he hadn't been back!

We finished this little trip just down the road at Talwrn (LL11 3PG) – after the very steep slope up to it, locals referred to it as 'The High Lion'!

But when you get there, the welcome is immediate and sincere – everybody saying hello from all directions and it wasn't because they knew I was coming. It just felt like that kind of place. Perhaps, too, if you have to climb a hill to get there, you've passed a test already.

They loved the Quest and were delighted to be part of the photos… That is when they could tear themselves away from the horse racing on the box and a little local betting thing they had going, explaining the scattering of yellow slips all over the place!

Janet had run this little gem in the tiniest bit of Wales for 18 years with the help of her daughter. She tried to buy us another drink and they individually bid us well on our departure. I can imagine they all went home that night and told tales of this madwoman, shaking their heads in disbelief.

The weekend ended on a high and, moreover, Paula had unknowingly notched up 36 Lions. Not bad for someone who just came along for a ride out one weekend.

THE LIONS OF LEICESTER

Three weeks later Paula was back for more! She was either very loyal, bored or hugely intrigued. Sometimes you were too far in to withdraw. She was going strong and so was I. After the break the impulse was on and Leicester's 15 Lions this weekend seemed more than possible. Our first was Lutterworth (LE17 5LT) some two hours from home.

Over hummus, olives and a lime and soda the bar lady flagged up Burbage, already an additional one not on my list. She gave me the address but first we called at Barwell (LE9 8DX) as this one closes at 2.30. With just two drinkers at the bar, the pub seemed old-fashioned and dated, and the barman appeared to be dressed like Manuel from *Fawlty Towers*.

Though he wasn't from Barcelona, had no rat and was very friendly.

At Hinckley (LE10 2EF) we laughed about the previous and its chipped Formica hatch amongst other things. It was stuck in time. Hinckley was lovely. I can highly recommend a sunny bay window and home-made ginger cupcake.

Just 3.7 miles away was Sapcote (LE9 4FG). It looked empty. It seemed dead. Were those prices for real on the blackboard outside? Starters and sweets were £1 each, mains were £4. It seemed too good to be true.

I got my pound out!

'It's only Tuesdays and Thursdays,' said the shy bar girl.

In some ways I was relieved. I had never seen prices this cheap. I envisaged the worst! Was this the reason no one else was in? Was this place full to overflowing on a Tuesday and Thursday? I should go back one day to find out. Amused by the skittle table, we clicked on the camera. Was this to be a new category? – Least Eventful Red Lion Day EVER!

That notion was halted, thank goodness, at our next Red, Huncote (LE9 3AU) – a great little Lion run by Georgina and her husband for 11 years, which, given much of what I had seen, was a decent innings in the current climate.

It resonated, too, because when a landlord takes the time to show you round every single room, you know how much heart and soul they put into it and their pride will outlive your visit.

They had reason, too. They had just won 'Beer Garden of the Year' and were waiting on their trophy! If you thought about it the same way I had on the Quest, the Beer Awards could literally run into hundreds of categories and this would be one of the better ones.

Only four miles away is the Red at Earl Shilton (LE9 7LQ), a village famous for, amongst other things, its shoewear, with exports as far as the Russian Army. You have to ask how a small community in Leicestershire were involved in Communism!

It was Saturday 5 pm and the pub was busy mainly with men warming up for the evening. As I popped into the next room to take a photo of the darts board, they all asked why.

This isn't just any old bullseye, it is a 'Red Lion Earl Shilton' customised dartboard! It opened the dialogue, though. One of the locals had read about me in the *Metro,* another had heard it on the radio; then I was asked for my autograph.

I really wasn't that famous. I was just visiting pubs. Red Lion pubs. Once on the train to London – yes, Red Lioning – I managed to find 68 words out of the words 'RED LION'. Obsessive, I know, but no claim to fame.

'Fame' one minute, hazardous roads the next!

At Desford, just four miles on, we found a very deep ford – in theory a great approach to a Red Lion. Paula already had her seat belt off and hands on the door handle just in case I attempted it, but my motoring past told me otherwise!

When I diverted off every possible turn off from the roundabout, I finally found the RL.

Then that sinking feeling.

Boarded up with not so much as a 'Business To Let' sign, it was Leicestershire's first dead Lion. All things considered, that wasn't too bad a record. We gained one, we lost one.

Finally we called into Rothley (LE7 7NJ) with its two small rooms and carvery, then called it a night.

The next day, Leicester had a busy air about it for a Sunday. You could wander into a city centre oblivious to its own agenda. Today happened to be the Leicester Marathon. Having run four half-marathons myself, I always feel the anticipation knowing how much training they have all put in. Each time I finish a half-marathon I think I would want to do it all again without stopping. No, so every credit to every participant! We left the runners behind en route to Sibbertoft (LE16 9UD).

This is a quality pub, renovated in 2004 with a compact and interesting inside and extensive wine selection. When I compare this to some Lions who didn't have much clue or desire, this stood doubly for not wanting for detail.

The owners had been in close to a decade and you can see that attention in the fact that the ingredients are locally sourced for a menu that changes monthly. Of course it's a lot easier to churn the same stuff out night after night, but the easy option doesn't get you far.

Andrew, the landlord, says nothing gets on the wine list or menu without him sampling first, which is great. The fact that he needs to point that out reflects on other pubs' standards. It should be the norm that people running pubs have the passion or the professionalism to do so, shouldn't it? Surprisingly, or should I say shockingly, it isn't! It naturally had been Red Lion Wine Pub of the Year.

There is little nearby. We're really out in the shires, but that's a plus point. There were three other Lions vaguely nearby which I hadn't been aware of. It was often the case that I had missed the odd one, but three?

It was time to explore.

It seemed we were now in big game of tag. Andrew had pointed us towards Thornby (NN6 8SJ), with its walls decorated with photos of the village from the 1900s, and from here, the owner told us to say hi to Nick at East Haddon (NN6 8BU). I could see why when we got there. At eight miles away, there was barely a house en route!

Once again I had been deceived! Paula agreed that this was possibly the grandest Red Lion yet – packed with people who had come from… Well, I don't know where!

It looked great for a wedding reception and has beautifully named rooms from The Pigeon Loft to Cherry Blossom, from Four Lions to Mail Coach. I have taken you through enough Red Lions by now for you to understand that nod and a wink to its history in the naming of the rooms. I guess the Mail Coach means this once was the Post Office.

I was afraid I wouldn't get Paula off the luxurious sofa by the fireplace. Paula likes an open fire.

And yes, I said hi to Nick!

We stopped for a quick drink at Brixworth (NN6 9BX) – a strange, big, old pub with an odd atmosphere, and if I said to you pool, darts and skittles and loud Abba music you would get the picture.

I had to meet Matt from BBC Radio Leicester at Great Bowden (LE16 7HB). Sure enough, this Lion was the total opposite of the previous.

You just never know what you are going to get every time you turn up, and whatever you may have read when Googling, you can never know what you will feel as you walk through the doors.

This is a great little pub that makes its own bread and ice cream on-site. A good indicator, too, of its warmth and quality is that some who had run the Leicester Marathon had chosen here to replenish after the gruelling 26 miles, and after something like that, you are only to go to a pub that you know and trust, aren't you? I felt their sense of achievement. Matt was easygoing; the interview was relaxed.

Our last Red Lion of the day was at Welham (LE16 7UJ). It is always a bonus to end on a good one and this is a cracker. From the outside it looks a typical Red Lion if there is a typical Lion. What I mean by that is no ivy, the big Lion hanging in the wind, and no clues as to what might be inside.

However, the slightly dated cream of the exterior does not match the beautiful wood of the interior. It feels clean, historic but chic, too, and that is a fine line to walk between being contemporary but serving up the past.

And it is in the middle of nowhere. Perhaps, the locals are used to it and take it for granted, but I fell in love with its thatched *bar* (!), comfy sofas and fires.

New category alert – a thatched *bar.* It had the wow factor. And as I contemplated across the fields the journey back to Preston, I realised how much Leicestershire had surprised me. I hadn't expected such affluence and such friendliness. I think I had seen the Leicester rather than the shire. The good news was that I hadn't done them all, so we would be back.

THE BIRMINGHAM SIX

It was now 20 October 2012. I had nothing on, so, with FMS driving off, we went to tackle West Midlands Lions. First stop was to be Hockley (B18 6NG), passing a Brown Lion on approach and a pub named The Actress and Bishop.

This Red has no other category. And I am not talking about discovering a pub with a murder, a conception, a playwright, or indeed a thatched bar.

This is now the UAB: Urban Art Bar. My previous Lion met contemporary and traditional halfway. *This* was a Lion that had ripped up the non-existent Lion rule book and gone Banksy.

Birmingham, or dare I say it 'inner city', seemed a good place to try this concept I knew nothing of. And whilst a UAB and Banksy might all sound a bit 'street', the pub also had wine-tasting groups, a Monday 'Cow Club' and jazz nights. It really is a different pub and you can only wish it well – something for everyone without that meaning bland compromise. Hats off to it!

'Welcome to Kings Heath' (BL14 7LY), said the sign accompanied by a massive gold crown around a tree at its entrance.

This building has to be the grandest yet… East Haddon just six days ago is still the grand establishment I described, though this architecture really is fit for a king! Steady British food is what Ember Inns are about, and as the sun shone through the window we relaxed until 3.30 with my favourite tipple and half an ale.

And from the highs to the lows.

Acocks Green (B27 6RA) was closed. I suspected this when I called. It looked like it had been a working men's club. It was no more. A dead Lion.

Next, Shirley! This Lion is at 171 Stratford Road. I don't always give the street names. It gets a mention as we joined it at Number 2205. It is a very long road.

Of course, we had already missed the pub once.

It is a unique one, this – with a Red Lion Folk Club and a Songwriters Circle visiting. It made sense. Drink and music went together. Folk was slightly old-school but this was rather cute and fitted with the traditional feel of the pub. That said, we stood watching the end of West Brom v Man City with the landlord, which disappointingly for him ended 1-2. I had seen live music in previous Lions, but they were essentially visiting acts rather than something that grew from within. I liked it.

A little over three miles away is Earlswood (B84 6AQ) – a vintage inn down a country lane, fenced in with a big beer garden at the front.

A couple of centuries ago you would know this pub for offering 'pony and traps to hire along with good stabling'. Today, you would simply say 'oozes rural charm'.

Ah next, a real gem and another category. The Red Lion at Alvechurch (B48 7LG) is on Red Lion Street!!!

I loved it.

What came first: the pub or the street? Presumably the street came as the pub was being built and the name followed. I am guessing. I don't know when Britain started having street names.

The pub *had* been a row of cottages. Before a police station existed locally, the local landowners used to meet here regularly to discuss thieves and trespassers.

I had become used to seeing churches next to Red Lions and did wonder which came first, the pub or the church, but I now believe always the church, as often the pub was originally built to house the materials and/ or builders when the church was under construction. Times had moved on. A group of wealthy individuals could haggle out justice from the comfort of the pub in the past. Now we would probably call them vigilantes.

Whilst one unexpected theme of the Quest had been the number of times a landlord had flagged up an unknown down the road, it was rare that I would have to wait some time before cashing in that info.

The Red at West Bromwich (B71 1RH) Tandoori and Balti House was the one alerted to me by the Punjabi landlord at Cyffylliog some time ago!

I had actually passed here last year but not mentioned it, as it wasn't open! I also wanted to return when I was hungry, and this had been whetting my appetite for a year.

As we entered we were overwhelmed with The Pogues blasting out in the front bar. Some wobbly, rowdy people were a sign that the beer was good. But where was the food? Through an opening behind the bar I spotted it: we walked round to the back of the pub into the large, noisy, canteen-type room, and the SMELL...

The time had come to order. Chicken bhuna, chilli mushrooms and garlic naan came in at £12. The Asians certainly did not disappoint: the queue for tables was growing, and it seemed everyone around loved this place. The recommendation was worth the wait. It's an amazing place and well worth the visit. A perfect end to the Birmingham Six.

Top 5 Buildings:

Kings Heath
Eaton
Parliament Street
York
Cromer

NOVEMBER IN COVENTRY

Aspatria, Wigton (CA7 3HQ) – what else was there to do on a clear, bright winter's day? Why not go for a drink? 115 miles actually to this solitary Red Lion! FMS just loved Red Lioning, so it wasn't a chore.

I made the mistake of going to Wigton first to find a 'Lion Hotel': surely this one hadn't lost its colour! A quick phone call to the Red Lion informed us it was eight miles west of Aspatria.

Only three people were in as darkness fell – 4.30 pm and two of them were leaving, as was the bar girl who was just getting ready to feed the cows! We chatted to the landlady and the other man who left knew Preston, like most people seem to. Possibly because it is where the first motorway was built… The good old M6, or it could be the prison!

When I commented on the 'Red Lion dartboard', it turns out it has a history all of its own! Someone had seen it in an antique shop in Cockermouth and snatched it up. The plaque on it stated it had been presented to the officers in the officers' mess in Carlisle Castle! The plaque has been removed and kept safe. We supped up and left. Some people pop round the corner to the pub. My 230-mile round trip meant a new pin could be placed in my map!

Paula was back for more and our friend Sharon was now on-board. We had a long list of Lions ahead and some unfinished business. That meant Ruddington (NG11 6LB) from the Leicestershire trip was keenly ticked off.

Shepshed (LE12 9RT) looked like it was catering for everyone with pool table, bandit machine and a little dance area in the middle.

That was Red Lion Number 250.

Dropping south down the A447 we found the busy, welcoming pub at Market Bosworth (CV13 0LL) in a town famous for the Battle of Bosworth, the last struggle in the Wars of the Roses. Towns, pubs, churches, war!

We ordered a fish platter in this warm, traditional pub as you never know when the day is going to end on this Quest.

The Red Lion at Ansty Road, Coventry (CV2 2EY), is a large Ember Inn, yet another where the glasses didn't meet the wine ordered: the landlord of four months told me he had no flutes yet; he was new but it wouldn't take much to pick some up from Morrisons at £2 for four. Though I am sure he had many other things to get in order first.

The following morning, I was live on the BBC with Malcolm who has interviewed me before. Someone had text to say that Hunningham Red may be flooded, and one of the presenters' husbands was the chef at Ansty Road, which is the pub I visited the previous night! It is like a Red Lion network.

Malcolm asked me to introduce the next track, which I chose, so I left the building on a high listening to The Killers 'Human' blasting out and thinking I may have to swim up to Hunningham.

Our first of the day was Kislingbury (NN7 4AQ), which was now an Olde Red Lion!

This pub stands out for the landlord, a natural comic who had placed his favourite sayings around the pub. Such gems as 'You pay for the drinks, the abuse is free' stamped his identity on the place. We stood around the fire with him and the villagers for a good half-hour before leaving for Fosters Booth which they had alerted me to. We opened the door to leave and he blurted out:

'Are you queer?'

We were unsure what he meant.

'You know, lesbianos?' he followed up.

We fell about laughing as we got in the car: he must have been weighing us up all that time.

Red Lion Number 254 sounds more like a hatch where Australians would get their beer on the sly. Welcome to Fosters Booth (NN12 8LB). The reality was that it defied any stereotypical Aussie drinking hole. The landlady confessed it was a quiet pub. With one man at the bar, it looked that way.

I was particularly looking forward to Upper Heyford (NN7 4DE). We had passed this earlier. It had been open since 5 am.

Wait a minute, new category alert… What Red Lion could be open at 5 am? Do not get ahead of yourself. This is a truck stop. The first and only

Red Lion truck stop!!! And certainly the first keeping those hours. If Alan hadn't pointed it out to me in a truck magazine over a year ago, I would never have expected to find a Red Lion just off the M1 for this purpose!

In a way this broadened the mindset. I shouldn't expect a thatched roof or a ghost in the cellar. Surely, this was just about an all-day breakfast! It literally was a fuel stop.

To be fair, there was a big refurb underway. But when I arrived, it had burnt lampshades and random furniture, a canteen area and a blackboard menu that offered the predictable, large drums for tea and coffee. But that was OK. You would expect nothing else.

And, even though this was very much a truck stop, the half-African, half-Indian owner came to chat and proudly showed us the improvements they were making including female showers for the lady trucker and a chance to bed down for the night for £12. We got into truckers' mode and ordered fried egg butty, sausage butty and steak baguette with tea and coffee, and two headache tablets for Sharon! It was unique, a million miles from your average Red Lion, but I admired its ability to provide the truckers' essentials whilst feeling the need to better itself. It clearly had a passing trade and wouldn't be a local to anybody, though you might choose to make this your stopover if you were passing this way every week or so.

It is a respectable Lion that served an entirely different purpose and community. I admired it.

Whatever followed this would, of course, contrast. It just had to.

20 minutes later we were in Hunningham (CV33 9DY), a 17th-century pub next to a 14th-century bridge over the River Leam by waterlogged fields. The car park was almost covered in water true to the radio listeners' alert texts, but they were prepared. A yellow dinghy moored on the car park indicated more rain was on the way.

As we sat at the bar drinking Prosecco, something was intriguing me. Behind the bar was a strange-looking plastic tube that circled above, just below the ceiling. It was a real eyesore and an odd contraption.

It was their method of transporting the food orders and added to the general feel of eccentricity that I noted when I spotted pages from the landlord's childhood comics in frames around the pub!

We dropped Sharon off in time to catch the 4.40 train back to Preston, while we caught one more for the road before heading on to

Corley (CV7 8AP) which was quite tough to find. Hindered by the rain and by being out in the sticks, it took us about half an hour longer than expected, but was very pleasant when we got there with its cute, little snug bar and beer garden. That was enough for today: back to our hotel to wind down and chill. Paula and I often just relaxed in the hotel after a day on the Quest as I caught up with my notes.

The following morning after a short run we edged north on our mission to conquer as many as we could, starting at Atherstone (CV9 1BB) – a magnificent, grand old hotel which welcomes you from the moment you arrive through its bright and warm entrance into its long conservatory and dining area. The Lady Godiva Room further along on the right is small with wooden panels and decorated with historical pictures. This was, after all, Lady Godiva territory – once, one of the most powerful women in the 11th century, she owned land around here. We sat comfortably with coffee watching preparations take place for the carvery and the onslaught of Sunday lunchers, but before Paula got too settled we moved ourselves on.

It's busy and full-on but oozes quality from the food to the function rooms.

I called ahead to Polesworth (B78 1DR) but all I got was a dead tone. Here we go again, the roller coaster Red Lion tour which flits from such beauty to such uncertainty in a matter of moments.

The road on approach was extremely flooded, too, and I just about got the car over the bridge without a second thought for how I might get back out!

The doors were closed, the lights were on, but not many people were home. On trying the door, a pleasant gentleman came out offering to take our photos: he was the new landlord's grandfather. Once inside I told them (just one lady and the landlord) how hard they had been to trace and how all a Google search brought up was that a woman had been arrested here for attempted murder in May of this year. He shrugged and said the attempted murderess still popped in for a drink sometimes.

I had been to quite a few where historical deaths had been relayed to me, but this was the first time I had found a Lion with relatively fresh blood on its hands.

A man and his dog had to be airlifted to hospital after a 47-year-old woman injured them outside in a traffic accident. She was charged with being over the limit and failing to stop. The drinks were as undesirable as the history here. This pub needs an injection of enthusiasm and much more.

When I looked at this pub again just recently I also found that it had fallen foul of the Hygiene Police, ending in a court date in November 2014 and a Food Hygiene Rating of zero and assessment that it all could have been avoided with basic health and safety procedures.

Some pubs are worth challenging the floods for. This wasn't one of them.

Now, back to the way out and the floods! It got worse at Wilnecote (B77 5BS) just five minutes away, forcing us to wade our way through to our third Red of the day to a hugely male-dominated pub, a friendly bunch of males, some with wives at home cooking their Sunday lunch, those with nothing better to do, then those who could not take a photo to save their lives.

Stuart had three attempts at getting me, Paula and the sign in, so I gave up and Paula took one of me and him. It is sometimes a bind getting the photos done if it's cold or raining or dark, but Paula has it down to a fine art, although it is a miracle that she hasn't been run over yet standing in the middle of the road to get me and the sign in.

This was Lion Number 260 – a fact I mention on this occasion only because the landlord was delighted to tell me that was also his house number. Quirky little stat!

Now, if you head to Brereton (WS15 1EB), watch out because the Lion just leaps out at you on the left!

The pub was busy; the manager very attentive. It seemed well run and my starter luxury fish pie in a shell hit the spot. Whilst we were eating, a voice from the adjacent table piped up, asking where my accent was from. The lady recognised my Northern tones as she was from Bradford.

Now this is where the Quest is fun. I explained what we were doing and, as was often the case, they added to it, recommending The Beer Train in Huddersfield where you buy a daily ticket and hop on and off as many times as you like for beers in the stations! What a great idea. Not quite a quest, but a possible detour in the future.

Just 1.3 miles away is Rugeley (WS15 2JH), pairing these two as the *now* closest Lions so far. This one, however, is tiny with three little rooms and a small bar packed with characters: it would be impossible not to get talking to someone, and we were on first-name terms before the Cokes had been poured.

Stuart explained to me how he had been an extra in *Max and Paddy* on the TV. I think he likes telling the story: it's the kind of pub where people chip in. Banter is king. One guy flagged up the Red Lion in Dubai, too, but I was ahead of him, having already been. It's funny that people might travel halfway round the world, remember that there was a Red Lion pub there, and not notice some on their doorstep. A plaque hanging above the bar says: 'Beer helps ugly people have sex'.

Our 15th of this weekend was Little Haywood (ST18 0TS) and, given that this is just 3.5 miles away, these three are probably also the closest *trio*. It sounds like I am making stats for fun now, but I think what it underlines is the historical dominance of the name.

Now, clearly when I turn up at the Red Lions, it is often my only experience of that pub on that day. Who is to know if what I find is the everyday or just a one-off? You get a sense after so many as to the answer.

When we walked in here past hand-carved tables and stools to the free cheese and biscuits and quartered doughnuts at the bar, it was quite obvious by 3 pm on a Sunday afternoon that most of the pub was rather merry.

Some time after this visit, I accidentally found a video on YouTube whose description read 'Just a normal Sunday afternoon in the Red Lion, Little Haywood, Stafford!!!! You don't get many like these!!' Sure enough, as the video shows, they were up and dancing (badly) on another merry Sunday afternoon! A great local village pub with a great atmosphere.

For Paula and me, this weekend hadn't failed to entertain with a wide range of Red Lions and characters.

CHESHIRE'S LAST FEW

Fireman was on another of his four days off and was eager to investigate a couple of the remaining local Red Lions. It was a second chance for Northwich, which had been shut last time I tried as it closes between 3 pm and 4.30 in the afternoon.

But Winsford (CW7 3AA) was first, as the timing didn't work once again. En route I was curious to know why a pub would have been named the 'Slow and Easy'.

Winsford is a massive pub, 250 years old and quite different from a typical Lion. Just next to a salt mine, when in the old days the wives of the salt mineworkers would wait outside for the husbands and more importantly his wages, giving him just enough back for a pint or two. It is now a music venue with quite theatrical décor; the main room with the bar in had a stage and another had a piano. Perhaps a miserable wet Monday afternoon is not the best time to visit! Quite clearly, this is one pub by day and another by night.

At Northwich (CW8 1QL) after killing some time, I couldn't have been more relieved to see the doors open. It's a warm, AA-rated B & B with a roaring log fire and, on my visit, lots of dogs! Cathy, the landlady, knew of the Quest and told me if I had rung on my first attempt, she would have opened up for me. We chatted to a few locals comfortably in the warmth the fire gave, as I collected a couple more Facebook followers.

Relieved to have ticked this one off, next Hollins Green, Warrington (WA3 6JT), was concerning me. I had doubts it still existed. And Manchester Road didn't help, being so long and changing on the sat nav halfway through to the A57, leaving Manchester Road running parallel and, lo and behold, hiding our doubted inn.

It did exist, but perhaps others had the same trouble as there was hardly a soul inside. Andy, the landlord, had been in just six months and was slowly building up trade; he had been expecting me after his brother tipped him off about a woman going to Red Lion pubs. He had come from The Black Swan, which we passed and was heaving. It looked like Andy was in the wrong pub.

I wonder how many Black Swans there were in the UK. I wasn't about to start an alternative quest! Though I did learn that *they* got their name because a black swan landed on the river at the back of the pub. It sounds an obvious choice of name for a pub unlike some.

The Red Lion at Ashton-in-Makerfield (WN4 9AG) has an outstanding front, dating back to 1863 in typical black and white Tudor style. It comes alive at the weekend, open until 2 am, according to the bar girl, who then tops up her shift by working in the club out the back until 6 am.

I am sure that was how the Tudors lived, too!

ANOTHER YORKSHIRE DAY OUT

Still on his four days off, FMS and I drove east. I called Mexborough: the line was dead. I called another pub in the village, oddly named as The Boy and Barrel. That's the name of the pub not the village, obviously.

On such moments of improvisation you can sometimes stumble across stories that count. The lady who answered told me The Red Lion had closed down in 2008 and she had been the landlady there for four years until Punch Taverns sold it behind her back. She said it had left her devastated, and then she had to suffer the misfortune of seeing it turned into a block of flats. She is now trying to buy The Boy and Barrel. I wished her luck.

At the heart of every Red Lion lay individuals, couples and families whose lives were on a knife-edge because of the unpredictability of the trade. This captured the moment perfectly.

I punched Wath-upon-Dearne (S63 7QG) into the sat nav. It looked strange and stands out in a category marked Broken Signs!

The exterior was painted cream. Its sign was a damaged blue and green neon announcing 'Red Lion Out O Town'. Letters were missing. My guess is it had been like that for some time. Inside it was sparse and scruffy, but the cheap beer kept it busy, though it isn't somewhere I would hang around: this old pub had somehow lost its identity.

At Conisbrough (DN12 2BY) we walked in on the Golf Society's prize-giving dinner preparations. It is a Sam Smiths with the trademark four rooms, cheap ale and own brand Cola. Humphrey, one of the two brothers running the brewery, is the area manager. It is a pity we didn't catch him as I have heard they are quite eccentric. One of the locals remembered driving by two Reds in Durham, Birtley and Ouston both of which I visited with Paula. (*Phoenix Nights*, remember!)

I rang ahead to Braithwell. The number was dead and so was The Lion.

The pub was no more, but as we pulled up it was being turned into a physiotherapist's. The builders said the Red Lion sign was inside, being kept as a souvenir!

At Thorpe Hesley (S61 2PY) I witnessed something I don't think I had ever seen before or since. Three men came in, and ordered three cups of tea. They didn't exactly get the party started but it was only 4 pm midweek. I beat FMS at pool again and we were on our way to Grenoside where there are two Red Lions, with a plan to eat in one of them.

At Penistone Road, Grenoside (S35 8QH), we were greeted by a huge chef statue at the entrance to the stone building.

Slightly old-fashioned, or perhaps traditional, I had never seen so many people eating at 5 pm. It was well run and orderly. We decided to eat at the next one.

This one on Main Street (S35 8PR) and the previous Lion had now just taken over the title for the closest two together. The bar staff confirmed people often got them mixed up. They were less than a mile apart: I wonder whether this will be beaten further down the line.

They did things at their own pace here – we ordered food, and obviously didn't mind waiting until the chef came back from walking his dog! It was worth the wait, we enjoyed the food, and as we left the place was filling up.

Heading home, we saw a sign for Dewsbury (WF5 9PE). FMS remembered seeing one on the list. How could we have nearly missed it?

Ordering half a White Lion ale and a small red wine, we plonked our money on the counter only for Trio, the landlord, to plonk it back. He already had a clipping of me. It has never been my intention to get any free drinks. That is why I always order and pay before telling them about my Quest, but I find it heart-warming how many landlords want to buy me a drink, maybe as a way of spurring me on or admiring my mission. Actually my sole aim was to satisfy my curiosity.

'Have you been to the Red Lion at Wakefield?' Trio asked. 'It's only five minutes away.'

I was pretty sure I had visited last year, the layout like a bingo hall.

When I described it, he didn't think it sounded the same and insisted on us following him there, tearing off as though he was trying to lose us!

It *was* the same Red Lion, though not exactly a wasted trip. I could compare it to my previous visit and it now had a new landlord who was making changes for the better.

One thing that had remained constant, though, wherever I was in the country was the number of landlords in the middle of a shift who were prepared to drive or point me to a potentially competing pub as soon as I told them about the Quest!

YEAR'S END

It was ten days before Christmas 2012. I had a free day.

That meant I could incorporate the mystery of whether the Red Lion at Urmston still existed into a visit to the Manchester Christmas markets.

If a physiotherapist seemed an unusual use for a dead Lion, I am sure you can only imagine what I felt when I discovered a care home! You can see why Google sometimes throws up uncertainty. Building a care home would take some time and obviously pretty much remove any signs of a pub being there, but I did have it on a list. Only by going there in the flesh could I know that.

That of course, could turn out to be an expensive problem when I continue to do the overseas Lions!

The festive markets replaced the disappointment but on the way home I was in for a surprise! No sooner had I been deprived a Lion than an unknown popped up on Bolton Road (M6 7GU) in Salford.

I quickly realised that this was Bolton Road, Salford and not Salford Road, Bolton where I had already been, causing a moment's confusion.

I soon learned the history of the pub from Brenda at the bar, pointing out a room that had been the living quarters and how it had been a typical Joseph Holt pub rebuilt in 1905.

Interestingly, whilst we know the effects of the recession on the trade, I hadn't really considered the role of the town planners. Brenda explained how the town had been torn apart when a bypass was built and they called this Irlams o' th' Height Red Lion, presumably cutting some people off from places they used to frequent like The Lion.

What I took most from Brenda is that she was 68 and had been drinking here since she was 17 years old. She had obviously been home in between, but half a century's worth of drinking mean 50 years of change within the pub and around the town. She was a lady worth listening to. I may be wrong because people hadn't made me aware, but she sits or should I say drinks in her own category of 'Longest-Serving Lioness'.

It was 21 December: as in previous years there was no stopping for Christmas, beginning at Nantwich (CW5 5QS) and with my friend Helena who had travelled the world with me, but so far no Red Lions!

I think Nantwich stands as the pub with the newest landlords. Andy had been in a week and was going for it like there was no tomorrow with quiz nights and bingo and the works. There was no time to lose!

My gut feeling was that he would make a success of it. With eight students living above the pub, I am sure he would be busy! My gut feeling was right, as I was contacted and invited back in 2014 by the guy running the rugby club there: it is an essential part of the community. We all piled in for a photo second time around; they bought me a drink and offered the chilli being served to the mucky, hungry rugby lads just back from a match.

At Wybunbury (CW5 7NA) we found that Lion Number 276 has newly reopened its doors after being dormant for over two years. The landlord, with four pubs to his name, was leasing it from Thwaites. How do you run four pubs at the same time?

If they are all at this standard, then that makes four great pubs. Wybunbury is a gorgeous building. They take pride in their fresh food and unique range of ice cream, with beetroot amongst the flavours. Out the back are rabbits and guinea fowl. It was clearly a favourite. When I relooked it up recently, TripAdvisor had rated it the Number 1 pub in Nantwich. I don't believe everything I read on there, but you couldn't go far wrong with that ranking.

Today was the shortest day of the year – of course – not a great one for chasing the Lion. There were still enough hours in the day but darkness was coming quicker than ever. Steady December rain didn't help either.

When we arrived on that final mad Friday before Christmas at Prescot (L34 5SB), I will never forget the anecdote of one of the locals.

She had been to the Red Lion in Benidorm and stolen a glass, and would tell anyone who listened. That just about summed up the pub – and Benidorm!

Sadly, I read after my visit that the pub had been closed and several arrests had been made for drug dealing, crime and antisocial behaviour.

Well, perhaps the clues were in the Benidorm theft. When a stranger puts that straight on the table, what else lies beyond?

Would Helena be back for more Lions? I think so.

As you might expect by now, Christmas Eve meant no rest for the wicked. I had – ahem – pencilled in four Red Lions for today's Christmas drinks with FMS.

First was Dudley (DY3 1RU) where they looked for me on Facebook whilst posing for photos. Five guys were drinking at the bar, assuring me that Gornal Wood (DY3 2PQ) was open, despite my concerns.

It was more than open, serving up from 9 am via a happy bar lady dressed in leopard-print leggings, striped cardigan, sparkly top and boots. Very festive, unlike the landlord!

I told them their phone number was dead. Her reply? The landlord was not interested and not sociable. Wow – he was in the right trade, then.

At Tipton (DY4 8LD) it felt like Christmas was really here. Finally.

This is the oldest building in Tipton and the only one remaining from the 18th century on the canal. Proof once again that the community starts at the pub.

I got chatting to a really interesting guy at the bar who had just had a stroke. He was a lorry driver who was not permitted to drive for a month. Then I noticed he had no finger on his left hand. He had cut it off at a sawmill. He had also lost the tip of his right hand middle finger in a different incident. This was an entirely new category, but for the life of me I wouldn't know what to call it.

Christmas Eve was the time to discover Lions that I hadn't mapped out, and the guys at Dudley had alerted me to Willenhall (WV13 2RN), but first passing Mad O'Rourkes famous pie factory.

It is a long building with a nice bar but a bit on the scruffy side. At the pool table were six kids; at the bar four men. You really wouldn't know it was Christmas.

You get a sense about some pubs. Most places have some festiveness going on at Christmas. In October 2014, I learned that the pub was to become part of the Hungry Horse chain, which seems to be a growing company.

It really was time to be driving home for Christmas.

In my mind we were done for the year. I laugh now looking back, never one to let an opportunity pass me by. I said to FMS on that nothingness day between Christmas and New Year 'just one more?' We nipped to St. Helens (WA9 3PB) for one more for the road on 27 December.

I don't mean that alcoholically but a spur of the moment decision meant ending the year on 282 Red Lions. We found a rough exterior and a 60s building but Happy Christmas, a landlady who knew about the Quest.

That was never the be-all and end-all but it always felt nice. It had a warm, seasonal glow about it.

An original Lion had stood in the car park, spittoons, sawdust and all, but was burnt down and rebuilt 50 years ago.

As the barman with missing teeth served us, the landlady asked me if I had been to any rough ones.

I was too polite to answer properly. After all, 'twas the season of goodwill.

And that was that for 2012. At 282 we were done.

There was still a long way to go. I wasn't even halfway through. Given almost two years of Red Lioning, I knew I could always expect the unexpected, but who knew what lay ahead? Bring on 2013, and Wales first of all.

LIONS, NOT DRAGONS

2013 had barely begun. The compulsion would never cease. Destination: The Square, Llanfair (SY21 0RP). Four days into the New Year and the sun greeted our entry into Wales – and so did a photographer from the *County Press*. It was becoming a habit now. My daughter Hayley was this trip's companion. This was one of those towns with two Lions, a Red Lion and a Black one.

The Christmas decorations were still up in this cosy, lovely pub. It was the kind of place were locals all wanted to chat about the Quest – as though the pub were a local news bulletin in itself.

Then in came Ivan, very keen to ply us with drinks, keeping us there for a little bit longer. It was one of the best 'little bit longers ever'. We were serenaded by a man with a beautiful, smooth voice in Welsh, a moving version of 'My Grandfather's Clock' followed by a local carol. It was still the season of festivities, though in Wales they need no excuse for a song.

It was one of those priceless Red Lion moments.

Reluctantly we made tracks at 5 pm to Main Street, Caersws (SY17 5EL), to the warmth of the log-burner at Lion Number 284, some 20 miles and 35 minutes further on. It was one of those places where winding, narrow, bent lanes in the dark made you feel like progress was slow. It was the closest thing to a toboggan run in a car. Tempting to say, do not go in January; I'm equally inclined to argue that this is the best way to arrive!

Tunnels were now the lie of the land as we made for Trefeglwys (SY17 5EL) through another dark incision into the land.

We were really where time didn't matter. It was dark and only 6 pm but felt so much later. I loved that illusion that the ambience could suspend the hours of the day.

A brass plaque by the fireplace read 'Free Drinks Tomorrow' – of course they were. And tomorrow never comes! I could never have imagined when I set out in the Lake District that my life would be bombarded by plaques, but every pub seemed to be quoting – each of them memorable in their own way!

We nearly missed the entrance at Long Bridge Street, Llanidloes (SY18 6EE). This time it wasn't the dark or concealment by tunnel. There was simply scaffolding over the front and I could just about make out a red lion statue over the door.

The lounge inside was relaxing – so much so, in fact, that the one barmaid on shift forgot to bring us our coffee! It felt like a pub for sports fans. A two-hour journey home beckoned. There was to be a return trip to more Welsh Lions the next day.

The final point of call was to be Cardigan where Brains Brewery offered Alan's daughter, Robbie, and me an overnight stay. I hadn't envisaged anyone chipping into funding the Quest other than myself, but it was certainly appreciated! In Wales opening times are a law unto themselves, so I took an extremely long route back via the M6, M5 and M4 to Burry Port.

I had never been to that part of the country before and even the £6.20 charge to cross the bridge didn't dampen the experience. Over the Swansea Bay Estuary, I hadn't realised how close I was to Morriston (SA6 6JA). I knew there was a Red there.

Driving through quite a basic town and passing the DVLA that every driver at some point has communicated with, my expectations weren't high until I encountered a large Wetherspoons (they all are) with interesting décor, friendly staff and a big crowd already at 4 pm. It integrated the décor with pictures of the surrounding areas from yesteryear and a stained glass window over the side door leading onto a patio door which had Red Lion written in both English and Welsh… A decent welcoming touch.

With dark falling so early, we made tracks, and again I hadn't realised we almost passed another RL at Hendry (SA4 0UN). I still loved discovering Lions either unknown to me or unaware that they were right in front of me.

Hendry faces another pub opposite and stands on the corner of a roundabout. I guess as people flitted between the two over the years one or the other would have been the favourite. Sadly, this lion needed work, in and out – its sparse clientele sat around watching darts. I was made welcome and didn't feel uncomfortable, even though I was a strange female in town.

Dropping down to the coast and taking the A484, we reached the lovely Red at Burry Port (SA16 0UB) – an excellent stopover at the day's end.

Robbie was shattered and it was time for Cardigan (SA43 1DB) and the Angel Hotel where Brains Brewery had offered us a bed for the night.

At check-in, we found we were above the nightclub! We decided to walk round the corner to the Red Lion – which had been closed for four months!

Thankfully, the excellent refurb done, it had just reopened. It seemed to be the way – close or reinvent.

Downstairs had retained many traditional features. The landlord was from Leicester and running several businesses at the same time; he still had to start on the upstairs which was a wreck. I chatted while Robbie was invited to play in the next room with some children. She is an absolute pleasure and always engages people wherever she goes. We were both acutely aware of how Wales had defied our preconceptions. They didn't hate us and didn't revert to speaking in Welsh when the English turned up!

A new day meant new Lions. The Lion at Llandysul (SA44 5UH) was tough to find. The address did not agree with the sat nav! Only after ringing the pub a few times could I find it. I was hoping to get a light breakfast but they did full Sunday lunch, so we decided to hang on. The bar girls were extremely friendly, and as we were about to drive away they came running out with some crisps for Robbie. Small snippets of generosity like this leave a warm feeling.

Tregaron (SY25 6BH) suddenly appeared as I drove round a bend. The sign only says 'Llew Coch', but as I was now familiar with Wales I instantly recognised it as a Red Lion, plus it had a worn-out painting of a lion on the wall. This was a Lion who had been in court. Maybe that's where those preconceptions began. The then owner Dafydd Evans was once refused permission to hang Welsh-only name signs outside the front! With signs on order and only in the mother tongue, six Welsh-speaking members of the bench had rejected the application!

The owner, from London, had planned to spend considerable cash converting it to its former look of the 19th century! Most of the regulars referred to it as 'Y Llew' as it was known in Welsh, and here was a man from London who wanted to bring its Welshness back to it, and his own neighbours had knocked it back. I don't know what followed, but it was in need of much TLC.

Wales had that air of mystery about it, and the names were all but impossible to pronounce, from there to – Pontrhydfendigaid (SY25 6BH). What a find with spectacular views over the nearby Cors Caron Nature Reserve and across the Cambrian Mountains. It is a perfect stop for walkers and mountain bikers overlooking the River Teifi, one of the best salmon-fishing rivers in the UK. Birdwatchers love it, too.

It was a beautiful end to the start of the year, and a special trip with Robbie.

OUT IN OXFORD

It was just past the middle of January 2013. Sudden snowfalls cast a white spell over the entire country. Against advice, and digging my way out, I made for Oxford.

A hotel booked and interviews ready to go, fireman said he wasn't even going to try and persuade me to cancel the trip, so we left early in search of Bloxham (OX15 4LX).

The M6, M5 and M40 were deserted – the quietest I have ever seen – and when we arrived we witnessed the most beautiful sight of the new landlord shovelling snow from the doorway, preparing to open up. We couldn't just watch, besides there were lots of Lions on my list, so with another shovel I got stuck in.

Christine and Mark were barely into their first five weeks running a pub – something they have not done before.

The village comprised three pubs in a triangle around the church. It was very old-school England, and just how it was meant to be. Christine was the first Red Lion landlady I had met who confessed her passion for women's cricket!

Out the back was an Aunt Sally amidst a sea of white. We slipped and slid as we tried to leave the car park, and with a little push we made it. One down, 15 more to go!

Sadly, I read in 2014 and 2015 that the pub was up for sale with Fuller's looking to sell for between £300,000 and £400,000 and the community attempting to buy it with donations coming in from Shanghai, Vancouver and Sydney: this would be more than a community-owned pub, it would be global.

Clearly, it meant a lot to many people around the world, but their absence could not save it on a day-to-day basis.

Just six miles down the road at Chipping Norton (OX7 5BJ) we found this stone pub without a front entrance – the smallest in the village. It bore a sign saying 'Hook Norton Ales Est. 1849'. The pub actually dates back to 1684.

Hook Norton Brewery comprises around 40 pubs serving its own Hooky Beer. They now do a Lion's Ale, one of their bestsellers, and they kindly invited me to the brewery in the most picturesque thatched village possible. I would recommend anyone to take a visit here. It is like going back in time.

At Deddington (OX15 0SE), 11 miles down the road, John at the bar described the pub as a 'drinkers' pub'! It was just that. Thankfully, he also pointed out the Red Lion at Adderbury (OX17 3NG), which I didn't know about, though I was delighted to be rerouted here to this lovely, welcoming stone building with a coating of snow.

I was surprised I could not find the pub on my list and when I quizzed the staff, all very busy running between the three rooms, they told me they were part of the English Inns Group and offered me a key to check out one of the rooms. After a higgledy climb up the old stairs, I unlocked the door to discover the most idyllic, small but beautiful room, overlooking the snow-covered front, with a four-poster bed. Just perfect. Close to Banbury and with thatched roofs, it dates back to 1605. This is a must to revisit.

Just four miles away, Mel the landlord was running the pub at Steeple Aston (OX25 4RY) which was also a Hooky pub. He had been there for the last seven years and was aware of my Quest. With a beautiful add-on dining room and log fire we picked the perfect time of year, looking out onto snow-covered gardens.

And so to Red Number 299. The excitement was building. My new biggest number was looming just down the road but Kidlington (OX5 2BP) does not deserve to be written off as the one before a landmark! It's a decent pub with a pizzeria at its helm, and part of the Orchid chain. Jamie at the bar also knew of my journey. It is a busy pub: pizzas were tempting, but time was of the essence. I was to meet a journalist in 20 minutes.

And so to the triple ton – Red Lion Number 300. Congratulations, Gloucester Green, Oxford (OX1 2BU): it's you.

I just made it in time with a couple of minutes to spare to meet John from the *Oxford Mail*. I bought two halves of Brakspear Blonde cask ale to celebrate and for the photos, and then went inside to relax, sharing a delicious garlic bread topped with caramelised onion, tomato and goat's cheese. My glass of Prosecco tasted extra-bubbly today.

I couldn't believe I was nearly halfway home. Cheers, Salut, Skoal, Iechyd da, Gan bay, Prost!!!!! (I will need cheers in these languages for the worldwide Red Lions at some point!)

And I was fortunate, too, to have done the maths! The next Red was closed and does not count. The builders were gutting Garsington (OX44 9JT), about to turn the empty shell into a private house, still with the sign outside. From an extreme high to sadness, such is life.

And it didn't get much better initially as we pulled into Chalgrove (OX44 7SS) as darkness drew in. The pub was closed.

Whilst we were debating whether to beat the snow or hang around, the landlord and his son pulled up and let us in. How many times had this happened? Yet another Red Lion had shown us kindness. I note that the acts of generosity, helpfulness and kindness are symptomatic of the more successful pubs. In other words, grumps and misery don't belong in this trade.

It is a great local pub: his son soon had the open fire raging. It transpired that the church owned the pub! So many Lions were just a stone's throw away from places of worship, but for one to own the other? The link between alcohol and religion was unquestionable.

The Irish landlord alerted me to the Red nearby at Britwell Salome, which was not on my list. He even rang to check so there was obviously some doubt as to its status. Indeed, I learned it had been the Red Lion then The Goose, and was now a Red Lion again. We had 35 miles to travel to Newbury and our hotel, so unfortunately we could not squeeze it in this trip, I was in for a treat when I did eventually get there, 267 Red Lions further in and two years later! Hotel, check-in, shower, and one more Red Lion today.

Chieveley (RG20 8XB) and this Lion is technically Ye Olde Red Lion! I loved that and you can see why on approach, marvelling at the 15th-century building that just oozes character.

And inside, modern-day attitude met that sense of historical perspective halfway – I spied a sign at the end of the bar announcing 'Bullshit Corner'. It was clearly for locals who let out steam night after night, or for anyone who happened to be over-egging their case of an evening. What a great way to diffuse a fight before it has even started. Send someone to Bullshit Corner.

The food, too, did not disappoint – Thai fish cakes and a Red Lion burger hit the spot, and by the time our South African taxi driver James picked us up, we left with gifts of home-made jam and chutney from the landlord's girlfriend. James was forced to leave his farm in South Africa with nothing, abandoning everything he had ever worked for to strive for a new life in the UK. The Lion tour certainly threw circumstance in our faces many a time. Bizarrely, he also knew Doris the landlady at the Red Lion Rodney Marsh, miles away in Kent, whom I had yet to meet.

The next day we headed for Theale (RG7 5BX). In thick snow, we arrived to find a crowd of – none!

Darren and Dave had taken over the place just a few months earlier. It is difficult to judge how well it is doing since we were first in and first out. Who knows, we may also have been the last in and last out! You rarely found a pub empty, so I did some Googling.

Online I found a disturbing tale of previous landlords ripping off customers in a Christmas Club Saving Scheme. It seems like most people got half of their savings back and are still waiting for the remainder. In essence, they positioned themselves at the heart of the community, whilst robbing it on the blind side. How could the person who served you a pint every night be secretly deceiving you behind the bar? It ripped out the soul of the notion of having a local. Hopefully this Red Lion will eventually lose its bitter taste.

On we went for Woodcote (RG8 0SD) – a picturesque drive through a coating of snow and across a 40p toll bridge! At the bar, a contrast to what we had left. A regular notching up some 40 years of drinking here! That is a lot of lifetime to spend at The Red Lion! Busy, friendly and with food smelling great, this is a cracking little pub. The landlords of the last six years also filled us in on an unplanned Lion at Peppard Common (RG9 5LB). Another diversion on the crazy trail.

It was busy but we managed to get a table. My microwaved baguette nearly broke my tooth and was replaced, so not the best.

Upper Basildon (RG8 8NG) is one of the trickiest Lions to find. But tricky Lions often prove a treat and, through more snow and negotiating icy, hilly lanes, we arrived to a gorgeous smell of home-cooked food. I wished we had waited to eat here now!

Lions like this must look at the Quest with amusement. Why, in the dead of winter, would a Lancashire lass persevere to seek out this pub just to tick it off the list? We hardy Northerners are not to be underestimated!

Rustic, rural, thatched, warm, glowing, friendly – it ticked all the boxes. You would be happy to live in the village near this pub and wander in for a quick one every night of your life. I looked back as we drove away to see children playing in the snow. Ah, the village life!!

Red Lion 307 was one I had been anticipating, as much for all that went on around it as in it. It had stood as a pillar in the community and had been on the news so many times. We were in Royal Wootton Bassett (SN4 7AQ).

In 2011, Princess Anne gave it its royal title – only the third British town to be so adorned. We had all become accustomed to seeing it on the news as the bodies of our deceased military came home.

Always poignant and respectful, the town had fallen silent too many times. At its heart stood a Red Lion. And 'Bassett' seemed to be a classic Red Lion town if you revert to how communities grew up around a pub, a church and a railway line.

Inside, it was home from home. The landlady Sue had ended up here… from my home town Bamber Bridge. That was one of the beauties of the Quest – finding a little piece of home on your way.

By the time we arrived at Chalford (GL6 8DJ) it was dark and the snow was so deep that the pub was not accessible by car. It looked every inch an Alpine ski resort. Seeing deer on our approach and gorgeous houses, you could be forgiven for thinking this was not England. A rare moment of beauty.

Abandoning the car, we walked up the hill to the pub, to find it… closed. It was 5.10 on a Sunday afternoon and the note on the door said 4.30 closed! I knocked on it as I could hear voices inside. It was like a lock-in but at teatime! The landlady emerged to explain they were having a family meal and the pub was shut, otherwise she would have let us in for a drink. Disappointed, we hiked back to the car and headed home – the only consolation was seeing the village beautifully covered in snow: it was magical. This was fireman's 79th and final Red Lion: he never did catch Paula up!

ONE AFTERNOON IN BURTON UPON TRENT

It was now 19 February 2013. My friend Fred – well acquainted with the Quest – joined me for his maiden voyage, with 308 lions behind me! No time like the present.

On the spur of the moment and with the top down on the car for the first time this year, we decided to go to Burton upon Trent only at 4 pm and some 76 miles away. It was late in the day to chase the Lion. Sometimes you just got in the car and went.

This is a cracking pub but left me wondering! Tracey, landlady of just eight months when we visited, told me we were in the snug, but the other, nicer half was where the cows used to be milked many years ago. That is worth replaying in your mind a couple of times. We are well aware that locals would come to their locals at the end of a hard day, but what I had not experienced was the mental picture that the pub was also an agricultural home!

There really was a lot of history and culture entwined in the Red Lion world.

Strangely, I had a massive allergic reaction to the man next to me at the bar. Then I found out that he put shoes on horses, which is the worst thing to trigger me off! All in all, an old-school ambience in the pub!

At Barton-under-Needwood (DE13 8AA), as I ordered a pint and a Diet Coke, the landlord reminded me that I had met his father-in-law on the Isle of Wight! I loved tying up the loose ends. It was constantly great when the Quest had assumed its own life through the people you met and the people you met came back into the story at a later date. I loved that.

This is a friendly pub with a small, cosy atmosphere. It was always odd how people at the bar could be ahead of the Quest – one local adamant that the next one at Burton upon Trent had long since gone, then replaced it with another at Repton.

Sadly, I left on a sad, thoughtful note. Mike the landlord told us his father-in-law had passed away in September. I only found out by asking how he was doing. The Quest had completed many circles. It was always upsetting when the circle of life began and ended in my tour.

Repton (DE65 6FL) meant reptiles. Standing at the bar, I jumped for my life as the huge, dangling tarantula came my way. Rubber tarantula: it frightened me to death!

Anthony, the very laid-back landlord, revealed a grin on his face as he reeled the thing back up to the ceiling on its fishing wire, a stunt I am sure he had pulled a thousand times before. And that is before we got to the rubber bat and the unscary fluffy lion.

Then he introduced me to the Red Lion statue at the bar wearing glasses! Apparently, it used to be in the pub, but when the previous landlord left he gave it to the Chinese restaurant up the road, then when Anthony took it over they brought it back in for him! Even statues come full circle.

When Gizmo the cat jumped up to the bar, I wondered what else was to come in this box of tricks. (Gizmo was real.)

There was no food, no sport, just tricks! All in all, though, a friendly place to hang out and with a born entertainer in our midst who had somehow been deprived of a mainstream talent show on the TV!

Bye, Burton!

I later learned that the Lion at Burton upon Trent had indeed been closed for a couple of years. As was often the case, the man at the bar was right. Local knowledge prevailed.

A SCOTTISH EXCURSION

My friend Denise joined me on her first Red Lion outing. She fancied Scotland. We were heading for Hexham (NE47 5AR) in Northumberland and then passed the border.

We pulled up at the old stone Lion at 14.30 to discover one of my oldest Lions ever, built in 1190!

At the bar lay a tray of drinks. Tragedy followed tragedy. We had descended upon a funeral party of some 60 people, celebrating the life of a local farmer.

Keen to leave without intruding, we noticed a wooden posser at the side of the wood-burner – a true throwback to yesteryear, used to stir the washing in the old days!

We made for Bonnie Scotland before the funeral party arrived.

And our first stop was Low Causeway, Culross (KY12 8HN), racing against the sun as we crossed the Kincardine Bridge and arriving at the beautiful pub standing on the estuary.

The landlady Ann had been in place for 20 years and greeted us with drinks, explaining that the pub had started out as a Gothenburg pub which did not serve alcohol! This is a system which – no surprises – originates from Gothenburg in Sweden in a bid to curb the control of spirits in the 1860s. Today, north of the border, they still exist and are known as Goths! Clearly, alcoholism is not just a modern-day disease!

There was something quaint, too, in the fact that time stood still at this pub – the ceilings, hand-painted and telling local tales. The staff, too, had time for you and had been with the landlady Ann and her husband David for years. I loved Red Lions where stories were told and the rat race hadn't overtaken real life. Best, though, was the painting of the Scotsman wearing a real kilt behind the toilet door in the Ladies.

The temptation to lift the kilt was one I could resist but clearly a pattern had been long established. Any such action would notify the clientele by a little mechanism unbeknownst to newcomers in the pub! It was a touch that meant you would never forget this pub.

As we left, we were given a bottle each to take for later. We couldn't leave in a hurry, though – the gift of a Red Lion sign from our hosts produced a pantomime just trying to manoeuvre it into the car. I was always grateful for a Red Lion sign. It seemed there were quite a few just hanging around the country. However, with space limited, it's not the easiest thing to accommodate. As we drove away, I looked at Denise almost partitioned off from me by the sign, clutching her gift of beer and shaking her head. She would soon adapt to the Red Lion way!

We arrived at our final destination of the day, where we had two nights booked at Balkerach Street, Doune (FK16 6DF), by 7.30 in the evening, just half an hour before kitchen closed and dinner stopped.

I guess we stood out like a sore thumb – two guys smoking in the car park came to take our suitcases. You sometimes got this out in the sticks and this pub dates back some 200 years. The town's name derives from the Gaelic word 'dun' meaning hill fort, referring to the mound on which the castle now stands on the banks of the River Teith. Originally a hunting retreat and lodge for Robert Stewart, Duke of Albany, around the 14th and 15th centuries, the castle has been restored and is one of the best preserved medieval castles in Scotland.

Mary, Queen of Scots was imprisoned there and the castle was used in the movie *Monty Python and the Holy Grail*. Every year hundreds of fans flock to celebrate the anniversary with occasional cast members. For them, the Red Lion is often the first port of call.

For us, it was a peaceful retreat where you can sleep like a log after a long trek to get here. Mackerel and haddock dominated our food choices – fish being a must in these parts.

The next morning we were on the road by 10.30 through snow-topped mountains in glorious sunshine. We wouldn't get further north than this.

Up the A9 and then the A95, not too far beyond Aviemore lies Forres (IV36 1PH). In fact, you could be forgiven for stopping several times along the way. The route is lined with distilleries!

The Red Lion is known locally for its Beastie Bar, built in 1838 but now a home to live sport, dominoes, pool and darts.

At the bar, the distillery mentality has come home! Water jugs sit there to add to your whisky. Inside are clever compartments just for the ice to keep the water chilled to ensure no ice cubes drop into the whisky.

The barman offered me the jug in exchange for a £7 donation into the charity bottle. It already had £700 in it on their way to their target of £1,000. I duly obliged. The jug now sits in my Red Lion garage bar, although whisky is scarcely drunk there!

Lion Number 316 was Fochabers (IV32 7DU). This has to be one of the great mini-tours in the Quest. Where, for example, Oxford has many Red Lions only two miles apart, we were now doing 20 miles between Scotland's two closest ones.

Fochabers is a small town with the River Spey running through it in the heart of the Moray countryside.

As we entered, the bar is to the left with a long bench on the other side. The old adage was true on this occasion – just one man and a dog sat there. There are ten rooms here and it would be a peaceful retreat.

The bar girl knew well our next port of call – the Aberdeen Red Lion (AB24 3JU), and we were grateful for her knowledge as the pub had no landline. I hadn't been too sure it still opened its doors and you didn't want wasted trips in this part of the world.

The sign at the bar was true even if the company was small:

'There are no strangers in the Red Lion, just friends we have never met.'

Suddenly the dog began to bark loudly.

'He does it every day when I have had two whiskies,' the loner explained.

'It's a clever dog,' I replied.

'Worse than the wife,' came the response.

You could always spot a man who came to the Red Lion at the same time every day for his peace – his dog a trusty servant.

By mid-afternoon we began the 50 miles to Aberdeen. In these parts, that meant 70 minutes to Spital where I recognised the Khyber Pass Takeaway! I had rung *them* to see if the Red Lion was open in the absence of the landline.

Just across the road, it was indeed – a little dusty and rough from the outside but warm and welcoming as Stan, who was standing outside smoking, took us inside. Two people recognised me from the local paper and Stan bought us a drink. It was loud and we laughed in this wonderful traditional pub against a background of darts, dominoes, football on the screen and Echo and the Bunnymen blasting out of the jukebox.

One thing that is striking about this pub is the effect of the smoking ban. The landlady pointed out the lovely ceiling with ornate lions painted in small squares. It had taken her husband months of cleaning to restore the original red and gold once the ban came in. They had turned a filthy dirty brown.

Stan did tell me he was coming with me to have a cigarette in every Red Lion. He also warned me not to expect a 'family atmosphere' in Glasgow the following day!

That was to come. First, as daft as it may sound, we pursued one of the beauties of the Quest – after any recommendation the detour often followed. We were about to drive the 118 miles back to Doune for a Chinese recommended to us with good reason by Ann at the Red Lion in Culross!

Before we parted, I heard a first.

'Why is there no landline?' I asked.

'The druggies used to sneak in and use it for their deals,' the landlady replied.

And so another solid sleep back at Doune Red Lion after our Chinese, a quick morning run up to the castle, and then on to Glasgow (G51 1LQ) in search of that friendly atmosphere.

Down the M9 and M80, we learned from the local radio news that there had been a big, all-night fire in Paisley in The George pub. Then, when we found the Red Lion, it was the most scruffy flat-roofed pub, with once tenement flats sitting above it. It stood padlocked up and looked a bit scary. I had called ahead to learn it opened at 11.30 am, but by 12.00 there was no sign of life.

I counted it in my list because it was meant to be open, even though we never stepped foot in it. Here is where the Quest throws unexpected situations at you.

Over a year later, Red Lion Glasgow contacted me on Facebook saying, 'What about us????' Oh heck. Either I got their opening time wrong or was told wrong, but they open at 12 noon on Sunday.

We loved Scotland and the Scottish people get 10 out of 10 for friendliness and warmth.

WOLVERHAMPTON WANDER

It was now 28 February 2013. I was probably still some two and a half years away from completing the Quest. Fred was back and first stop was the Red Lion at Wombourne (WV5 0JJ), a village often claimed to be the largest in England.

It nearly didn't happen at all after an MOT failure, so two new tyres later we were away and this became visit Number 4 to the Birmingham area. This Quest is even taking its toll on my car!

Wombourne is hard to find for an outsider, with the dual carriageway running alongside the original A road. Inside, wooden beams and a small bar comprise this 17th-century inn; the bar lady was enjoying a quiet moment after a busy lunch trade.

Six miles away, we arrived at Brierley Hill (DY5 3AB). This is a pub that has done the rounds in terms of ownership and a number of notable breweries over the years. It had once been just a Lion and run by the local blacksmith and later a glass-blower.

Today, it looks like a proper boozers' pub with cheap shots advertised. Furthermore, a couple of years ago, a previous landlady was convicted of selling cannabis in the pub and escaped jail by 'the skin of her teeth'. A court heard that her husband had lost his own job and had begun 'drinking the profits'. Surprisingly I hadn't met many landlords yet who were consuming as many as they sold. On this occasion the lady behind the bar avoided being put behind them.

This barman had previous Red Lion experience – in Crete. Point noted and added to the overseas file! History, too, was on the wane nearby – he also mentioned that Stourbridge Red was now a block of flats.

Passing the Starving Rascal pub on the way, we pulled up on Brettell Lane, Amblecote (DY8 4BA). It wasn't busy and didn't look like it was trying too hard. Even in barren pubs like this, someone always shared a nugget with us. The other Stourbridge Red Lion was now a supermarket, but there was one very close by in Netherton. In just a short time a few Red Lion mysteries had been cleared!

Discovering Netherton (DY2 9JA) we found a friendly little pub fascinated by the Quest. As ever when word spread, people were keen to pile in with their own Reds. One guy said he regularly delivered medication to a Red Lion doctors' surgery. I had witnessed Bromsgrove, which had been a surgery and was now a pub, and now was he saying that this was the reverse?

Go on then, just one more!

Bobbington (DY17 5DU) is a lovely place to end the day – a long pub with an inn and 17 bedrooms.

I stood there admiring a painting of a Lion when Mark, the manager of nearly two decades, asked would I like to see his 'big one'. I was expecting a stone statue or something, so imagine my surprise when I saw a stuffed lion and tiger standing tall just through the door. He paid £2,500 for them 26 years ago. Now this was a first, and talk about embracing the lion ethos!

He must have pulled that trick every time a stranger walked in, and never got tired of the delight it brought. There is a message here. A gimmick, just like the kilt at Culross or the drop down spider in Repton, creates a fun atmosphere before a drink has even been served. It literally sets the bar high.

And when it came to food and drink, it looked and smelled great at affordable prices. Mark offered me more Lion souvenirs to take on my travels in the form of a Red Lion polo shirt and… Red Lion golf balls. Is there a Red Lion merchandise department randomly handing out a not very obvious list of souvenirs? Maybe there should be: you simply never knew what you might get next.

Top 5 Unusual Features:

Stratton Audley
Bobbington
Great Wratting
Erdington
Woodbridge

AYLESBURY

The first of what turned out to be 16 this weekend was Claverdon (CV35 8PE) – the first of a few Proseccos undoubtedly, these served with fresh pomegranate kernels in beautifully shaped flutes. I thought of one of those early Lions where they didn't even have the proper glasses. If they couldn't get that right, it does not fill you with confidence. Paula and I only left Preston at 5 pm heading down to Oxford, and decided to stop in Warwick for the evening. This was a civil and elegant way to begin our weekend.

The next day the first Red, Ilmington (CV36 4LX), was initially shut when we arrived 15 minutes early, so we used the time taking photos. Percy, the landlord of eight years with long, silver hair in a ponytail, opened up dead on midday. Once he got the fires going he helped us plot our route from here. I had left my map at home! With its stone-flagged floor the pub was traditional but with lots of interesting artefacts, including another plaque promising 'free drinks tomorrow'.

Ilmington attracts the walkers passing through. Suddenly they just all descended on the place. You can spot them a mile off with their rucksacks all coming off their backs at the same time and stopping for a well-earned pint of ale.

The trip to Culworth is one of mixed emotions. We meandered through the fields of Middleton Cheney spotting beautiful llamas, deer, rabbits and the magnificent Elmington Countryside Hotel, but we could not spot its Red Lion. At the site where it once stood were a bunch of new houses.

Travelling on to Culworth (OX17 2DB) itself, we arrived early afternoon to find a pub brimming with eaters. Always innovative with its menus and daily specials, it prides itself on its food, serving fresh fish six days a week. As a non-meat eater, it was just my kind of menu.

Without our map, Google suggested Stratton Audley (OX27 9AG) next, some 26 miles away. With a charming courtyard and thatched roof, it is packed with rural Oxfordshire warmth. Inside, traditional board games will distract you (I hadn't played Frustration! for years), and outside, a beautifully carved, oversized wooden chair, perfect for the photo op. It had been skilfully created by the gypsies we passed as we turned into this old English village.

Overall you could tell that it stood at the heart of the community. They had raised £12,100 for Movember (the charity raising issues on men's health), and another £17,000 for Macmillan Nurses.

At Wendlebury (OX25 2PW), just five minutes away, we took the weight off our feet with two coffees in the beautiful, long, stone pub with wooden floors and a cosy wood-burner. The new owners run it well. I decided to pop back to Islip (OX5 2RX) next. It does not open all day, so we failed in our previous visit. Second time around was not the most exciting Lion of the pack. It could have been a one-off, but we found the atmosphere slightly morose and were nervous to speak. Yes, even I found myself whispering. People were pleasant but it was awkward. The sight of a big Lion's head with crazy hair broke our ice. We were just getting the hang of selfies, so we had fun with the pictures.

Red Lion 329 was three miles away at Yarnton (OX5 1QD). It was a loud, busy pub with a rugby team. That gives you some idea. It was the perfect contrast from Islip. We chatted as loud as we liked!

The bar lady was helpful, too, as ever pointing us in the direction of another Lion further down the road. This Lion is slightly unusual in that you think of Red Lions and beer. This Red had a rum thing going on. That may have contributed to the noise, but then again I have never seen a quiet rugby team.

Just 15 minutes up the road at The Green at Cassington (OX29 4DN) was the sixth today. The problem with so many Lions in one day was that we were drinking for the sake of it now. Not drinking per se, but coffee, water, Coke, polite halves. This has never been about alcohol consumption – if it was, why move from one to another? In fact, I think that the reason no one has ever visited every Red Lion pub before is that the intention would have been overruled by beer if a man was to try it!

Alex was smoking outside so ended up being involved in the photos. A young local wearing a random furry hat with earflaps explained all about the Quest to the other pub-goers once we entered. I mention his outfit as the chances are that, if you find this pub, he will be wearing the same.

He was well briefed in our adventure. I felt he wanted to be involved when he, too, pointed another one down the road. We were invited out the back to a room we would not otherwise have seen, and an old well with a glass cover over it making this Lion in a category of three with Birchover and Avebury, and possibly more in the future.

It was surprising there were so few or maybe others had just been filled in or lost. It would have been something you might expect to find as breweries need the best water supply, so many were built around wells. Was the glass cover a modern sign of health and safety, or an attempt at preserving the past?

And what a find Alex's Red Lion is, just five minutes away in The Square at Eynsham (OX29 4HW) and a beautiful stone village. I am grateful he flagged it up for us, but equally it would have been wonderful to stumble across it, too.

When I walk into a Red Lion I walk into the lives of strangers. One chap greeted us in the car park to explain it was his 'missis's 40th', and they were setting up inside. Countless times this had happened. Not, you understand, that this lady had her 40th but that a Red Lion was playing host to a celebration. In itself that was a good sign for the industry when there are so many choices these days. If it's your local, though, it's your local.

He grabbed our photos to see what the fuss was about, threatening to run off with the camera. That was a nightmare I hadn't foreseen. I had kept detailed notes and had hundreds of photos all backed up, and much of the Quest was stored in my head, but to lose it all at any point would be a tragedy.

But the goodwill of the Quest was always there. One lady in the pub had read about me and gave me a historical business card from the pub, and Alex from Cassington was obviously so enthralled that he had followed us on his bicycle and was waiting for us outside as we left.

Chinnor (OX39 4DL) was a bit further away, reached via the M40.

This pub is a regular in the CAMRA Good Beer Guide since 2006, so it comes well recommended. Inside, a beautiful, warm fire was up and running and it was crammed, and with us being the only females.

Then we spotted a curious sight. The majority of the men standing were hanging onto leather straps attached to the low-beamed ceiling as if they would fall over if they let go.

I don't know if it was some tradition, or if they were heavy drinkers and needed support, or if it was just a gimmick. I had never seen anything like it and so far haven't since, except the similarity of how people hang onto the yellow straps on trains on the London Underground. So far on this jaunt we had stepped into nine completely different Red Lions.

At Longwick (HP27 9SG) the colour hit us right in the face. Red carpet, red chairs, and half the walls painted red. It was the most *red* Red Lion!

Then I noticed the owner at the end of the bar with a wooden spoon in his hand with an air of well, authority, about him, marching around without a smile or eye contact.

Yet the pub was popular, with all the tables reserved under individuals' names – with red napkins obviously. I did notice, too, a first. Attached to each wooden box of condiments lay a small pair of scissors. That was so simple I wondered why nobody had thought of this before. How many times do you tear these sachets open with your teeth, for their contents to fly out landing where they shouldn't, if you can get them open at all?

Old-fashioned and a real step back in time, the pub was thriving.

We had never visited so many Lions in one single day. We freshened up in the hotel and took a cab to Brierton (HP22 5BU), our eleventh today and a fine way to end the day. The pub dates back to the 16th century and was particularly significant during the English Civil War when it hosted many Royalist officers, including Charles I himself.

Under low, dark beams in this traditional country pub, out came the Prosecco alongside fish cakes and sautéed mushrooms. At the end of the evening the waitress ordered us a taxi, so we retired to the bar while it arrived. It took forever but this was definitely not a problem, as one generous local handed out his delicious, home-made chocolate Malteser slabs. He gave me the recipe but I doubt I will ever make them due to the few thousand calories involved. It would be dangerous if this was my local... I would need to double my gym sessions.

The following morning, the next four would be my last for three weeks. First stop was Finmere (MK18 4AG). It stands in between two villages!

Beautifully thatched and stone, its wooden floors and contemporary furniture ooze English charm. We ordered coffee, and while waiting for our fish cakes Paula randomly selected a book from the shelf entitled *Adult Pub Jokes* and shared some of them. Has anyone eaten so many fish cakes in Red Lions as Paula and I have?

The Red Lion at The Green, Evenley (NN13 5SH), is one of those pubs that just says 'sit outside in the summer and watch the world go by' whilst equally wrapping you up in warmth in the autumn and winter with its open fire and fantastic food.

Its air of summer stems from its location. Apparently it is known locally as 'The Cricketing Inn'. It sits on the village green and *you* can sit and watch or ignore at your leisure. It makes up a beautiful snapshot of village life that is dying out nowadays. It doesn't matter if cricket is the dullest sport on the planet, in settings like this it creates a special atmosphere. These locals are blessed. To top it all, Angie the landlady used to live in Preston in the same road as my sister, selling her house to a friend of mine. Small world.

I am sure the odd cricket ball must have entered over the years, and I am sure the odd cricketer, too.

The old coaching town of Brackley (NN13 7AB) was to be our penultimate of this leg of the Quest. Some 19 miles from Oxford, and with two bars, it has stood for 400 years: this is a great pick if you are visiting Towcester Races or Silverstone for the Formula One.

Checkley (ST10 4NJ) isn't easy to find. They gave me a Red alert on Red Lion farm in Dayhills, but time was getting the better of us so we headed home to our own local which is not a Red Lion but Ye Olde Original Withy Trees.

And every time we returned from a venture they would always ask 'How many?' and this time I was proud to say 16 and one dead.

It had been a mammoth weekend.

BAR HUMBER!

My friend Helena arrived at midday, despite blizzard snow, with the intention of heading to Lincoln again and to my friends in Folkingham. They must think the only time I see them is when I am on a pub crawl. It isn't true but, because of the Quest, I actually go more often. We are all guilty of putting things off and sometimes years go by before you actually make the effort to see that distant relative or friend.

A couple of hours in we stopped at Barton-upon-Humber (DN18 5PU), which is easy to find just over the Humber Bridge. This Lion comes with certain local clout. Everybody starts their Friday and Saturday nights here, apparently.

Number 341 is Broughton under Brigg (DN20 0HY), although I only took notice of the Brigg part of the address and parked up there instead!

When we finally found our bearings a poster just stared at me from the pub wall. It read 'Puggie Wuggie Disco with karaoke and buffet' that evening.

There were lots of dog faces on the flyer. Eventually curiosity got the better of me. How would a karaoke for dogs work?!

That was barking mad.

The bar girl put my mind at ease. They were raising money for the local dog rescue organisation.

Further down the A15 and across the A631 to Market Rasen (LN8 3BB), and a chance for a pleasant surprise or disappointment.

I had been here before.

Market Rasen was closed in September 2011. Facebook's all-powering knowledge suggested it had reopened in the November.

Beyond pleasant surprise is the answer. It had undergone a total refurbishment into a classy yet traditional mix of brick and natural wood.

The menu was small but the odours emanating from the kitchen confirmed it would be tasty. I had noticed that fewer items seemed to

Stratton Audley – the amazing carved chair

Cassington, the guy who turned up at the next Red Lion on his bike

Paulton with brother Andy, Jon and Eve

Holt Heath – Mum and Helena for Mum's 80th

Lenham, with Braz

Charing, the child's shoe discovered in the chimney

Cranford, Clark Gable's initials are etched on one of the small glass panes

Penderyn, a big favourite near the distillery with Natalie and her Dad

Builth Wells – the oldest pub in Powys with Helena

Little Missenden and a Morris dancer

Studham – 499th with Robert the lodger

Dagnall, my 500th

be becoming the norm these days rather than huge, long menus which couldn't all be absolutely freshly made. With five rooms, too, the licensee was moving on from this being a drinking pub towards quality dining and overnight stay. This irritates some people, calling it gastro nonsense, but as long as it stays alive and kicking it has to be better than a boarded-up drinkers' pub.

I was glad to have revisited.

It was still freezing when we arrived at Dunston (LN4 2EW), 22 miles and 40 minutes on from Market Rasen. Kindly, the landlady opened up early for us and we sat near the bar in old-fashioned surroundings cluttered with horseshoes and tacky ornaments.

The unusual backwards clock with the numbers on the wrong side threw me totally. We left at 6.15. Or did we?!

It was well below zero with fresh snow falling by the time we arrived at Wellingore (LN5 0HW), and we did not stay long.

One hysterical detail remains with me from this empty pub with the hoover plonked in the corner.

'Julie welcomes customers old and new,' said the blackboard.

'Are you Julie?' I asked.

'No, she went on Monday and I arrived. I'm Millie but I haven't got round to changing the board yet,' she replied. She only needed to rub out the 'j' and 'u' and replace with 'Mil'??? She wasn't even busy hoovering.

She had run 20 pubs in five years and now landed here in what was a tatty décor.

Perhaps her Number 21 was just around her corner.

We awoke the next morning, freezing but keen for a short jog in the snow. We slowly made our way to Folkingham where we met our friends Denny and Val for lunch, but not in a Red Lion! The snow continued as we watched through the window: the road and pavements were all one sheet of white. It was good to experience Red Lions in all conditions and next on our list was Bourne (PE10 9LT).

That said, it was one of the rare occasions when I had diverted from my original route. People had often diverted us, but we had barely let the weather do so: abandoning Skegness, we decided to stay more local.

Bourne was like an old-fashioned working men's club. With pool tables at the back and bandits at the side, I would barely say there was a lounge. We had no choice but to brave the elements after 15 minutes!

And now it was severely limiting our movements. Just stopping briefly at West Deeping (PE6 9HP), though, this is a nice long pub with exposed stone, and the window seat gave us a lovely view to watch the snowfall. A reminder, too, that the pub still served as a community noticeboard from bikers to chess players, from bridge club to book club.

On reflection, 16 miles across fields to the listed building at Gedney Hill (PE12 0NN) might have been a bit daft, but was probably more sensible than going home in this weather.

Two big dogs greeted us from behind the bar in a pub hogged by men and lacking in atmosphere. On the ghost pub website it says that a former Turkish general called Pasha haunted the place. I don't know how the Turkish military ended up here but it could have been entertaining.

And at Market Place, Spalding (PE11 1SU), it didn't appear to get any better, looking rough from outside at the back. Helena didn't fancy going in, but she knows the rules so in we went.

Inside was a warm and cosy, traditional pub and open fire. How could two faces of a pub so contradict each other, and what if Helena had run? How many others had, too?

Not Jimi Hendrix. He stayed here in May 1967 when for one day only Spalding became the rock'n'roll capital of the world! Eric Clapton was also on the bill.

Tickets were just a pound. Nigel Hawkins, the then landlord, told a BBC programme that Hendrix was trying to woo girls back to his room in the Lion, including the landlord's own girlfriend at the time. Hendrix was reported to have tied them in bedsheets and dangled them from the window. Naughty Jimi! I can't imagine Spalding has seen the like since.

We survived the snow and made it safely home, laughing about those groupies.

A THURSDAY IN WALSALL

I collected Fred, did errands in Blackpool, and then headed south towards Stafford. I didn't like to waste time on the Quest, so I rang ahead to check the Red Lions' opening times.

Worth doing – one closed at 3 pm, and the others were only open in the evening. Goodbye, Stafford then, and hello, Wolverhampton (WV11 1LE)!

I remember growing up to 'opening hours', but then pubs weren't permitted to open all day. It may seem strange to some people whose locals open all hours that some pubs still close but I can see why in some tiny villages.

And we arrived late, as a lorry had spilled its load on the M6. Yes, when did that not happen? It's a decent, big Red Lion on the corner with meals half price between 2.30 and 5.00 pm Monday to Friday.

The Red Lion Walsall (WS9 08L) is not to be confused with The Lion Bar and Club in the area. That is the area's premier gay bar and club, but Google might take you that way.

Instead, head to Station Road and the village of Aldridge on its suburbs, and you will find a place valued at 15 shillings in the Domesday Book!

Its Red Lion is the only pub in the village and seemed a male-dominated establishment, but equally one enthralled by the Quest. It prompted the usual discussion about the most common pub names: I believe the White Hart and the Rose and Crown come in at second and third. And whenever you came across a group of men in a pub to whom this was all new and that conversation followed, I suspect they all wished they had a reason to tour the UK's drinking holes.

I was way ahead of them!

I tried to ring ahead to Walsall (WS1 1NW) but there was no number – often the sign of a dead Lion.

Instead, we found a lovely fronted building of red, cream and brick and an inside dominated by a large wood and iron spiral staircase leading to an upstairs looking down onto a slowly closing down town. It was almost 5 pm.

The wall above the bar was adorned with a really unusual mural of a river scene and a red lion with two proud lion statues filling the wall above the bar.

Plenty of lions and definitely open. Not all landlords put any importance on a landline with so much social media and internet, but often Google information is way out of date.

On to Bradley (ST18 9EG), travelling along narrow, windy lanes which were merely dirt tracks and ran for nine miles. We needed something at the end of this assault course!

And such a struggle turns to delight afterwards when you arrive at a gorgeous, 16th-century inn with low ceilings and beams. I like a challenge especially when there is a reward at the end. That feeling of 'it had better be worth it when you arrive' was always wonderful when it was.

Three cottages had been transformed into the bar, restaurant and a few small rooms, with fire and comfy leather chairs, and it was one of those pubs where the relaxing atmosphere made the food smell even better.

The pub is over 500 years old and now bears the sign 'Beer is the answer but I can't remember the question'. So many Lions had their own particular catchphrase or saying. You noticed them once and then never again. A sign in my local says what if the hokey-cokey really is what it's all about?

By 7 pm, we were at Derrington (ST18 9LR), ordering from a barman who could not speak so he wrote down the amount due on a white board. Then he sat down to continue his crossword.

He was pleasant enough but, when the next couple came in, it all seemed too much of an effort for him to serve again. It was all very odd.

I have since learned that this Lion has now closed and was being sold off possibly for houses. The village had also previously lost its shop.

It had been there since 1779. I wish the closures would stop.

BRISTOL WITH BROTHER

On the spur of the moment, I decided to visit my brother and family in Bristol, beginning with a girly night out with my sister-in-law Jess at The Red Lion Wine Bar on Worrall Road. It was boarded up and closed – another dead Lion. The Quest even dominated my genuine social activities, and disrupted them, too.

My brother and kids drove us in from Clevedon and deciding to give the other Red Lion a try, with him pointing out that the area was not great and if we decided to move on there was nowhere very suitable to go. Unfazed, we waved them goodbye, jumped in and my sister-in-law entered her first Red Lion on Whitehall Road (BS5 9BP).

It was rough, almost seedy – a no-frills pub. Male-dominated, and with the band setting up, this pub knew what it was. They really didn't expect us and the Quest, though they were quite charming about it, especially John who had been drinking since Friday evening. It was now 8 pm on a Saturday. I have barely mentioned the hardened drinker. Most pubs have theirs, and here it was John. He takes the crown for sure.

It looked like the kind of place where anything could happen but came with a huge dose of fun, too.

We thanked Anita for the drink, summoned a taxi to leave, and headed towards the harbour. The cabbie called to say he was outside and I promptly tried to get in the wrong vehicle but thankfully it was locked. It was the wrong area to get in a strange car.

We crept in late. The harbour is a great night out.

By the next morning I had roped in more family members, including my brother Andy and my niece and nephew who soon got into the swing of things. It was a thumbs-down for last evening's closed one, and today's two got a big thumbs-up!

For my new recruits, their first was Bishop Sutton (BS39 5XD), and for my sister-in-law Jess a complete contrast in the cold light of day with old photos dotted around the place.

Surrounded by greenery and encased in beautiful stone, we couldn't have visited two pubs at the opposite end of the scale to last night's, and this would have been a lovely place to eat but it was still a bit early.

Next stop was Lion Number 356 at Paulton (BS39 7NW). I had been here before in July 2012 on my way to Devon and Cornwall on that tour!

Another lovely stone building in a cute, small village, it offered an under 5s eat free option with other kids' meals at a mere £2.50... Excellent food and value yet they only took payments by cash. Perhaps this was still a hangover from the previous regime under which the pub had closed but they had applied for a card system and were working hard. At 2.15, after a really enjoyable weekend with the family, I took myself back to Preston.

DERBYSHIRE DAY OUT

It had been a whole month since the last outing because I had begun dabbling with some overseas Red Lions. That's another story for another day and not part of this Quest. In fact, that could be a never-ending one. If you think how many times I had been in a UK Red Lion only for someone to point out an unknown one, it would present serious issues overseas. It's not like I could suddenly hop five minutes down the road. Fun issues, all the same.

So, inspired by a victory in an Ebay auction to purchase a gas hob at £2, collecting it meant only one thing – more Lions.

In tow this time: Fred, Cooper and now Bradley, my friend's 19-year-old son from Australia. We set off for Ilkeston on a two-hour drive. Bradley came from Australia to pursue a football career, temporarily staying with me. 'Temporarily' meant for a year!

With the hob packed up, we passed Ripley, which I had already visited, and Clay Cross, which was closed on a Monday and needed a revisit.

Also shut was Shirland (DE55 6BB).

We did stop for photos, causing the landlord to pop out and question why. When we mentioned the Quest, we were invited in. The hesitation arose from a development across the road which had used photos of the pub for advertising purposes, so he immediately assumed the same for us. Inside sat the funniest-looking Churchill dog ever. Oh yes.

We stopped briefly at Sheffield Road Chesterfield (S41 8LX) before taking the road to Sheffield itself with a couple of Red Lions in mind.

In the end there were three, with the first an unplanned stop at Heeley (S2 4HT). The landlady knew of the Quest and wondered why this had not been on our list. I liked it when people knew we could just turn up at any point. I wondered, too, why I had missed it.

A quick scan of my notes found that London Road *was* on the list but I had crossed it off as dead, replaced by a Chinese takeaway.

How had that happened? Seemingly, there *was* a Chinese close by that was a Red Lion, hence the confusion. Both *were* Red Lions and both *were* open. I was grateful for the knowledge. I never wanted to complete the Quest and have misplaced the odd Lion, though obviously as time passes the Red Lion map was always both evolving and shrinking in front of me.

Heeley recommended Gleadless Road, Sheffield (S12 2LL) next. Starving and with no food being served, we were then told that no children were allowed. The pub had been recently done up but remained an old-school drinkers' place.

Brian had been the landlord of 21 years. There was nothing ornate or historic or quirky about this pub, but he did insist on taking us to his back room… full of Sheffield United memorabilia. A few days after, he kindly emailed me the postcodes of all the Red Lions in the Sheffield area.

11 miles into the city we arrived at Charles Street (S1 2ND) – a large but cosy, clean, traditional pub with little else to report.

And then two weeks passed before Fred, Bradley and Cooper picked up the Quest with me again, heading to Stoke (ST4 6ER) for a rarity – a one-off, a Red Lion all by itself.

And there could have been so many in theory. There are quite a few Lions listed around Stoke but no live phone links, and whilst Stoke is easy enough to find, it is one of those strange half-town half-cities with not much identity and no obvious centre.

I had a pretty good idea of the whereabouts of two Lions and was really looking for either to avoid a wasted trip. The sat nav indicated they were close to each other.

We stumbled across the Famous Lion on Church Street, but that unfortunately does not count, and after asking countless people we eventually found this Lion tucked down a side road, Stoke Old Road.

The pub opened on the dot at 3 pm and Graham, landlord of two years, said he had been waiting for us to visit since following the Facebook page.

He is affectionately known as Grumps, though there were no obvious clues why. I found him and his partner friendly and down to earth, just trying to make a crust. The pub had been an Enterprise Inns business, but Graham said his turnover was now very much on the increase since he took it on. It was an eternal problem for landlords. You have the support of the brewery but are then restricted, especially in terms of profit, or you go alone and nobody really knows until then if you can sink or swim, and many of these pubs need refurbishment and often it is better to get someone else to pay for that… if they will? This Red is relatively young, built in 1930, though a pub had stood on the plot for many years.

Graham took me out the back. By now, I was used to this 'code' which often led to fresh insight, areas not open to the public, or souvenirs. And this time I was offered a sign he had just replaced from outside. Of course I wanted it. That garage of mine was filling up!

They suggested we try Burslem. We weren't convinced it was open. They confirmed it was. But when we got there, it wasn't! With opening hours just for evenings, we would have to return.

NORFOLK

I had visited 362 Lions. Not one of them was in Norfolk. Yet, I had made several journeys to areas like Birmingham.

It was time to fix this.

At the end of May 2013, I set off with Helena, deliberately targeting Norwich City of Ale Week! In glorious sunshine at the end of half-term week, I should have known better, stuck in traffic immediately into our three-hour drive.

By the time we arrived some five hours later at Swaffham Prior (CB25 0LD), it was one of the rare occasions when you really did need a drink the moment you got out of the car. Helena, who had my map on her knee, spotted it just two miles off the motorway. Perfect.

And it is a beautiful village dating back to at least the Domesday Book and with its two churches towering above the landscape, you can pinpoint the place from miles out, with its two operating windmills equally delighting your line of vision when you pick them up. The Lion is next to one of the churches. With a large BBQ in the lovely, long beer garden, it's another which has 'perfect summer's day' written all over it.

We actually still hadn't made Norfolk – Swaffham Prior is in Cambridgeshire, but we didn't have long to wait, arriving at Thetford (IP24 2AL), a Wetherspoons just about half an hour away.

Some reviews were hailing it after its refurbishment a couple of years back, with one citing the choice of real ales in the Thetford area to be poor but the Red Lion broke the mould. That was encouraging.

Indeed, when we passed through the new part of the town to reach the lovely old centre we found the pub by the town square and a décor incorporating local tradition using very natural materials – the rooms full with pictures, photos and quirky design features. It really was a bit more than I expected from a Wetherspoons.

It had been a long day by the time we arrived at Caston, Attleborough (NR17 1DE), another 30 minutes down the A11.

Again, this had just been renovated but nothing needed fixing about its location – sitting idyllically on the village green. I never tire of seeing Lions like this.

Oddly the original pub sat just round the back with its old sign still hanging. I am sure I only had to ask to add it to the collection!

That evening we checked into our second-floor hotel room in Norwich city centre to open the curtains to discover we were actually looking onto Carrow Road, the home of the football club. The youth team were actually playing an end-of-season match. I was told it was impossible to book during the season. I didn't know Norwich were that popular.

The following morning we took the A14 north towards Cromer – the 20-mile trip interspersed with numerous vans selling strawberries and asparagus. It seemed to be the thing around here!

By chance, and we would have missed it otherwise, Helena spotted a small sign in the grass pointing to the Red Lion up the track on the left. It was Aldborough (NR11 7AA). I was not expecting it, but the surprise was well worth it. A mile and a half down a narrow road brings you out onto a small village green and a gorgeous pub at the far side. On approach, you couldn't tell if it was open but it definitely was, with a massive open fire, plush leather chairs and plants everywhere in no particular arrangement. Trudy made us welcome with a good pot of coffee.

I would have been disappointed to have missed out on this Old Red Lion, as it is called. The discreet sign and the little track were almost deliberate. You are rewarded if you find it. Your loss if you don't!

The Red Lion at Cromer (NR27 9HD) is a distraction for all the right reasons. It's a real grand old Victorian affair on the seafront just overlooking the old pier and it took us ages to reach the bar as the entrance from the rear held so many interesting features. Without appearing in any way dated, it's a definite throwback. You cannot walk into this pub without imagining how we used to live.

Nothing exemplified this more than the traditional bar but there is also a bright conservatory, a tearoom, cabinets selling handmade jewellery, many interesting pictures, and a life-saving ring made into a

Lion's face. Like many Norfolk houses, the walls also caught our eye – made traditionally from pebble.

Friendly locals frequented the bar, the food looked and smelled delicious, and visiting families would pop in and out en route to their sea walks and rambles. In other words, in terms of clientele, it crossed that rare divide – something perfect for both visitors and those who grew up and lived here. That was not always the case with a seafront pub with accommodation.

Genuinely, this is a cracking place. I expect it was a highlight of a wealthy British family coming down from the city in the post-war years.

By the time we arrived at 2.30 at The Skiffkey Red Lion, Wells-next-the-Sea (NR23 1AJ), we were chasing the clock. That remains a shame because this, too, is a beautiful pub with each of the three rooms bearing a fire and a cool, tiled floor. The smell of fresh fish dominates throughout.

But our hastiness was down to a conversation I had with Amanda at Bishopsgate (NR1 4AA). The Norfolk press were waiting for us!

This is a traditional pub on the River Wensum, dating back to 1760. So far, I don't think there has been a better location to do an interview, perched next to the old bridge just by the river itself. Once the photographer started snapping so did everybody else – passers-by who couldn't have had a clue what we were doing began taking our pictures, and Helena snapped them back.

Inside, Amanda handed me a T-shirt from the previous year when one guy had cycled round all 13 of Norfolk's Red Lions for charity. That made me think. There was him and there was me. Had anyone else warmed to this theme? It made a handy little Red Lion list.

Across from the pub was another called Lollards Pit. This is haunted by a ghost from when locals used to throw witches in the river just by where I had been sitting. Such behaviour seemed all so normal back in the day!

On Fakenham Road, the Red at Drayton (NR8 6PW) was easy to spot. By 5.30, the pub showed it was obviously very popular with a queue for the carvery.

This pub had been an old farm and become a Lion in 1678. The date was painted in black on the pub to stand out. Peter, who had run the pub for 13 years, showed us his handiwork. His is an interesting story, the likes of which I hadn't yet heard on the Quest. He was an Australian backpacker who arrived 25 years ago. He liked the area so much, he never went home. It is usually the other way round!

We had just one more Lion to do for the day and that was five miles down the road at Eaton (NR4 7AB).

This is quite a unique Red. It is a very old brick building with an interesting, Dutch-style gable end and a very formal interior focussing as a restaurant with oak-panelled walls. It was friendly but a bit posh! – a little Hooray Henry.

It seems, too, that over the years they had attracted interesting acclaim.

They had been awarded a silver plaque by The Red Lion, Bangor, Maine, in the US by a Professor Bernard Yvon on 4 July 1982. I am not sure why or what you had to do to get one, but there it stood.

And its story began in 1652 when it was owned by the Sheriff of Norwich. The Dutch influence from just across the water stems from the start.

Today the pub is very much embedded in the family that run it. The landlord and his wife had been in six years and took it on from their parents.

Red Lioning Norfolk had been nothing but a delight to this point.

The next morning that changed at Halvergate (NR13 3QB). It was dead and drab, and my abiding memory is of the landlady wearing an England polo shirt ready for an England v Brazil match that evening.

Curiously, and I had seen this before, for five years as late as the year 2000, the pub had also been the post office!

There was a fair trek ahead to the next one, so we had the perfect excuse to make tracks. Red Lion Number 373 was 26 miles away at Needham, Harleston (IP20 9LG). This is a picturesque village between Norfolk and Suffolk.

It would be easy to miss this pub, and its extensive decked terrace at the rear – a real suntrap. And when it wasn't contributing to a classic English scene, perhaps there were clues in some of the street names around here as to what this area could be like in the winter. I may be wrong but Freezin Hill and Snow Street meant either that a Mr Freezing and a Mr Snow had been prominent in the local community, or that the community had often been cut off through bad weather!

We ended our weekend on one of the best at Kenninghall (NR16 2EP). It is now run by Bruce and Mandy Berry, but it had been closed for seven years until 1997. That is a long time for a pub to be taken out of its community and to find its customers again.

Now it was thriving through food specials, live music and their annual Go-Kart Race! The interior has been completely redone, mostly in oak, and its snug is one of only two in East Anglia. Bruce had done much of the work himself, to his credit.

It was hard to leave and it had been one of the great Red Lion weekends, almost without exception featuring top-quality pubs, again all different but all with character and quality with just the odd exception.

Bruce and I have since been in contact via Facebook, and since then he told me he got divorced from his wife and she got the pub!!!!

It had taken so long to head east but only because I had been trekking north, south and west.

LET ME ENTERTAIN YOU

Operation Overseas Lions was a reality. Since Norfolk, I had also visited one in France and was planning further afield for later in the year.

I couldn't get ahead of myself, though. There were still over 200 to go in the UK and some unfinished business.

The first of these was at Burslem (ST6 1DJ), which had been shut on the last Stoke visit.

Before we could crack on, I had to revisit Graham at Hartshill to collect my Lion sign which he had given me the previous month but I had been unable to fit in my car.

Then finally we could see Burslem. It had been built in the 60s with the sole purpose of accommodating Port Vale supporters!

Since then, it had taken its place in rock'n'roll history. This used to be Robbie Williams's local.

It's worth saying those words a few times over. Here I was standing in the pub where Robbie used to drink. His DNA was very much among us, in a fag end or in a glass or by a machine. Everybody had a local and this was his!

In fact it goes beyond that. He had lived here, as his mother Jan had been the landlady, having taken on the pub from David Wolstenhome, a relative of the sports commentator Kenneth who gave us the legendary 'They think it's all over. It is now.'

This place was steeped in history.

Someone inevitably had written 'I am loving angels' on one of the walls.

Beyond that, at 6 pm on a Thursday night there was no sign that the next Robbie Williams would be found here. In fact, the pub was pretty empty. Of course, it didn't necessarily follow that a pub where someone very famous once drank would be thriving, but equally the tourist map was always littered with such cases.

Robbie hadn't put Burslem on the map.

We made for Chesterton (ST5 7ER) just four miles away, a big betting pub with racing from Haydock on the TV. On the way, curiosity got the better of me. I spotted a place called Saggar Makers and Googled it. I found it was the name of a skilled person who held the pottery on the kiln while his less skilled helper was the Bottom Knocker. You can write your own punchline here.

This was, of course, the Potteries.

After Chesterton, there was nothing. I had come to an abrupt end for no obvious reason. You would think I would be on a high after toasting Robbie and returning with a new sign. The truth is I didn't see another Red Lion for a further two months.

It was now August 2013.

Much of my absence can be explained by the annual arrival of my Belarus visitors. So, back on track, I texted my sister Debbie to see if she was free and within 90 minutes we were heading to Wrexham (LL13 0NT). It was her first Red and there were also very few left within an hour or so of home, so these spontaneous opportunities were diminishing in front of me.

We arrived by 5 pm at a Grade II listed building but it was actually a long, tatty pub with its only entrance at the back. This was true of so many Lions and I had never got to the bottom of why you would build something that was after all a social focal point and yet would encourage people to enter almost discreetly!

The landlady had been in charge for the previous 18 months but had worked there all her life, a total of 19 years. That must have been a massive transition from just being staff.

Now, she had been given three months' notice and the pub had been sold for £35,000 – a tiny amount and a depressing tale of one individual's dreams going up in smoke.

It was no surprise, then, when she told me they had few customers and the pub was often shut by 9 pm. That really was a very bad sign.

At Buckley (CH5 3AR) we found a much tidier pub and a landlord of just six months, and Foster's at a remarkable £2.30 a pint. We had a long chat about how some breweries had regularly stitched up the pubs and he should know – when I told him which other Red Lions he had visited, he seemed to have run them all in the vicinity at some point.

Two weeks later we were back in Wales at Rhyl (LL18 2TN), Paula having booked a friend's cottage for a couple of nights at Pwllheli.

There was just one woman and two children in this jaded, large, open pub with three areas hosting a pool table, sofa and bandits. Outside, the beer garden was overgrown.

Tom, the barman, told us that the pub used to have narrow corridors before it was opened up. That sounded like it had an aura of mystery and character about it. Now, it didn't feel very homely away and Tom told us he really didn't expect anyone to be walking in that day on a Red Lion trail. Those words alone told me that not much went on here. Every day people told stories at the pub. I got the feeling that for Tom it was same old same old.

He pointed to the B & B sign outside as he helped with the photos, but confirmed they no longer did it. He told us how, when people came in to enquire, only to be declined, they invariably bought a drink out of guilt. It had clearly seen more prosperous times.

At Ffordd Talargoch, Prestatyn (LL19 8LA) it was the exact opposite, with a full-on B & B, a gorgeous interior, the exterior a mass of colour with plants and flowers just about everywhere, all interspersed with little surprise ornaments, Lion statues, trees with faces, and seats, benches and swings. At Lion Number 380, this wins Best Garden so far hands down. Indeed, the bar lady explained that someone was specially assigned just to maintain the garden.

It was odd the way the Lion list suddenly evolved. I had no way of knowing that these two today would provide such a contrast as back-to-back Lions. The roof terrace on the tiny cottage at Llanbedrog gave us an hour of sunshine to end our day.

The next morning we awoke to an overcast Wales and headed for Dinas Mawddwy (SY20 9JA). Part of the joy of reaching this pub is of course the 80-minute drive through Snowdonia National Park – despite the massive puddles in the huge dips in the road.

We received a typically hearty Welsh welcome from both the friendly staff and the huge open fireplaces. They didn't know anything about the Quest but were delighted to be included, thinking how they would use this in their weekly quiz!

Their bar is very interesting – adorned with 300 pieces of shiny brass.

I explained that the next stop was Machynlleth (SY20 8EB), but wasn't sure if it was open. One local confirmed it was, having popped in for a pint just the day before – but only because he had gone to Machynlleth for a tin of peas as the Spar here didn't have one! The distance was 19 miles – a long way to go for a tin of peas!

It turned out to be a drinkers' pub. With a partly slate and partly grotty-carpeted floor, you could always tell. Drinkers' pubs didn't tend to worry too much about what was going on at ground level.

One redeeming feature, though, is The Red Lion Wall of Records behind the pool table. A dozen black records were stuck on the wall, each naming someone who had achieved some sort of bragging rights feat.

These events you would not find at the Olympics – who had ever heard of 'keeping a Malteser afloat' or 'going round the darts board the fastest' or 'putting the most marshmallows in your mouth'?

I thought I may revisit and add 'most Red Lions visited' as a new category, but I have since learned that there is no need. They have done it for me!

Last port of call was Old Colwyn (LL29 9PL). I had been here before in 2012 only to find it closed. Second time lucky. Geoff, the landlord, recognised me. He had been in for a decade, and he would have opened up for me had he known about my first visit.

This Lion did not serve food but did run a Thirsty Thursday where all cask ales were £2.30 a pint.

Geoff, I am sure, was very much under the thumb. I did not meet his wife but 'she was the one who kept everyone in order', fondly known as the Wicked Witch of the Red.

I had wandered into so many people's lives and my own existence had changed along the way, too, but now it was time to make a Red Lion centre stage in my own world.

I had eyes on overseas Red Lions – in particular, Australia – and I knew I would be away for my mum's 80th, so I decided to pick out an awesome Lion to celebrate in advance. Helena was in on the celebration and I couldn't have picked a better one than Holt Heath (WR6 6LX).

I had seen Lions of all shapes and sizes but this one actually meant something to me as we approached it. Their website looked good. I was desperate not to be disappointed.

I didn't need to be. Everything was perfect from the preordered champagne cooling at the table when we arrived, to the Lebanese owner himself celebrating that he just had become a father to a baby boy.

Sharing your emotion with someone else was a very natural thing. And a long banner across the front of the pub proclaimed 'It's a boy'. Like many babies that year, he was named George, though not through any allegiance to our newest member of the British Royal family.

What's more, it's not every day your mum turns 80, so we dined out in style – sea bass, pepper risotto, and pork. The champagne didn't stop all night, topped off with Baileys and Tia Maria nightcaps – on the house!

I was hugely relieved on a personal note. It was a new experience in close to 400 Red Lions.

The next morning we left for Cradley, Malvern (WR13 5NN), reflecting on the previous night.

We began the day with a short walk along a nice footpath, and especially for my mum this meant no hills!

An hour later we arrived at the white-brick, painted pub which opened its doors early for us, having seen us doing the photos! We enjoyed our drinks in the lovely garden surrounded by flowers and hanging baskets.

This one had sadly been closed for two years due to flooding, only to open again for the same to happen. The owners persevered and it was now, thankfully, coming good for them.

A three-mile, scenic, hilly route followed to Malvern (WR14 4RG). It's possibly one of the highest Red Lions and with that you get a fantastic view over the valleys. It is a Thai restaurant and, like everything round here, standing on a slope. It's a terrific Lion with awesome perspectives across the valleys. My mum, who at the beginning of my Quest just thought it was another of my oddball ideas, was beginning to understand the draw to being led through Britain's beauty spots such as these.

And that was 23 August 2013. There would be no more UK Lions for two months. I was off to the Melbourne, Geelong, Ballarat and Kilmore Red Lions down under with of course my friend Sammy. I would be back in the UK in time for more Roaring Lions by October.

And so it was (after as yet unpublished Lions!) that Ealing (W5 5RA) called. I sneaked it in after attending a charity ball for breast cancer at the House of Commons with Andrée, Kevin and family.

Taking the overground train from Clapham Junction to Shepherd's Bush, I jumped the Central line to Ealing, arriving just as they opened.

I was the only customer – in a London pub – so chatted to Jonathon, the landlord of 12 years.

Funnily enough, he told me he used to drink in the Red at Old Colwyn where I had been pretty recently. It is a small world when Red Lioning.

Beautifully, it is just across from the world-famous Ealing Studios, and they nickname this Lion 'the sixth stage', presumably as many of the UK and indeed the world's finest actors bailed out of the set and into the bar.

As I left chasing a train back home, I realised The Red Lion and Pineapple was less than two miles away. Not solely a Red, but definitely worthy of inclusion.

ON A RIDING TO NOTHING

Post-Australia, I needed to pick up the pace and Fred came a-calling. Yorkshire needed to be dealt with. In the second weekend of October, we headed for Spalding (YO43 4AB) near York.

We had differing interesting experiences in Yorkshire, so I was delighted to find a well-maintained Red Lion with beautiful smells coming from the kitchen.

The landlord had been in just six months, also running a successful pub in the next village.

The walls in the entrance and lounge were dark and wood-panelled, but not in a depressing way, as is sometimes the case. It is a good pub, some 500 years old and the landlord Chris is good at what he does.

Four miles later, Red Lion 389 is Market Weighton, York (YO43 3AH). This is a lovely area in the heart of East Yorkshire, and a rarity – we arrived as the Foster's lorry was doing a delivery.

This was one of those odd moments when real life took over from the Quest. As we walked in, the TV news was showing footage of a plane that had landed thanks to a passenger after the pilot had died.

As we left this beautiful village, I was conscious that our next stop was Anlaby, Hull (HU10 7AN), which normally implied Bradford- or Sheffield-type run-down Lions.

The route there was pleasant enough along the 16 miles of the A1079, passing through churches and fields along the way to Bishop Burton, a pub called Altissidora, round a roundabout with a jockey and horse embedded on it, and the famous Beverley Racecourse.

We were lucky as it had just been reopened in the previous six weeks, having been a dead Lion for the last 22 months. Indeed, Google still implied it was a goner. Once again, no phone number came up.

Since they had decent live music to promote, I urged them to set up a Facebook page. If only businesses, especially social ones, realised the benefits, I am sure more would do it. It really wasn't that difficult to do.

And they had a lot to shout about. Chef and landlord Steve could probably write a book himself, having catered for some of the most famous people in the world, including Queen Elizabeth II as he worked up the catering ladder aboard some of the great ocean liners. He had seen it all and served them all, and now had come home to Hull. I am sure he could tell stories all night long.

I had never actually been into Hull myself on all my previous trips around here, or in fact ever in my life. Passing the signs for Hull Arena, we came to the docks and there it was, The Red Lion on Clarence Street (HU9 1DN), on a small road to the right in a very unlikely place. I presume it had a history of being a dockers' pub. I hadn't seen many of these, if any, though Plymouth would have been had it not changed its identity.

I couldn't tell if it was open or not until a painter fetched Maggie the landlady who explained they were only open at the weekend and were doing it up in the week. Strange to be in a state of half-open, but she was looking after her regulars.

She had been there 16 years and it was overdue a refurb but, as she was still in the process of buying it from Hull Brewery, she was sort of in no man's land at this stage and up to her neck in paint and tools. She took time out for us, even buying us our drinks, having read about the Quest.

The pub's location is unique – almost like an island with four streets around it in Church Street, East Street, Alma Street and Clarence Street. That is a first.

We ticked it off and headed back to Beverley which is a fantastic, lovely racing town and home to the oldest grammar school in the country, but also the town which gave Beverly Hills in the USA its name, though it's hard to see why!

Driffield, which literally means 'dirty field' (YO25 6SS), is a relatively young Greene King pub built in 1910. The landlady and husband had been in for four years. Before that, it was once again the sorry tale of having been shut for an entire year.

Curiously, though, this Red's website says it is one of the oldest pubs in the town, which does make you wonder what on earth they did before 1910. Five Lions were enough for today as I needed to get home to cook for a friend – a rare moment where I put real life before Red Lions!

DERBY'S LAST FEW

Another landmark was looming. I was now seven short of 400 as I headed to Silkstone (S75 4JR) in Barnsley. I was actually on my way to Calow Hospital to visit a friend and left early, hoping to drop into Rotherham and Clay Cross Lions along the way. It was only when I pulled into the M1 services that I realised how close I was to Barnsley. We were such a small country but I still had this habit of stumbling on places and not realising how close I was to a Red.

It did make me think regularly – would I be sure at the end that I had done all the Red Lions? Let's just say now that I would have done all the Lions I knew of. I couldn't really be any more certain than that.

Silkstone is a beautiful village at the foot of the Pennines, and Glen the fishmonger was parked up in the car park when I arrived, wasting no time in introducing me to Rob, landlord of 12 years.

This pub comes with its own unrivalled story. It is haunted by a child ghost after the Huskar Pit Disaster of 1838 in which 26 children upwards of the age of seven were killed in a notorious flood. The bodies had been laid out in the pub for the inquest. It turned you cold when you found out.

It is impossible not to look around you in the pub and visualise the scene. Locals, of course, all knew what happened – the victims are immortalised in the town in a stained glass window – but many people will have been in this pub, too, and not known where they were standing. It is understandable that it created an aura. It is fitting is that the plaque outside tells the story. That is a decent tribute.

You would be right, of course, to be aghast that I write that children of seven years of age were killed. Thankfully, the law changed as a direct result of the disaster but it was always the way, wasn't it, that people had to perish before others could see the danger?

The 1842 Mines Act became law four years later.

This was one of a small collection of Red Lions I had visited on my own. In a way, that was fitting. I was glad to sit there undistracted to hear this moving tale.

On leaving I had another chat with Glen. It turns out he had worked round the corner from where I live in Bamber Bridge for 20 years.

Backtracking onto the M1, I headed to Rotherham and hurried to the Red Lion (S60 5SR). This one fought for my attention with hospital visiting time.

Sadly, the pub appeared a bit dilapidated, though very down to earth inside despite not being able to produce a Diet Coke. They had none: very unusual. Instead I opted for a soda water. There was none. Finally, I claimed the only bottle of still water standing alone on a shelf in an otherwise bare fridge. The toilets had no paper, though I wasn't really expecting any. Even one local asked me if I had been to any worse than this. The truth is, I had. What a contrast to the entrance to the pub – an arch round the back through which the horse coaches used to pull up. I know this pub had seen better days, but still, the folk were friendly.

Some things didn't matter, though, as I headed to Clay Cross (S45 9DX). My friend Sheila had been fighting for her life in intensive care, and on my visit I learned she was finally going home in the next few weeks. Hopefully my next visit had to be to her house.

I made the 15-minute trip to Clay Cross, but missed it twice as the sign was unnoticeable. Bizarrely, they do not open on a Monday or Wednesday, so I had missed my chance to go on a previous visit to Derbyshire. Who doesn't open on both a Monday and a Wednesday? Either was not abnormal, but both were practically unheard of.

Parking at the rear, I received a few odd looks as I entered. I am pretty sure that is the sign of a pub with regulars. They know every face that comes in, and any new one gets attention! Sure enough, once I explained the Quest, I was introduced to Nodge, he liked a drink and claimed to own all the Red Lions. Two things are certain: that he doesn't own all the Red Lions, and that he *will* be in this one daily! Well, five of the seven days that they open! I was feeling positive about Sheila on the drive home through the Peak District with my music blasting!

I did indeed go back to see her after staying with Andrée and Kevin, and much to her frustration she wasn't yet out of hospital. I was just able to nip to Kegworth (DE74 2DA) whilst waiting on visiting times.

Kegworth, I am afraid, for that reason I can't do you justice but I do know that you are the rare example of a Lion with a lion tale. In the 1930s one escaped from a circus and had to be enclosed in the garden!

I know, too, you claim to be haunted with nocturnal sightings in hallways and doorways. Pint glasses have flown off the shelf. Paintings have reappeared in other rooms. True or not? Who cares? Pubs needed character. However you got that, did it matter?

So, November loomed and so did my 400th pub and who better to celebrate with than Paula? Red Lion 397 was to be on the High Street, Histon (CB24 9JD), some four hours from Preston and along the dreaded A14.

For once, we were lucky and the road was clear and the locals were expecting me, having heard about the Quest on BBC Radio Cambridgeshire earlier in the week.

This Lion is a collection of old signs that took me back to the TV commercials of the 1970s – who remembers Double Diamond, for example? It works wonders!

The exterior of the pub bore one saying, 'Bottled ale and stout, 2/6d, per 12 bottles'. If only they were today's prices!

Technically, you could probably argue that you didn't realise it was memorabilia and you felt it was an advertising message to get you in. Good luck with that conversation!

Next came Grantchester (CB3 9NF), beautifully thatched with a landscaped garden and lots of gorgeous exposed wood. Sitting at the bar with a glass of Prosecco topped with pomegranate kernels, I knew I had to get Paula out now before she settled in for the night. Then the same again at Hinxton (CB10 1QY) with the cutest little smoking area as you enter from the pink side of the 16th-century inn with fantastic panelled features! It is a brilliant pub with a tremendous walled garden and frankly does not feel like a Red Lion, but it does feel like a revisit is on the cards to make the most of these two. Tomorrow was to be the big one.

The next day, we pulled up at Stretham (CB6 3JQ) at 11 am. Halloween pumpkins were starting to wither. The *Cambridge News* photographer was waiting but wondering if it was the right Red Lion, as the landlord knew nothing of my visit.

That is probably because I hadn't told him.

Much as the press was fun, I did prefer to go in anonymously. It was simply the best way to be objective. Allan, the barman of 20 years, had seen at least six landlords come and go.

Now he had a new one. Just one week into the job, he sat there eating a big breakfast, didn't bother glancing up, and I had the press in tow! It didn't look good.

His wife, however, compensated, telling us that the area used to be filled with windmills and had all been drained away as it had been a flat county.

With all the big airbases around, the walls were adorned with pictures of aircraft and pilots. *This* was Paula's 90th Red Lion – no mean feat.

But significantly, of course, Stretham came in at Number 400.

Poor old Lion Number 4 or 40. It wasn't realistically going to match the high of 400, even if it had been the greatest pub in the land.

Next was Soham (CB7 5HA), a place that just sends a chill down your spine because of the monstrosities that went on there. It's almost impossible not to see the sign and think.

The pub is a strange set-up. The car park is next to the annex, which is called Saucy Meg's Red Lion Diner.

The month after I left, an ex-con smashed a window in the pub. In January 2015, the landlord pulled its last pint to make way for a play area. It was a sorry end. And as we left, we passed the notorious school of such tragedy. It just seemed so unlikely in what was a small, friendly village.

Next stop Brinkley (CB8 0RA) – an interesting Red for what it had done with the name. I had seen Red Lions, White Lions, Olde Lions and simply Lions, but this was now known as The Brinkley Lion.

Just six miles short of Newmarket and ten from Cambridge, I couldn't not count it. It was obviously a Red until recently and with its expansive garden and delicious coffees, I learned from chatting to the landlady of just 18 months and the locals that other Red Lions nearby had actually changed their names completely. She also warned us about George, landlord of our next Red.

As we were leaving, I watched one local (a retired chimney sweep) shockingly inject a full pint of beer directly into his stomach. He made no secret of it either. I had never seen anything like it. Everyone else took it as the norm, but I couldn't get over what we had seen.

Red Lion 403 was the best laugh of the day by a mile. At Great Wratting (CB9 7HA) the front door was framed by two massive, 400-year-old whalebones, which was a first.

They are jawbones, occasionally found along the coast, and they stood proud at its entrance without anyone really knowing why.

And then there was larger than life George Sykes who sat at the bar with his huge sideburns. Minutes later he had me behind the bar pouring a pint for Nigel, shouting at me to do it properly. Immediately, we were laughing and joking and felt like we had been there for years. Leaving was not something to do in a hurry, but before we did, we were shown the piggery!

This was quite an incredible collection of pigs! Not live ones, you understand, but quirky ornamental ones and hundreds of them, too, on every shelf and the fireplace, even to the point of salt and pepper pigs. Somebody's OCD had got out of hand.

This was more Red Pig than Red Lion.

We arrived at Sturmer (CB9 7XF) in the nick of time, as Roland the landlord closes at 3 pm and was winding down with a red wine. It was Andy, a local at the bar, who confirmed they were whalebones at Great Wratting. This one is without doubt a good, well-run pub but not wanting to hinder them from closing the doors we hopped off pretty quickly.

By the middle of the afternoon we were at Horseheath (CB21 4QF). I can't do this pub justice as the rugby crowd were in – it was 20 minutes before the end of an England-Australia international, so you can imagine the volume! It was also now an Olde Lion. Oddly, from the heart of Cambridgeshire, the landlord used to run The Guild Merchant just six miles from where I live in Preston. Small world again.

By the time we got to Steeple Bumpstead (CB9 7DG), the rugby was over (we won 20-13) and the pub was in good spirits. This spilled over into landlord Jim who produced roast potatoes and sausage rolls to celebrate. I, too, was in good spirits because the football results showed Preston had just won.

I don't know if this was normal upon victory, but pubs rarely gave you stuff for free. I liked this touch. A few nibbles at the bar didn't cost a lot and just created a friendly atmosphere in such a small gesture. And Paula does love her nibbles. The time we were stuck on the forecourt of the petrol station when I put in the wrong fuel, she thankfully produced a little tray of goodies from her bag. Like a survival pack!

Just by Whittlesford Bridge (CB22 4NL) we stayed in a hotel as close to a Lion as you could get. Freshening up and popping in had never been simpler, and this time we stumbled across a wedding party. I witnessed yet another big day in someone else's life!

This is a top venue either way, much of its décor resembling the class of a Malmaison. Spacious, rural, clean, wooden, with attention detail: it ticks all the boxes. Strangely, the owner also owned the Holiday Inn we were staying at next door. He couldn't go wrong!

At Cherry Hinton (CB1 9JB) the next morning, the DJ was still packing up from the night before! Red Lion 408 was the second-oldest in Cambridge, going back to the 15th century.

Happy with my 12 Cambridge Lions and chalking up another big milestone, it was time to head north. This turned out to be the end of the road for 2013.

STOCKTON-ON-TEES

Just six days into 2014, and I was back on the Quest. I had taken on managing a function suite at a hotel for the Christmas bookings, which wasn't functioning well at all. Add to that a spell in bed ill: ironically I was more than ready to go again.

Destination Stockton-on-Tees on a rainy January with Fred! Thankfully our first stop was in the lovely town of Richmond – well, Langthwaite (DL11 6RE).

Coming off the M6 at Junction 36 near Nateby, we took the narrow track through hilly, windy, bumpy turns with not a car in sight. Even the sheep were sparse.

There was the odd tractor through the small hamlets of Thwaite and Muker against a backdrop of almost Cumbrian greystone. Then the road turned into a dirt track, over a ford and then finally we arrived at a 16th-century inn – a good place to begin the year.

A tricky Red to negotiate, it also came with a new category. Teetotal landlady Rowena Hutchison at the back-end of the previous year notched up 50 years in the pub. There was almost no topping that. Just think of all the things she had seen in life and in her pub. Hats off to the longest Red landlady on the planet until someone tells me otherwise.

Add to that the fact that this is probably the most filmed pub in the UK. James Herriot, *A Woman of Substance* and its follow-up, plus Walt Disney's *Escape from the Dark* and many other famous photographs told the story around the uneven walls. Pretty impressive.

The other two nearby pubs were the highest pubs in Britain and the one with the shortest name, the CB Inn!

There was a lot of quirkiness near Richmond that made this a great start to the year.

Then came Stockton-on-Tees, through the picturesque village of Barnard Castle, a place so cut off it really does not belong to anywhere.

In fact, it was so cut off it wasn't open until 7 pm, but I would be back. Barnard Castle was too good a place not to return to.

So, on to Norton, Stockton-on-Tees (TS20 1AU), over a lovely roundabout filled with pampas grass, the green still lit with Christmas trees right up to the cut-off point, and therefore a real village warm community feeling greeted you.

Following it round, it was a relief to find The Red Lion on the left. As we ordered drinks we enquired of Ramsgate, Stockton-on-Tees especially, as once again the landline was a dead number. It was open and she told us where to park.

To be honest, Ramsgate, Stockton (TS18 1BS) was nicer than I feared, even though the Red Lion was shabby on appearance. And when we arrived with just two men at the bar and a scruffy-looking carpet at their feet, we immediately asked the bar lady if Shildon was open, too, fearing the worst. It felt like we were part of a treasure hunt. She rang a friend who lived there, who rang someone else who rang back to say yes it was. People can be so helpful sometimes.

We found Shildon (DL4 1DX) at 6.20, feeling hungry. We ordered drinks, then I gave the bar girl my card as I always do, telling them they were Number 412. Next thing, the landlord came over to the corner where we were sitting and handed me a lion's head! He had been waiting for my visit and it was such a thoughtful gesture. I asked about food as something was smelling good. He pointed out of the window and said 'No food here but order from the Indian over the road and eat in here if you like'. Perfect! And rare!

After 40 minutes down the A1, it was a relief to find an open Cotherstone, Barnard Castle (DL12 9QE).

Inside – what a pleasure: no TV, no jukebox, no bandit. Just the crackle of the fire and some bridge players. Here was a Red Lion that had stripped backed the years. It was almost as though it was 1738 again when it opened. Its bestselling feature? – Hannah Hauxwell, a neighbour and host to the final sketch of *The Fast Show*. The pub also has the last heather-thatched roof within the village – an inability to maintain was often the problem. They demanded care and finance, and often people didn't have both, or either.

Barnard Castle, though, is a town built for a pub. You can still visualise market trading if indeed you don't turn up on market day. You see shops that are still local not entirely quashed by big-brand big business, and you see road signs leading to places around.

It remains a little pocket, a hidden gem, in the UK map and the Red Lion hasn't conformed to type, and that's a very good thing.

The next day and closer to home, Staffordshire was still unfinished. Bradley had another Australian friend over and they positively *asked* to do a Red Lion outing! There was something in this – just click here for Cathy's Red Lion tours!

I had actually been to Stoke three times now, but the lovely town of Leek (ST13 5HH) – if you like a slighter larger Barnard Castle – bears no resemblance to the half-town, half-city atmosphere of Stoke.

Again, it is one of those places that doesn't really belong, except to itself, and is not really reachable by anything other than a slow road. In that lies a beauty.

When you arrive, it is easy to spot. As I tried to park, the hand-painted, flowery, purple smoking area stood out a mile.

Standing in Market Place, though on market day this time, it just says community. I envisage a lot of people come in the Red for one in between everything else they have to do. That's how pubs were, I think, before binge drinking!

It's large with wooden floors. The toilet area upstairs and the spacious landing suggest there were once rooms here. If you were stopping at Leek halfway to somewhere, you would need a place for the night. There's not much nearby. I like the pub a lot with its old-town feel. I will return in a Quest-less capacity in the future.

As we left the bar girl confirmed my fear that the Red at Thorncliffe Road had closed, so on we went towards Cheadle (ST10 2NU), only to struggle to find it. Eventually, someone explained to us that we needed to head to Boundary, about two miles away and, of course, we had already passed it on the brow of the hill.

Finally, we found this cosy village pub and a bar lined with men. Old-school. To the side, the most inviting of restaurants in its presentation and odours. I know I have said this a few times but pubs vary so much. Not all Reds did food, of course; some claim to do so but the chef is actually the microwave. But, just like they say ground coffee can help sell a house, you know immediately on entering a pub whether the odours are those of real food!

By now, I clearly should have some pretty basic ideas and beliefs about running a pub. For the moment, I am happy with my own Red Lion garage bar for the occasional party.

But here, too, was a first. This Red Lion is notable for its ceiling. At some point you will look up and notice them – the beams are covered in foreign notes which locals had brought back from their travels along with a bottle of foreign drink that was saved for a big party once a year.

Obviously, once upon a time there only stood a handful of notes and the habit probably just evolved, but I loved the notion that you could be down to your last few 'pounds' on holiday and rather than downing them all in airport bars or shelling out for departure lounge tat, the little voice in your head told you to keep one back for the Red Lion.

Although the euro has wiped out some currencies, it is amazing how many are still remaining.

It's a talking point, too, and soon the locals were telling me that Waterstones nearby was open when I believed otherwise, and Dayhills Farm is a quirky pub *and* farm with random opening hours. The latter sounded fantastic but I needed to visit each on a Wednesday – predictably market day! Failing that, they said I could just knock on the door, which has by and large (the odd Londonian aside) been a pretty successful technique!

Delighted with my new information, we left for Ipstones (ST10 2NA), an 18th-century coaching inn overlooking the Churnet Valley.

Alas, there was but one man at the bar with whom I had no option but to engage. He set me thinking, though.

'I have been in more pubs called The Ship than any other,' he said.

I immediately asked him if he was a sailor.

'No, I am a coastal walker,' he replied.

That put my mind at rest and made sense. Pubs on the coast would be called The Ship or The Nelson or other variations. Despite being an island, Britain was definitely more inland than out. The Ship couldn't touch The Lion.

On the way home, knocking did not work. At 6.28 in the evening, Cheddleton Red Lion was closed, opening at seven. Despite the Ozzie Boys saying we should wait and do it, it was getting late so I would leave it for another day.

I didn't want to be leaving too many for another day, though.

BICKER OVER LINCS

It was six weeks later when Helena and I called at Donington Road, Bicker (PE20 3EF) and Red Lion Number 417. What a place to pick up the Quest in this picturesque village in a beautiful, old building which had been reopened only a year. It had once been a lighthouse with the original wall still at one end, and Donington Road itself had been the river where boats used to dock.

I loved it. Originally it was believed to be called 'John Drury' and dates back to 1665. That is the date of the Great Plague. Then it was perhaps called Mariner's Rest or possibly Sailor's Rest. How it went from nautical to a Red is unclear.

But the Red Lions that captured the most amount of imagination were those were you can see and smell history without it being explained in full to you. That is to say, when the odd thing is pointed out, as in 'this used to be a lighthouse and that was a river', your own mind takes you back through the years. What's more, this kind of pub works the magic twice because not only do you sense that historically, but also when you are there in real time it has the effect of casting that spell and making time stand still: before you know it, you have been there so long you have almost become a local and are genuinely reluctant to leave.

When I Googled Digby (LN4 3LY) it took me to an article suggesting there had been 2000 Red Lions in the UK, then another implying it was 900. Some, as we know, have reopened, but the general trend is diminishing.

Smart, with a restaurant on one side and lounge on the other, it clearly had a decent Friday evening clientele.

With night falling and time beating us before our hotel check-in, we finished the day at Caythorpe (NG32 3DN), a cosy, low-beamed pub with delicious food.

Being in Lincolnshire meant the usual diversion to see my old friends from Spain, Denny and Val, whom Helena knows through her trips out there with me. We had a lovely lunch with them in the quaint village of Billingborough followed by a meander for an hour down the country lanes to Withern (LN13 0NB).

Scruffy and for sale, I didn't give it much hope. The abiding memory is the smell of burning. Not a log fire or a chef cooking up something, but old papers being burnt – it just said 'closure imminent'.

At Mumby (LN13 9SD) I sensed the cruel side of the pub trade. Shane had been there for five and a half years and they were forcing him out on 27 March, just five weeks away. I didn't ask the details.

He was divorced and was giving his children their dinner. I really felt for him. For many, of course, the Lion was both a job and a home.

'Snowy' at the bar explained that he had once lived in Cornwall and knew Red Lion St Columb Major, which I had been to in July 2012, a lot of Lions ago. There was always that eagerness to exchange Lions knowledge, but Lincolnshire to Cornwall was a heck of a way.

At 68, Snowy was a true Red Lion character, and the pub seemed to breed them. You could of course enter on another day and not find it so, but characters in pubs tend to attract the same. If it weren't Snowy, it might have been the guy who won the lottery nine years ago but also lost his wife three years back. I felt like he had been at the bar ever since. You couldn't help wonder what he would have done with himself if his local pub wasn't there.

Mumby's contribution to Red Lion memorabilia? – a funny knitted Red Lion with goggly eyes. I took a picture so my sister could copy it for me!

15 minutes later we arrived at Burgh le Marsh (PE24 5LR) – a very posh name for Skegness. In terms of character, rather than characters, it was the best of the day with an open fire and lots of brass. The staff, too, wore very smart Red Lion T-shirts.

There had been many polo shirts embroidered or printed with 'Red Lion', but these stood out in a good way.

From here, we headed into the town centre to find Wainfleet and the large town centre Red Lion closed and looking in need of repair – not good for a town centre. I couldn't count it, so we progressed to Stickford (PE22 8EP) where we found a free house with a jolly landlord of three years. Some just had that cheery disposition.

And with that came that gene to experiment in the shape of the Stickford Stumble. That could sound like anything from a Bank Holiday three-legged race to a home-made sticky toffee pudding! In fact, it's their very own cider.

Though we preferred the Strictly Stickford!

It's a good touch, though, and gives a pub an identity and newcomers an icebreaker.

For some, I am sure, a few Stumbles later leads to a few stumbles later. They do have their own festival on 3 May. I can imagine it's a riot.

On the way out, we noticed how incredibly dark it was, I jokingly asked Nick the landlord whether he was trying to save money. He was, but put the lights on for us anyway: it helps with the photos!

As we left, we took in the sense of history at Bolingbroke Castle where the Red Lion benefactor John of Gaunt once lived, and noted too, that war had played a significant part in this Lion's role in the community.

In 1643 Cromwellian soldiers were billeted here up until as recently as World War II, when the 617 Dambusters Squadron from RAF East Kirby frequented the pub.

Since returning from Australia in September last year I had been bothered with constant pain which had led to various scans and hospital appointments. Eventually five months later they discovered a hernia.

My mum always says, 'If you are going to do a job do it properly'. It turned out to be a big, fat double hernia. I never have done things by halves! Still, I was over the moon that there was finally a diagnosis, an explanation for the pain and an operation date. This all slowed down the momentum of the Quest a little, but now, two months on, it was Good Friday 2014.

Enthusiasm was still as high as ever but essentially with just over a year left in theory, I was getting to the point where I was looking at leftover pieces in the jigsaw.

From reopened Lions to those where I had simply run out of time, to isolated ones or those with random opening hours, we were now looking at clutches here and there and that meant a bit more planning. Kent, of course, still awaited in almost its entirety.

Early into the Quest I had printed off my list of Red Lions which contained 32 per page, whereas some pages in the North and North-West were done, others were completely untouched. I felt a sense of achievement each time a new page was boxed off and I put it to the back of my folder.

But first, Easter and, of course, a rarity not to make a day out of it. The Red Lion at Cloughton, Scarborough (YO13 0AE), stood out on a limb with not another neighbouring Lion in sight.

I picked up Fred at 10.30 and for once allowed someone else to drive so I could truly relax along the Scarborough to Whitby road, and at 2.10 the inevitable obstacle ensued.

It was shut.

There was no sign of life; no opening hours on the door.

'I will try again in an hour,' I thought.

We passed some time with a drive to the bay and what a beautiful coastal view. Killing time meant a browse in the gallery of tearooms and an ice cream, until we noticed we had a flat tyre. This just looked like one of those days.

It was the garage which informed us that the pub opened at 4 pm – a lucky twist and one of those occasions when beer in the sunshine of the garden became reward rather than research. Satisfied, we made the long journey back to Preston.

Seven days later it was another trek up to the North-East and beyond the remote town of Alnmouth (NE66 2RU), not too far from the Scottish border and looking lovely on the estuary. You could sense Berwick was not too far away.

This time, Denise was my companion. She had loved our Scottish trip and was back for more fun and games. We headed north just after midday. Again, I was in the passenger seat, which allows me time to do the plotting and make my notes and, more importantly, take in the scenery giving me a different perspective of the Quest. Driving there is always a big part of the task and, whilst having a ball, I was always on a mission so today was a little more relaxing.

We were due to stay in the once great seaside town of Whitley Bay – with its once 'legendary' Spanish city which wasn't really very Spanish at all – but first headed up the M6 and off the A69 then onwards further north. We laughed at some of the eccentric place names along the way – 'Wide Open' winning first prize – and finally made it to the gated, stone-walled town of Alnwick. You didn't see too many places these days that still had that sense of border, of physically entering a town. And the mist added to the mystery of this historic market town. You can see why some of *Harry Potter* was filmed here.

The gate took you towards Alnmouth on the estuary. It was a real film-maker's dream, a *Doc Martin* of the North. And inside the pub was overflowing with typical North-East banter. You could hardly move for witticisms.

'My wife and I were happy for 20 years,' read one sign, 'and then we met.'

Another simply stated 'Alcohol is the answer. I forgot the question.' I had seen that one before, unsurprisingly.

Alnmouth has the lot. From the route in, to the arrival at, the atmosphere of, and the character within. Refreshed, we made the 22-mile coastal route south to Bedlington (NE22 5EZ).

Through the mist and the rain of late-April, it was strangely pleasant, passing the odd castle on the way in a part of the UK that is a lot less congested than many places.

At 5.30 we walked through the doors of a large Wetherspoons pub. It seemed that Bedlington had a lot of pubs. It was a throwback, really, to a time when small communities still did, and these days that is quite unusual. How many times, for example, could you cross a street and walk into another pub? There had always been a lot of pubs. Less so now, but Bedlington was bucking the trend, and the Red was busy and not just a drinkers' pub.

I had already earmarked East Boldon (NE36 0PZ) for dinner as the webpage looked enticing, although I was fully aware that these can be dated or just too flattering. Nothing is certain in my Red Lion world.

We were fortunate to get a table by the window in the unusual wooden, tall–back, hand-carved chairs. At 'two courses for £9.95' you couldn't go wrong with fish cake and prawn cocktail starters and coley with lemon butter sauce and chicken kebab. What was the fish cake count now?!

It did not disappoint in any way and the friendly staff gave you a sense that it was a family-run business, and indeed it had been for six years. Many of the staff were related. You picked these things up.

News of the Quest ensured a complimentary ice cream sundae, which we politely turned down, but they insisted and it was devoured.

In November 2012, they had been awarded first place in the Northumbria in Bloom Awards, and that was for the third year running, honouring the best effort for upkeep of external premises, public houses and hotels.

We left glowing, for our hotel for the night – our only doubt being if we were in East or West Boldon! (Neither is a very big place!)

Our route as usual was not the most logical. The following morning we made for Berwick-upon-Tweed (TD15 1JS). Probably we should have gone here from Alnmouth, but a night in Whitley Bay as the pre-booked accommodation caused the sideshow!

After a brisk walk along the prom and a good dose of sea air, it took us two hours to do the 66-mile trip right up towards the Scottish border. The road is not the best, but the view is pretty decent up the coast.

Amused by a sign for 'Pot A Doodle Do' (some sort of glamping-cum-wigwam retreat), we arrived in the walled historic town of Berwick to a surprise.

Up the street was a Red Lion that had been closed for a while, and when I last checked 15 months previously looked long gone. As a bonus, the other Red that I was looking for was just across the water at Spittal.

I was overjoyed to tick it off because it was a long way to come back just for one. Carlsberg, too, was ridiculously tempting at £1 a bottle, though so early in the day it was breakfast we wanted. The landlord was on his fifth Red Lion.

Berwick is often a place people see from the train. It's a little gem of a town with its own quirky ways. Very much in England, its football team play in the Scottish League. You can see, as a border, it has been a political pivot over the years. But it is a cracking little secret often only glimpsed by those who fly by on the way to or from Scotland. We couldn't have picked a better location and almost poetically, as we made our way over the river with the long aqueduct to our left, the sun shone for the first time as we pulled up at Spittal (TD15 1QY) on the estuary next to the church.

There is a real peace and serenity about this place. Quest or no Quest, I would visit here anytime.

The owner was Paul – a veteran of 25 years in the Red, initially doing B & B. That had stopped. It was haunted.

He had never seen a ghost himself, but he had witnessed the aftermath. He had seen an indentation on one of the beds after his wife had made it up for the next guests. No one else had been there.

In real life three men sat round a window table noisily playing dominoes, nattering and bouncing off each other with a very dry sense of humour.

Next, we were looking for two Red Lions in Wooler, an RAF town in Northumberland, just six miles from the Scottish border. Iain, the owner and chef at Milfield, Wooler (NE71 6JD), told us he had been there nine years, firstly as a tenant but then buying the business six years later, his business coming from the five surrounding hunting estates.

The pub dates back to the 1700s when it became a hub for sheep drovers of the north and major last resting point for the mail stagecoach carrying mail and passengers between Edinburgh and London. A lot had passed through here over the centuries.

Now, it is home to the Village Leek Club and the Borders Gliding Club who operate from the airfield! Heaven only knows what the Leek Club have to talk about week after week!

The second Lion at 1 High Street, Wooler, presents a problem. Iain had told me that it had changed its name to Bar 1 three months previously.

Interesting. We spotted the large ex-Red Lion on the main street. Clear evidence was there of where the old Red Lion sign had been. I weighed it up for a minute and decided that it could yet go back to being a Red and it had been when I started the Quest, and judge and jury Lord Google still said it was. So it was.

The inside walls and ceiling were carpeted with an unusual display of branches and tree twigs entwined with blue twinkle lights. Really pretty. Not many Reds serve Kir Royale. I could see this was moving in its own direction.

But yes it counted. I had done too many miles to get here not to!

And we were far from done on this, one of the longest round trip days without actually going back to Preston.

Nearly an hour later we were back in Whitley Bay (NE25 9JU) and a large brick building high up from the road. That angle clearly helped us spot the next oddity of the Quest. This was the first Red Lion with a large statue of a man praying in the side garden. I wondered whether it was significant or it was just a statue from a garden centre. There had to be an explanation.

The owner told me it was one of the Three Wise Men. Naturally, I asked where the other two were. Stolen was the reply.

'How terrible,' I sympathised.

'It's OK,' he countered. 'This one was the stolen one... from somewhere else.'

Little scenarios like this give you a snapshot of a place that may or may not be representative! The mindset of the owner dealing in, er, stolen wise men, the attitude of the thieves who pillaged but only took one, and then the lack of urgency to reunite the group... Well, it was beyond me, I still didn't find out where the other two wise men were! Who knows: after reading this, someone out there may be able to solve the puzzle!

The last Lion of the day was no such thing. Peterlee is another of these places that are tricky to get to – a 25 mile-long road of nothingness arriving in a town of even less, and then almost no surprise to find the pub closed. I had been told it opened on Friday and Saturday at 7 pm. I took a photo without really knowing why, then set off back past this sad and sorry Lion through the Tyne Tunnel for only the sixth time this weekend! We still had one more to do in the morning.

Fish had taken over by the time we left for Coxhoe (DH6 4AL), just a few miles outside Durham. We detoured to the fish markets of North Shields in search of more. Breakfast was delicious crab.

I did not know if Coxhoe would be open. I had read all sorts about its future, including British Gas obtaining a warrant to enter the premises over an unpaid £8000 bill in a long-running dispute.

Enquiries on Twitter suggested yes – the bar girl was half-expecting me. I arrived to find that the only pub in the village was still going – most men watching the football and eating Petee's Pies from the pie warmer on the bar! The gas was clearly on. It said old pit village pub to me, at least it was still going, and after nine and a 'dead' Lion we were going home. This final one coming in at Red Lion Number 433.

STOKE AGAIN

It was now 5 May 2014 – Bank Holiday weekend. Even though Coxhoe had just been a week before, there was no slacking. The rearing of a holiday weekend on the calendar really was not to be wasted.

This time my lodger Robert joined the Quest for the first time. I guess that tells you that it had got under his skin!

Not the first time, it felt like I was saying to myself 'This will be Stoke for the last time'.

At Chadderton (ST13 7HN) we found a ceiling dedicated to twigs and fairy lights not dissimilar to Red Lion/Bar 1 in Wooler! We made it a quick stop as the landlord was about to close at 3 pm.

Waterfall, Waterhouses (ST10 3HZ), may have had the monopoly on water but was hard to find. Obviously, I was looking out for the giveaway clue of a waterfall which never came.

Sometimes hard to find is a very good thing and this is a cute, small Red. I arrived to see its two sides in all their glory. Three dog walkers with pooches sat at the bar at what was clearly a dog walkers' pub, whilst the remains of a stag do were looking slightly jaded at the other end of the bar. Outside there are stunning views of the Peak Park.

20 minutes down the road is Rocester, Uttoxeter (ST14 5LF), just past the JCB headquarters which anyone leaving Alton Towers will always see!

I got chatting in the big bay window to a Scottish couple who had read of the Quest and had also lived in Spain. Perfect. I could not have imagined during my 12 years there that the tapas and sangria would one day be replaced by Red Lions and more Red Lions!

And the next Red Lion was one I had been anticipating for some time. This was Dayhills, Stone (ST15 8RU), that had been flagged up to me on my last visit as the half-pub, half-farm Red!

Except it was really a farm and opened rare hours.

There were 60 sheep in the field to the right and tractors, barns and hens aplenty. It was a full-on working farm with a small room to the side, and that was The Red Lion!

Yet it was packed with locals who could spot a stranger a mile off. The bar girl's grandparents ran it, it served meat and eggs over the bar, too, not cooked or on a plate, but butcher's cuts.

I am unsure how it became it a Red, but this is a very special place.

There had been some confusion about High Street Red Lion so again I went looking for it with no luck. Moving on to Ruxley Road, Stoke (ST2 9BN), and arriving at 7 pm, I was assured from them that High Street was no more and a dead Lion pushing up the daisies. We got chatting to a couple who were visiting all the canal pubs – not the first time I had heard of alternative Quests, but this one sounded fantastic.

The Domesday Book records this one as a coaching house and a court. Imagine that today. So many people have had so many incidents in pubs. The next day, you find yourself back in the same venue – this time facing the arm of the law, not the arm of the barman.

A new day and a new Red Lioner, Braz. I decided on Wales.

As I looked through my list planning the route, he said, 'How hard can it be to go to a pub for a drink?'

Little did he know.

I opted for Halkyn only an hour away: we arrived at 2.30 pm, but it only opens at 4.00. Not too fazed, we drove on to Alveley. There we found not so much a dead lion, more a demolished one. Not counted!

So on we went to Kidderminster. It was always a slightly different feeling when a newcomer came on-board. Someone like Paula knew what to expect – basically the unexpected – but anybody on their first outing could experience any set of unknown circumstances and that, frankly, could determine if they came again, though they always did!

Braz's first outing meant one shut and the other gone, and before you say 'Why don't you check these things before you go?' – well, you do!

Often the info online is out of date, the phone goes unanswered or does not exist, and sometimes you think (in the case of an ex-Lion) that you had better just check to be sure if you are going that way. When I asked people at Alveley where the Lion was and they offered me two alternative pubs, they just looked at me like I was mad when I explained it had to be a Red Lion as I was visiting every one.

With Kidderminster (DY10 3TB) just 15 minutes away, I needed to break this duck and Braz needed a drink! Four hours after leaving home we found this large corner pub. Finally demolishing a beer, we sat on the benches at the front in the sun before heading to Bewdley, which was also closed. Two out of three ain't bad, but one out of four is terrible!

Braz went to the pub across the road for a quick half and to enquire.

What he discovered was a rare tragic moment on the Quest. The landlord had passed away three weeks earlier at the age of 80. His two sons were living there and had no intention of opening up again. They were obviously still grieving and presumably had a lifetime of memories in that place. Very, very sad.

So Wolverhampton and Bilston Road (WV2 2HU) seemed the next obvious place to go trying to forge a route back to Preston.

After this quite unforeseen day, we were obviously delighted to find this cosy, traditional family pub, whose Asian landlord had been in since 1999 and his own father before him in 1995.

We found a real cross-section of society – an equal mix of Asians and non-Asians, all speaking Brummie in a pub that you could tell was a hub and devoid of any racial tension. Braz spotted the casual plate of lamb samosas on the bar and could not resist, saying it was the best. I was specifically eyeing up Tuesday's Curry Night where a meal and a pint came in at £4.99. I had rarely seen better value.

It was a positive end to a disappointing and thought-provoking day. I couldn't know if Braz would come again! Wolverhampton was Number 440.

Nine days later it was Fred who rejoined me, calling to say he had just passed a Red Lion at Bispham and would finish work early, so should we hit the road? First port of call was actually Halkyn, Holywell (CH8 8DL), which hadn't been open on Easter Monday.

It was just an hour down the road and on this occasion we timed it to knock on the door five minutes before opening to be greeted by Nat and Lu, who had only been in six months and were still getting the place together. They had been up since the crack of dawn fetching a Husky Cross rescue dog from Manchester Airport, and were gutted I had caught them on a bad day.

That was just their perception. They had had a long day but sat with us at the front on the benches over a beer, and this is something you must do to experience the amazing views over the Welsh valleys.

They were making swift progress and I would expect to hear really good things about this Red by the time you read this. A lick of paint and a menu were in the pipeline, and they had already found themselves on the Real Ale Trail with a footpath running through the land, enabling many walkers to stop for one.

They had added more real ales and beers, offering me a delicious Purple Moose Elderberry Ale! I loved it and it was often overlooked that one of the things that can bring character to a pub is a quirky beer with a quirky name.

As we left, I suddenly had a flashback to a tweet I had received about Fagl Lane, Hope (LL12 9NG). I had been here in April 2012 but it was closed. Social media was telling me it was now open.

I could picture it. I had not forgotten that this Red Lion stood opposite... a White Lion. It is not the only time the two species have sparred together and history does not record the moment of inspiration when somebody said 'Well, if they are going to have a Red Lion, we will have a white one, or vice versa.'

There surely had to be something in the decision-making process that implied rivalry, humour or one-upmanship.

The bar girl was delighted when we told her about the Quest. As often happened, it led to instant fame! One customer bought us a drink and she didn't hesitate to tell the landlord that they were Red Lion Number 442, taking pictures for their Facebook page. It is not as though they were one of the landmark numbers like 400 or 500, but they were more than happy with their status at 442!

After overcoming the predictability of Preston North End being defeated in the play-offs for the ninth year, running a mini-Red Lion tour was my distraction as I was still debating whether to go to Wembley anyway and watch Rotherham give it their best.

With the sun out in the middle of May, I put the roof down on the car, my lodger didn't need much coercing to join me, and we headed south to Sutton, Newport (TF10 8DG).

90 minutes later we were there. I had few left to do that were under two hours' drive away.

Trish was running the show and had been for the last decade. Mark, her son, was the chef. Behind the bar was simply the biggest Great Dane I have ever seen, permanent resident, aged seven and answering to the name of Ben. It is a nice, friendly, 17th-century pub with stables at the back.

As Bewdley showed, the unknown in the Quest is when you walk into other people's lives. The décor and the clientele of these pubs will seldom change, but the day-to-day lives and the circle of life continue to evolve around them.

As Tom proved, interrupting my small talk, being the pub's only customer. He was pleased as Punch to have just passed his motorbike theory exam and was in to celebrate.

It made me think. If I have another five years to spare, might there be time for *Red Lion Revisited*, where all the individuals who shared these moments and all those landlords who told me of their plans get a second Red Lion visit and we see exactly what materialised and didn't. I loved these moments.

Only six miles away was Great Chatwell, Newport (TF10 9BJ), and you reach it through one of those lovely countryside drives past fields of rapeseed dotted with tractors and houses covered with ivy and weeping willows.

It's a big pub with a restaurant at the back and an outside terrace. The landlord had been in a week. Imagine if I had turned up seven days previously on day one. That was something I had never experienced. He clearly had to learn on the job.

He was already up on his knowledge through sharing with me that the pub opposite had been the Old Red Lion and that he also ran the White Lion in Kettering.

I was starting to think he had a bit of Lion thing going on like myself.

I had one more Birmingham Red Lion to slay, assuming there were no gaps in my information, which, as we know, was always possible.

Pulling in just before 5 pm, it is easy to spot the grand, large corner Red Lion on the right. It seems a bit scruffy when you enter, first seeing the curved tiled bar in front of the door. I soon learned that the bar was listed and so was the glass dome over the entrance porch. The man who told me this was the son of Betty who had worked there for 35 years!

Her photo sat behind the bar accompanied by a plaque saying she was greatly missed. His pride shone through, and every time he sat there with his pint, she was looking out towards him. These recent Lions really did underline how some of these places were entire lives and not just pubs. Some people came to drink to forget about life for a while. If you were at all associated with the running of the place, then it was all-consuming and all your memories were made here.

I passed my card to the girl behind the bar as I usually did. This remains one of the few occasions that I received no reaction! Normally it provokes something but the girl said nothing.

We finished our drinks and said goodbye.

Just as I was walking out, there was a tap on my shoulder.

'Are you the Red Lion lady?' the man asked!

'Would you like to go out the back and see the mural?'

I followed him out to a large back room where almost the entire wall was being stripped to reveal a massive ancient painting of the pub and what had been the old theatre next door with billboards amongst the people in long dresses mentioning Jack the Ripper.

They had nearly finished and had summoned a local historian and a restorer to preserve it and its astonishing detail. Slightly brown-tinged from the smoking era, it was another example of how much of the past was locked inside the Red Lion story.

To think I was seconds away from getting in the car and heading off! I am so grateful they were able to share this landmark moment with me, and the bar girl obviously told them about me quietly.

Learning that the landlady of five years was due to complete on buying the pub that Monday, I left a worthwhile 20 minutes later, pondering how many other hidden treasures were concealed in cellars, wells or behind old wallpaper.

COME ON THEN, KENT!

It had been a long time coming. It was a long way away. Finally, with 445 lions down, it was time for Kent! The bottom of England was still untouched.

And it was now because my friend Braz, who drives lorries, rang to say he was going to be parked up there all Monday afternoon. Yes, Braz was back for more!

I decided to set off on the Sunday and stop over in London to visit Andrée and Kevin. With traffic slow heading south, I pulled off the motorway for a break and eventually found the Red Lion at Fenny Stratford, Bletchley (MK1 1BA), on lock 95 of the Grand Union Canal.

I rarely went to Lions alone but this was a perfect centre and, a cool beer in hand, I strolled outside by the canal as I am sure many people had done before me. Waterside pubs were a magnet and a must stop for anyone driving barges up and down the country!

Some never moved, of course, and were home to permanent residents. Three such characters took it upon themselves to entertain me – all of them animal rescue workers.

One of them, Mike, was an avid vegetarian similar to me, with fish being my only 'exception', and he was keen to push his case. He didn't need to. I was already in his camp!

Tattooed Martin with his random grey beard and rescue dog from Turkey quizzed me as to my upbringing. Sure enough, he had been in my village driving a Waitrose lorry, some three hours away, the previous day. Coincidence was a constant on the Quest.

For a random unexpected stop, it was difficult to prise myself away, but they left me with some of their eccentric wisdom.

Vegetarian Mike told me that if you were to put a two-year-old child in a pram with an apple and a live bunny and it played with the apple and ate the bunny, he would buy everyone a new car which Martin would

197

service, as he was so convinced it would never happen and it proved that humans were not meant to eat meat.

This was their logic.

Martin also explained why locks existed, which I had never even thought about! Obviously, it was so boats could go uphill. He directed me to the website www.narrowboatworld.com to check out how natural longboat people were being priced out to make it just a holiday thing.

The Grand Union Canal is the longest of all the canals with 167 locks. This lock is the smallest and only exists by accident.

I finally left. Arriving in Putney to meet Andrée, I was stopped by Nick Clegg's policeman guard for going the wrong way up a one-way street! What were the chances of that?!

Next day, 19 May 2014, and Braz is not quite ready! So, in between Lions I sneak in… a Lion. I had tweeted and Facebooked Gravesend (DA11 9AA) in advance. It is a long way down to Kent and it was well worth checking as much in advance as possible.

This is a strange Lion right on the shore, unexpectedly tucked away at the end of the road. It dates back to the birth of licensing records in 1702, though the building has been here longer.

I arrived just after midday as Terry the landlord was doing ten jobs at the same time! I suspect it was always the way. He was that type of character.

He would take a delivery, sort the Wi-Fi, empty the bandits, talk to me about the music venue next door and negotiate better prices for his Gatorade. It was like being a real-time fly on the wall.

Terry had been here since 1978 when he began as a DJ one night a week. Then he put on a few bands (he said he was well connected), and in 1983 brewery Truman's asked if he wanted to take it on and also the factory next door for the bands. Over the years, the pub has played host to anyone from Anthrax to Manfred Mann to Iron Maiden.

Frankly, I was blown away by this raw, functioning, fantastic place which even boasts a wild Lion head mural on the back of the stage which lights up. The drum kit was already set up for the next gig. Music was such an important part of pub life, but I could almost count on one hand those which could be written up as an established music venue. This topped the bill.

Just outside was a first – a fully branded Red Lion snack bar!

Finally, Braz of non-existent timekeeping fame, was ready just before three and eventually we headed off to Swanley (BR8 7NF). Despite driving for a living, he has yet to fully understand the nuances of Red Lion touring like opening times, inaccurate addresses and closed pubs, so ignoring all his advice, we pulled up at the lovely square of Swanley and its Cask Marque Red Lion.

This is a vibrant pub with something always going on, from live music to barbeques. Throughout the year they always seem to be organising something, from carol-singing to racing nights, and from Easter egg hunts to superheroes evenings. They really do run a full programme.

On Sevenoaks Road, Braz spotted the sign for Borough Green, and then I caught sight of the rest – all boarded up and going to ruin. A disappointing dead Lion, and even though I had seen quite a few deads, it genuinely was disappointing each time you found one.

Every time you start the engine thinking what will the next Lion bring, you believe in surprise, you have an open mind, and unless you know it is closed, you don't expect it to be.

The Square at Lenham (ME17 2PG) raised my spirits. Convinced he knew the way, I ignored Braz all the way, arriving at this historic 14th-century nugget.

It is a little beauty not far from Leeds Castle (which *is* in Kent, not Yorkshire) and not far from the famous Pilgrims Way.

You sense this is a real heart of the community pub and part of that is down to furnishings. Without being antique, the beams and the wood around the bar make it homely whilst preserving its history. Its exterior is a lovely garden area with a specially designated barbeque space which would be a big draw on a fine summer's day.

Some bar areas now do not provide any kind of seating as you order. It's just a void to move into and then disappear from once you have bought your drinks, and that can miss a key element in what the pub is all about. The landlord or the bar staff are the secretaries of the communities through which all knowledge, gossip and anecdotes are channelled. How many people have sat there over the years to answer the 'How was your day?' question. Bar staff are unqualified psychotherapists, too, as people let off steam. No stools or seating removes a huge element.

Next came Charing Heath Road (TN27 0AU) and an old thatched farmhouse built in 1562, it was granted its ale and cider licence in 1709. It has an interesting history on two counts.

It once doubled as the post office, and a child's shoe was found in the chimney – at least the second occasion the Red Lion history book preserved the awful memory of child labour laws, or the lack of them.

The shoe is on show in the pub and local legend suggests that if it ever leaves the pub, things go downhill fast. I liked the power that the shoe held – a reminder that we must never go back to such primitive ways. This is where I first noticed the appearance of dried hops hanging around the pub – very typical, I was to discover, of Kent where they are grown. Old photos on the wall showed hop-pickers on stilts, and the table we sat at was an original hop press.

The Red at Sittingbourne (ME10 4PB) is definitely haunted by both ghosts and some of the friendly locals who frequent the pub, especially FOD with his endless quotes! We had a great laugh with them: they follow my progress on Facebook and even sent me an invite to their Christmas do seven months later.

The Lion has stood here in all its timber glory for over 600 years. We know this because King Henry V was entertained here on his return from the Battle of Agincourt. Seven years later, he died at Vincennes with his remains brought from France to Westminster Abbey. And many other kings and emperors followed, too, including Henry VIII.

The records show that in 1610 a Herr Zinzerling arrived from Germany. Legend reports that he drank the Scottish landlord under the table!

Today with my Diet Coke there was not a royal in sight, but my goodness they had all been here over the years.

As we crossed the huge bridge and were welcomed to the Isle of Sheppey, Sheerness (ME12 1RW), we found another pub steeped in age. At 600+ years old this didn't have the same guest list as Sittingbourne, but certainly had a history and remained one of only a handful of pubs left on the dockyard wall road. Sheerness began as a 16th-century fort protecting the River Medway, and later in that century a Royal Navy dockyard was established. In the 19th century it grew into a seaside resort, and today there are more caravans than houses. Only just finding the Red Lion behind its scaffolding disguise, it was a world of its own. The landlord bought our drinks and told us how the local name Blue Town came about. Everyone in the town worked in the dockyard years ago and would steal the blue paint used on the ships to give their houses the annual coat of paint! They obviously made no secret about it and the shipyard bosses must have turned a blind eye to it – if that was at all possible, or was it the unwritten annual bonus? We got fish and chips on the way out of Sheppey, and Braz enjoyed this more successful Red Lion trip than his first. My bed for the night wasn't a Holiday Inn or even a Red Lion, but the bottom bunk/shelf of a lorry. This Quest certainly is varied.

HIGH SPIRITS, HIGH WYCOMBE

Five days after the long haul back from Kent, I made the mad decision to go to Wembley to the play-offs, even though my beloved Preston North End had been knocked out. After all, last year Kevin had kindly invited me to a Preston v Rotherham game in the Directors' Box so I do have an interest and, although that time we drew 0-0, they had beaten us in the play-offs.

Of course, I know what you are thinking – any excuse – and you would be right.

I set off with Robert, fondly known as Roger the Lodger and another useless address reader! The M40 was closed so we pulled off and found Southam and its absence of a Red Lion.

I checked the address and it was actually Northend (CV47 2TJ)… The lodger really needs to improve his map and address reading! I was lucky as it had only just reopened the week before after being closed for a year previously. It is snuggled at the foot of the Burton Dassett Hills, and a lovely place to dine. The owners also had a White Hart ten miles away, making them one of the few couples to be in the list for the most popular pub name and second most popular name!

It is a classic walkers' pub.

At Whiteleaf, Princes Risborough (HP27 0EX), we arrived at 8.20 to nothing but noise! Perfect timing. A marquee out the back played host to live bands; inside the place was crammed. We had just walked into the May Real Ale Festival.

Tony, the owner of 17 years, still had time to come over to explain the proud history of the pub. It had not always been a Lion. For six years it was named the Black Boy.

Better than that, you could tell he was passionate about the history of this Red because he went to the trouble of photocopying a list of the licensees dating back to the 1700s. I admired his passion about the pub and the village: he was telling us that The Upper Icknield is an old Roman road from Dorset to Norfolk, but originally had been The Lower until it clogged up! It was made of clay. So they made the Upper!

Sincere pride is a must for a landlord. Tony ticked all the boxes and was passing this on to his son who is now taking care of Red Lion business.

En route to the hotel for the night, the contrast at our next Red could not have been starker at Bradenham (HP14 4HF). One man stood at the bar with an empty glass at 9 pm on a Saturday night, talking to the owners Jackie and Pete.

Jackie was on her laptop. Food had ended for the night. I genuinely could not be sure if they had actually served any. We declined when she offered to put the fryer back on and she explained that it was a quiet area and this was a National Trust pub.

I don't know if that meant they were secure and funded, or if it was an explanation for their lack of business, but she told me it was never busy and they just wanted to run a pub! Fair enough, but there was no point if there was nobody in it.

They *had* always wanted to run a pub but strangely were happy with how it was. If it was ticking over, fair enough, but it seemed to lack ambition, perhaps summed up by the man at the bar ordering a solitary cup of tea.

My 455th was pleasant, oldey worldy, but empty.

The next morning with the May sun beating down on us, we drove the six miles with the top down to Wooburn Green (HP10 0EU). It's a good pub to look out onto the green just across the road and is typical Buckinghamshire leafy suburb territory. We ordered a couple of baguettes and I handed the bar girl my Red Lion card and told her they were Number 456, to which she replied 'Oh I have never done this before!' It sometimes took a while for the Quest to sink in, and even at 456 I was still coming across people who had no idea, despite being several years in.

This trip, though, was all about Wembley. My South African lodger had never seen a live game of football after five years in the UK and, despite Preston's exit, we had the tickets and it was time to follow Rotherham.

Next came Knotty Green, Beaconsfield (HP9 2TN), a lovely rural pub dating back to 1753 with authentic features.

This is a must pub to slot into the category of breathing in the DNA of the past, and nothing reminds you more of that than cosying up in the Enid Blyton Snuggery.

She used to live in the village in a house called Green Hedges, which has sadly been demolished, but her name and works live on. There is a selection of her books to browse and some original Noddy prints in the pub. She must have found inspiration here at the Red Lion. And now I was sitting in her seat.

It was another example of how much history these pubs held.

And yet the pub was contemporary, too – a room to the left hosting permanent drum kit, stage and mic for their regular music nights.

On the wall was a poem written warmly about some of the bands, too. Popular and friendly and with a variety of atmosphere to sample, from the contemplations of the snug to the thrash of live music, this is a great pub and deserves its success. As the excitement of the day ahead grew I began with a pre-match Prosecco in the garden. We parked the car at Beaconsfield train station and hopped on the train to Wembley Stadium.

Rotherham, by the way, won their play-off. The game went 2-0 to Leyton Orient, ended in 2-2, went on to penalties, and the final penalty kick determined the result. Was it a fantastic Wembley trip fitting in Red Lions, or the other way round?!

Just under a fortnight later, on the 70th anniversary of D-Day, I left home early for Hook Norton (OX7 5BJ). I was looking forward to my visit by invitation of the Hook Norton Brewery at noon.

Remember that double hernia? Well, two days after Wembley that was successfully operated on and nine days post-op there was no stopping me.

I don't think I have ever driven into such a picturesque village in my life – every house perfectly thatched. It could have been a hundred years ago or more.

Looking for somewhere to stop, as I was early, I spotted a first – The Red Lion Coffee Shop. It was not on my list and a wonderful surprise. It had once been two pubs, the Red Lion and the Sun Inn. I felt I had to count it! I paused for a coffee before heading along to the brewery up Brewery Lane to meet Adrian and the gang. What a fantastic building, some four floors high. Brian was waiting for me on the steps when I arrived and escorted me inside where one of the employees was just leaving to get married.

James, fifth-generation family of the brewery, was driving him in the big, orange brewery delivery wagon. You could see how embedded in the community this brewery and family were.

Then came my tour starting at the top, where everything is taken, then gradually changes form making its way down to the bottom floor. I don't think all those steps are recommended in hernia recovery programmes, but I managed. They do a brewery tour, but I felt honoured to have such a personal one.

I left with souvenirs, too. There were three polo shirts with the Lion Beer embossed, a Lion Bar runner, 12 bottles of Lion Beer, and a glass.

Outside, Roger and his shire horses had just pulled up. They still deliver barrels to local pubs, and every day Roger brings the horses back here where I witnessed him order two pints – one for him and one for the horses who literally drank from the pint pot with their tongues!

After a couple of hours, it was time to go so I drove the 25 miles to Litchborough (NN12 8JF), passing Culworth which I had already visited, not realising how close I was to this one. Litchborough served the Hooky Lion Ale.

The staff was oblivious to the Quest but a local, Peter, was intrigued, informing me that the landlord had died and the pub closed for 18 months only to reopen a year ago by local farmers.

What a positive turnaround. It said a lot about the pub that the Red Lion hadn't been forgotten or abandoned after the landlord's passing – and it said even more, I think, that the community had stepped in. It was obviously hugely important to the area with no desire to see an outsider coming in. And now it also had a farm shop and the food was good. What was once the barn is now a beautiful oak and stone restaurant, they have done well here in what is an idyllic village.

On 18 July 2014 I hired a van with a plan. First go to Nottingham to pick up a table I bought to refurbish on Ebay. Then meet Braz at his truck stop in Rugby and blitz four Reds around Rugby, then set off at 5 am to pick up another Ebay table from Bourne and return the van within 24 hours! Where there is a will, there is a way!

Red Lion Number 460 was Brafield-on-the-Green (NN7 1BP).

With the traffic terrible, I didn't reach Rugby until 8 pm, and that's when we discovered Little Houghton Red Lion, 20 minutes away, was no more. It was called Four Pears, because four couples have bought it together, though I later discovered that one pair had dropped out, so it was to be renamed Three Pears. It sounded like a recipe for a disaster! Perhaps call it The Red Lion. Just a thought.

Then, when trucker Braz and I arrived at Brafield-on-the-Green two miles down the road, I was expecting Denton Red Lion. I think Braz is a bad omen: it got worse. Braz came out with a Prosecco and half a lager only to receive 5p change from a £10.

Needing to get this right, I went back in to ask if this was Denton to be told it was indeed Brafield-on-the-Green. Handing my card to the landlord, he asked me how it compared to the other 460 Lions.

'Beautiful,' I replied truthfully, 'but at £7.95 a glass, the most expensive Prosecco I have ever had.'

Denton was just two minutes away, hence the confusion.

As we turned into the village, the first thing we saw was a peacock wandering the streets making a hell of a racket. It distracted us from the pub but there it was, The Red Lion, high up on the left.

We were greeted by a man leaning on the railings wearing a T-shirt, who immediately told of his recent accident there. He raced sidecars. People always told you stuff at the pub! People always wanted to explain their T-shirts. I suppose some people wore them dying for you to ask. He clearly wanted to tell everyone.

Most importantly, a stone's throw away, the mini-bottle of Prosecco (so a glass and a half) was a mere £5.95!

Interestingly, some locals showed me a book on The Red Lion written by a historian. This work was only about Denton, the one surviving pub (from three).

Friendly, cosy, traditional, contemporary, it was purchased for £69,000 in 1984 by Charles Wells brewery and is still family-run by brothers Paul and Peter, whom they spoke highly of.

Three minutes away was our second Charles Wells pub at Yardley Hastings (NN7 1ER). Within striking distance of Northampton, you could almost be in Brittany. From thatched roof to its isolated hilltop position, it looks like a farmhouse from the approach. Inside, though, its classy interior is mirrored by a well-dressed clientele making it one of the busiest Wednesdays I have seen at a Red Lion. Dressing up was a dying art and there weren't many pubs you could say this about, but you sensed a quality and a respect for the food that people made the effort.

We stood out like a sore thumb and my Preston accent immediately attracted the attention of the bar girl who was also from the North. Her aunt had bought the lease a year ago and they had plans to develop, even though it looked untouchable.

One building over the drive was to be converted into accommodation but was currently a shop selling shabby chic furniture and handmade clocks, some of which were displayed around the pub.

After a game on the Northampton skittle table in the back room, we returned to the Eddie Stobart truck stop for a five-hour sleep before our early starts, mine driving to Lincolnshire to pick up my table and get the van back in time, and Braz to pick up a load from somewhere! That was a very productive 24 hours!

CLARK GABLE

Six days later in June 2014 I set off at 3 pm to meet Braz again, but was slightly ahead of him down the M6, A50 and M1, so I detoured to Crick (NN6 7TX). I waited a quarter of an hour before it opened at 6 pm. I was in but you knew locals would follow at their own pace as well as canal visitors and those nipping off the motorway like myself. It was a sleepy, thatched roof, village life kind of place and clearly everyone knew the landlord. Tom had been in for 34 years – so pretty much all of most people's working lives. Nowadays his son was mostly in charge but, into his fourth decade at the helm, the urge to potter around never left him.

In fact, this Red had stability written all over it. Tom was only the 19th licensee since 1760. On the fireplace sat a large brass Lion – the emblem of Phipps Brewery which had recently reopened.

I picked up Braz and half an hour down the road is Middleton (LE16 8YX). It had been closed for years but a tweet drew my attention to its reopening in December. Social media had certainly had a terrific effect on the Quest both in filling in my gaps and alerting pubs that I was coming. It was a huge part of my story, I put pictures of each Red Lion on my page which in turn generated information, contacts and banter!

Outside, hens peck around the beer garden. Inside, I will remember this as the pub where Luis Suárez bit Chiellini in the Italy v Uruguay match. The pub dubbed him the Hannibal Lecter of Football.

Most people were staying put in the pub that night. Braz wanted to, too. I had other plans. There were two more to go and the first was Cranford (NN14 4AA).

What can I say about this great-looking pub?

Clark Gable, the legendary Hollywood actor, known indeed as The King of Hollywood, was stationed here in the RAF.

Gone with the Wind came out in 1939, the year war broke out, though of course, America did not join the Allies immediately. At arguably the height of his career and on his third marriage at the time, he was persuaded to join the US Armed Forces in 1942, against the wishes of his studio back home. By 1943, he was in Britain, seemingly flying missions.

Six days after D-Day in June 1944, future US President Ronald Reagan signed his release papers from the Army and he returned to the movies.

In one small window of this Red Lion we were shown his engraved initials. I don't know if that was his touch or someone else's. You would like to think the former. It was extraordinary to match up a Hollywood Great with the Quest, especially when you consider that Hitler had offered a sizeable reward for anyone capturing Gable unscathed. Braz asked the bar girl whether they minded the damage to the window. Her response – 'Frankly, my dear, I don't give a damn'.

The final Lion at Broughton (NN14 1NF), despite no famous engravings, has a lot going on, from a twice-yearly beer festival to 'Carry on up The Red Lion' evenings to a 'Christmas 2' night in June, which I had just missed!

This was a midsummer chance to relive the festivities and trimmings of last December, just in case you hadn't noticed it was Christmas.

And at Christmas the pub is home to the Broughton Tin Can Band who roam the streets after dark banging on anything vaguely musical from dustbin lids to pans anytime after midnight in the run-up to Christmas.

As character goes, this pub always delivers in its entertainment – humour and community are right at the top of their list.

The following week, June was almost over and I found myself back in London for a celebratory lunch in the Houses of Parliament for my friend Kevin who is an MP but had just been knighted.

With that, of course, came a couple of London Reds, the first of which was Kennington Park Road (SE11 4RS) just across from the Tube station. After an early start getting to Westminster for noon and lunch, followed by a private evening meal, Sheila and I had crashed out late in our hotel. Due on the 16.30 train back to Preston the next afternoon, we hit Covent Garden for the shops then, saying goodbye to Sheila, I made time for this and Walworth Road Red Lion.

Kennington Park is brimming with character. There are two rooms downstairs with interesting alcoves and quirky furniture, and doll's houses decorating the back wall leading out to a beautiful, walled beer garden.

The manager told me that the pub had been rebuilt in 1929, having stood here for many years, and once had an aviary in the garden. It was owned by the Antic company who owned another Red Lion in Deptford which no longer opens. Their ethos was to keep the character of the pubs as their own, and it worked here. It's a good pub. I walked around the Elephant and Castle and 25 minutes later I stepped into Walworth Road (SE17 2AW). A typical old-fashioned boozer best describes this, again contrasting with the previous Lion. In fact, for good, old-fashioned you can almost read 'scary'. Packed by the early afternoon, there was plenty of drinking going on and as I ordered I felt that tension, clearly taking someone's spot as I stepped back from the bar.

Sure enough, a hardy Irishman and Jorden, a younger Glaswegian, were talking at me, swearing a lot and offering me drinks I daren't refuse. They were well on the way and clearly made a habit of it. They were also in for the long haul with a plan to set off Chinese lanterns at midnight for no obvious reason, but not able to do so as the Chinese lantern shop was closed!

Good company, but not my kind of company. I posed for photos, tore myself away, and was relieved to make my train home!

American Independence Day 2014, and it was time to head back to Wales for a weekend of nearly ten Reds.

First was Llangynidr (NP8 1SR), travelling steady through constant drizzle. Again Helena joined me. We are frequent travel buddies and we have been to faraway places like Peru, Sri Lanka and India together, but this was her first visit to Wales. It was the World Cup quarter-final between Germany and France, and I provided a minor sideshow as they bombarded me with questions, wanting to know where I had been and where I was going next. When I mentioned Merthyr was on today's agenda I was blasted with an overdose of Merthyr jokes! The atmosphere is good in this pub. Everyone knows everybody else and we left not before having our photos with Ray, the teller of even more Merthyr jokes…

Just 20 minutes over the mountains lies Tredegar (NP22 3PX), ten miles from the Brecon Beacons National Park.

We were watching a game of football kick-by-kick through the eyes of the Red Lion. Technically, this was a Ye Olde Red Lion, but Germany v France was still on with Germany still winning 1-0. It is a long corner pub, honestly looking old and tatty. They had warned us at the previous Lion that this one was not the best. But you can't deny a local his local, and one man, Shirley Evans, had been coming here for 40 years.

On the outskirts of Merthyr is Heolgerrig Road (CF48 1SB). We loved this pub and you just knew that it *was* the village, crowded with men this was their Friday night. The landlady of seven years assured us that Merthyr was not as depicted by the joke tellers of Llangynidr. I had heard some of them before.

'What do you call a Merthyr man in a suit? 'The accused.' And so on.

Home-made cake was being passed around and we were not left out. They had their own football team, the 'Llew Coch CPD', and next week saw the leaving do for one girl who was moving to Washington. You could be forgiven for thinking it was the furthest anyone had been from here.

And when it was our time to leave, the bar gently broke into song, singing: 'Oh won't you stay, just a little bit longer'. I think we were the highlight of this Friday evening: it was probably how all pubs were once and a delightful little wander into another era.

The next morning started badly. The Red at Llannon was dead. The Welsh brewery had told me to tweet them beforehand to meet them inside. Only just remembering now, I arrived to a To Let sign and couldn't count it.

And when we arrived at Llandyfaelog, Carmarthen (SA17 5PR), we found an almost silent village. That is perfectly fine, of course, except the fear that nothing might be open. After a lovely drive through the beautiful hills and valleys and a last mile that was literally a track with no room for passing cars, Wales proved again that it has the best approaches to Red Lions, albeit potentially unpassable in the snow of winter.

Hungry, we were relieved to find this friendly, open Red run by Marjorie and David Price for the last 20 years. It would have been an excellent place to overnight, too.

Now, Marjorie had read about the Quest a couple of years before and was not the first to think I must have given up. Well, I still had 150 or so to do and she was happy I made them my 472nd Red.

Catching the sun in the cute garden at the back with good old home-made egg and chips, a totally crazy encounter happened as one family were leaving.

They were laughing about the madness of the Quest only for one lady to pipe up that she was visiting every Marks & Spencer in Britain. So far, she had been to 127.

I loved to meet other people with quirky pastimes and their own missions… but I always preferred my own! Marjorie refused payment and we continued winding through the Welsh valleys.

In contrast, Port Talbot (SA13 1HN) is a run-down, large corner building backing onto the railway station. Having paid £4.40 to park the car, we then noticed empty bays with the words 'Red Lion Customer Parking' on them. Heading towards the back door of the pub where a run-down caravan was parked, our expectations were at their lowest.

Inside, just two men stood at the bar in an empty room covered in music memorabilia. Within seconds, Pat was bombarding us with stories and information about the pub and the area, quite interesting but a bit wearying. He owned all the memorabilia and lent it to the pub. Amongst his facts and figures was the Olympic swimming pool that was built six inches too short and then burned down! Across the road was the closed-down old cinema with graffiti art depicting the images of Richard Burton, Anthony Hopkins and Michael Sheen who all hailed from here. Despite Pat's offer to take us on a tour in his car, we attempted to leave. Not letting it go, he wanted to buy us a drink but we declined again. Instead, he thrust a fiver in my hand towards fuel!

Just off the M4 is Pendoylan (CF1 7UH), an altogether much more pleasant experience, immaculately maintained with benches outside at the front and a lovely upstairs terrace with amazing views over the valleys and hills and looking down on the old church next door. When it comes out, the sun casts a beautiful aspect on the pub. They also have a Lion Suite! Peace and tranquillity were restored.

Peter Tennent had tweeted me to tell me that Penderyn (CF44 9JR) was the best pub on the planet.

As a result, cyberspace exploded with locals and distilleries piling in. I had been totally sold on a place before my visit, so much so that I thought if it is this good then I had better make a night of it!

But first we drove into Aberdere to eat. Aberdere, once 'the Queen of the Valleys', was now sad and run-down. It didn't have one restaurant: the best we could dine out on was a Subway sandwich! We got a cab up to Penderyn but when I arrived, there was no Peter. Everyone else turned up, but he had come down with a bout of conjunctivitis and was unable to get out.

Penderyn sits across from an old church and is small but compact inside with regulars from all over – Swansea, the Rhondda Valley, Merthyr and Cardiff. People made an effort to get here and sample the huge range of real ales.

Mum Beryl, Dad Keith and daughter Natalie were at the helm as the family had been in there some 34 years. It had been a wreck when they arrived, and into their fourth decade of running it they were still improving and adding onto the old 14th-century building.

It is a fantastic pub and Natalie tells a brilliant story (more than once over the years, I am sure) that one evening she was upstairs watching a movie with her mum, while Dad ran the bar. The following day, the papers had a story about Johnny Depp who was in the area making a movie, showing a photo of him. Her dad pointed to him and said he had been in last night for a good few hours! Mum and daughter were left gutted; Dad didn't even get Johnny to sign the visitors' book, something he would always ask a stranger to do.

I can see why it is dubbed the best pub on the planet. That is a hard accolade to award but is certainly one of my favourites. It is a special place.

After a good sleep, the last Welsh Lion on this tour was to be Builth Wells (LD2 3PN). Alan, landlord of more than eight years after finding it derelict for two, stood incredibly tall behind a very small bar. With low ceilings, the inside is very compact and believed to be the oldest pub in Powys. The pub can be traced to 1188, though essentially it was also a farm-based business. It has remained in the same family for 350 years.

Ordering two home-made leek and potato soups, we sat outside as tractors chugged by with their large bales of hay.

Despite the odd eccentric and one dead Lion, it had once again been a brilliant Welsh weekend.

FULL-ON AUGUST GUSTO

After Wales, there were no Lions for five weeks before a jaunt out to a singular one at Swadlincote (DE12 6PZ) on 10 August 2014.

I was itching to get going again, and conscious that there were a fair few Lions to get in before summer was out. August Bank Holiday was not far away.

Lion Number 477 was another Ebay-inspired jolly, having bid for a table from someone in Derby, I used this ammunition to coerce my youngest brother David to join the Quest, as it would fit in his car. It was about time he understood what this Red Lion thing was all about instead of just thinking his sister has lost the plot.

He and my nephew picked me up late in the morning. Also along were my lodger and his daughter, making it a full house for just one Red.

With traffic slow along the A500 and A50 we pulled over next to a butcher's to phone ahead to check the pub was open. Then I saw it up the slope ahead of me.

The snug was full of men – all lively characters, each bantering away.

They were delighted that I had driven two hours just to visit their pub, adding to the thousands of miles I had already notched up!

I didn't meet the landlord and the landlady. They were upstairs having a rest. But the barman was good enough, spreading the word about the Quest and to every new customer he served, he picked the baton up at 477 and exaggerated the number of Red Lions we visited.

As we left, I could have sworn we had done 692! Dave was shaking his head but I didn't doubt it wouldn't be his last Red Lion.

BEACONSFIELD WITH BRAZ

Now for a mammoth few days, starting on 21 August 2014: first stop Tetsworth (OX9 7AS). Oh my, what a pub!

En route to meet Sharon and Paula in Kent, I had set off a day earlier to meet up again with Braz and do a few around Beaconsfield. It was to be a busy few days, meeting Stephanie from Inapub to discuss the Red Lion app! What had this become?

But Tetsworth sprung out on me. Just short of Beaconsfield, I was diverted off the motorway onto the A40 and through this beautiful village.

The first person I ran into was a chap called Dave from a micro-brewery called Loose Cannons who told me that Red Lions were where people used to pay taxes. It may be true for some, but many Reds had served plenty of purposes over the years. He took my photo as I was a lone Red Lioner.

This pub sits opposite a cricket green – always the perfect setting. It has a really small but quaint bar and is also a fully stocked store at the back, as there is nothing else in the village. There is even a library with a dining table seating 12 in the middle of it and extending out to the patio, as though you were eating at someone's home. It's just gorgeous and another Old Red Lion.

Leaving the village, I passed The English Rose which also was a Red Lion in the past. I collected Braz from Beaconsfield Services, from where we took the short drive to Coleshill only to arrive too early, then setting off for Chenies (WD3 6ED), to find the same but due to open in the next quarter of an hour.

With wisteria climbing the walls and hanging baskets aplenty, it made the perfect photo.

As we waited outside I noticed a sign labelling this pub as 'autarkic'. It means a genuinely run private free house! This was a first.

The landlady popped out of the little attached house called 'The Banners Rest' to say they would be open soon; I mentioned I was chilly so she came back with a blanket. The landlord had come in for a bit of stick from a couple of guys at the bar when I asked if there was Wi-Fi.

Mike refused to install it, saying it was antisocial. He is right, of course.

At Little Missenden (HP7 0QZ) we discovered a real gem. Out the back, there was a stream/large pond with ducks, swans and trout and a lovely little bridge running across it. You could only be happy here. This is tranquillity defined. It wasn't yet dark but when it was, the area was beautifully lit up.

Inside, the parkin floor was amazing, in the pattern of the game Jenga. All around, notes and coins adorned the bar and you could never want for a lack of signs from the old-fashioned 'Horse carriages and pony traps for hire' to the wittier 'Everyone who passes through this door brings happiness. Some by entering. Some by leaving' to a Red Lion first – a notice announcing that the morris men were in town. We were too early to see them perform, but one morris dancer did say he lived at our previous Red, Chenies, for three years!

I was not surprised to learn that this Red had featured in *Midsomer Murders* on the TV. It fitted perfectly.

A couple of miles down the road was Penn (HP10 8LF), a lovely fronted pub sitting on the green and another with an old parkin floor. We sat in a cosy half-circle area said to be the only one in the district with curved seats and an open fire. Much of the clientele were eating – we joined them, sharing a fabulous goat's cheese and sweet red onion pizza.

We then stopped for half an hour at Great Kingshill (HP15 6EB) – a beautiful building, warm and inviting with wooden tables and menus written on chalkboards. Kim, the landlady, had been in only a week but had previously run the pub between 2007 and 2012. I am not sure what happened to her in the interim, but she was now back with her chef husband Chris who came to chat and bought Braz a drink. It is an affluent area and a decent pub. I think it will go from strength to strength.

As darkness fell, we returned to Coleshill (HP7 0LP), which was not open earlier. It looked very different at 9.30 pm. Just one car – a pink Cadillac was parked in the car park.

The pub was old and traditional but not very up to date, and the landlord who had spotted me earlier through the window told me he had run Shepperton Red Lion, which was currently closed and I had yet to visit.

He said he was in the process of doing Coleshill up but equally hinted that he had bought the pub to make a profit on the building. I wasn't entirely convinced it had a future. These Red Lions more than made up for Braz's first outing, and Beaconsfield Services by the way are brilliant.

The next day began early with my meeting about the Red Lion app. It was extraordinary really that it had come this far, especially as many Red Lions don't have webpages and Google info isn't updated. Now indirectly on my way to meet Sharon and Paula, I veered off to the Red Lion at Chobham (GU24 8RG), not the first to actually find itself on Red Lion Road.

Whatever state I might find a Lion in today, that tells you that a town or a village was built around the pub. And here the landlord was just in his first year but running an organised, friendly rural place. Chobham gets a nod and a wink for being the first to say they wanted the book when it comes out.

Ten minutes after, I pulled up at Lightwater (GU18 5RP), a large, detached pub covered in hanging baskets and flower troughs with a very large Lion emblem in the centre front, all quite symmetrical. If Jason and Kerri took that much care over something that probably isn't a priority, it was a very good sign for what lay within, and the Lion emblem – a large, proud indication that the Red Lion did mean something to its owners, staff and customers.

And within the pub is a bright space, windows on three sides and a decent-sized bar with the landlord's pig mascot at the end wearing a uniform! The staff were friendly, which makes a big difference being on my own in a new neighbourhood.

As I left, nobody was smoking at the entrance, which meant I had to juggle with the timer on the camera with no one to help. Maybe I should just give in and get a selfie stick!!

My next Lion at Betchworth (RH3 7DS) was nearly a 30-mile trek away, not helped by getting stuck at the level crossing while two trains came and went.

This was one of those quaint little railway stations that went hand-in-hand with the village. Betchworth is still a rural, old English village and you will find The Red Lion on a slope just close to the North Downs Way, but actually only 15 minutes from Gatwick.

Timing is everything, and when I arrived I found it mid-refurb with the only bar girl covered in paint from head to toe!

They had removed one wall, were changing the downstairs function room, and it was already looking brighter. I took it as a good sign. The pub remained popular, especially for its seafood. Indeed, next to go in was a seafood and fish stall with all the produce coming in from Kent. I liked the sound of that. Uniquely, you could take the fish away for yourself or have it cooked there and then on the premises. What a novel idea, the likes of which I had only seen in Dubai, of all places. A terrific Lion, clearly going places and very forward-thinking. Congratulations, Betchworth! It has got to be top of my 'must return to' list.

I arrived at Maidstone just as Sharon and Paula pulled in by train. After a night in the Hilton, it took 90 minutes to reach Hythe (CT21 5AU), entering along the Military Road to an impressive, white-stone building, spotting The Red Lion Clinic at the side of it.

What? The Red Lion Clinic?! Offering all sorts of acupuncture, osteopathy and physiotherapy, it had clearly decided that the Red Lion was a good name. Paula thought about checking me in!! I wonder which came first, the pub or the clinic, or did it begin as one joint venture where you could get everything under one roof???

I loved all these little Red Lion spin-offs and Hythe (the pub) did not disappoint. Relaxed and airy with wooden floors and large fire, it is perhaps more hotelly than hard drinkers' pub, and such establishments tend to have a calmer pace about them.

Now Dover (CT16 2PS) was one I had been looking forward to for some time. It is a place steeped in history from the song about the White Cliffs to the huge number of people who pass through the port and have done over the course of history, including those now trying to do so illegally.

The White Cliffs do impose. There is an air about Dover. Seaside towns do feel different, and sweeping down into the town with port below is an awesome experience. With the cliffs ahead and Dover Castle to the left, it was 2 pm when we spotted the old, long, dark stone Red Lion.

The pub is in two halves with a little raised area with a roof window leading out to a small garden where we sat under the dried hops running along the beams. How wonderful.

A couple at the bar told us our next Lion at St. Margaret's at Cliffe (CT15 6AZ) was a good one. Literally on the cliff, though I have no idea who Saint Margaret is, this small corner Lion has a blue plaque by the side door – one of those heritage acknowledgements.

It says simply that James Bond drank here in 1959! The inside is covered in James Bond posters. Ian Fleming, who wrote the Bond stories, lived on the cliff and mentions this pub in one of them. Wow, oh wow. Arguably the biggest movie franchise in the world ever and now I was drinking in one of its inspirations. As you know, there had been a few of these types of moments and they all took my breath away, but it never escaped me that I was sitting at the bar where a genius invented his stuff, and years after his death its legacy lives on.

This Red remains one of the oldest in the village and if Bond were not enough to make it stand out, imagine my reaction when I learned it had been a morgue, too! I had been in that one Red Lion where bodies had been laid out after a mining disaster, and I had seen pubs double up as all sorts.

There is more! The National Express bus through to Canterbury is the number 007. And finally, all those crazy channel swimmers about to brave 21 to France set off from here. As anecdotes go, this Red Lion must be near the top of the list.

En route to Ramsgate, Paula made contact with her cousin Peter who suddenly found himself joining the Quest. Paula's spur-of-the-moment text and his spontaneous reaction found him joining us outside Red Lion Ramsgate (CT11 8PN).

His first suggestion was to go somewhere nicer than the Red until we explained that we hadn't just looked him up out of the kindness of our hearts, but that we were on a mission!

It turned out to be a typical towny pub with lots of drinkers and lots of pool, but I did have my photo taken behind the bar with a Red Lion number plate – a new first! At Red Lion 490, there were still 'firsts' to be achieved.

Peter, Paula's cousin was not getting off lightly with just one Lion! After a stroll along the front, we made for Broadstairs (CL10 2TL). This pub had a wall dedicated to all sorts of mirrors – outside we sat at a little table and shared chips from the chippy next door.

What was going on in the Red Lions of Kent? Broadstairs was once a mortuary, too! We drove Peter home, met the family, then headed for our sixth Red Lion of today, promising Sharon she wouldn't be disappointed with the food.

Milstead (ME9 0RT) was a revisit. I couldn't be making too many more trips to Kent. It was important to get them in and get them open after such a long drive. I had been here three months ago on a Monday with Braz; it doesn't open on Mondays. It looked so lovely and had been recommended by the guys in the Sittingbourne Red Lion three miles away that I made a special note to return here to eat! I only just managed to get a table, which is always a good sign.

Jo, the landlady of nine years, had done the place up herself to her credit and turned around the business, following on from a 30-year stay by the previous landlord. Some people really had lived their lives in pubs.

This had been thatched but was burnt down in 1862, then rebuilt. A local author, Lena Jordan, had penned a book on Milstead in 2001 and of course, The Red Lion featured, underlining that pivotal role in the community.

Paula asked if there was Wi-Fi. Jo replied that she hadn't bought it, but if it was in the air, we can have it. Few pubs left modern life behind. I liked it when time stood still, and in a place like this who would want to be distracted by the outside world?

I ordered haddock and leek tart. Paula opted for chicken and chorizo, and Sharon the lamb. It was just divine and well worth the revisit and the retravel. That always filled me with a glow. At 9.30 we still hadn't checked into our hotel so we forced ourselves to leave.

We were slowly and indirectly making our way back from Kent taking in Salford, Milton Keynes (MK17 8AZ), the next day.

Taking photos outside, we were ushered in by the landlady who assured us they were open. Here was another Red, and another first. The interior had a New England theme – blues, green and wood, all very relaxing.

Bob, the landlord, had got a designer in and was a bit worried at first but it worked. They had been here for 20 years, but had almost taken a pub in Samlesbury near Preston. So often there was a home link.

This is a very handy Red Lion for many locations, with six rooms at £59 per night, and there was a lovely beer garden at the back overlooking large, open fields scattered with cows. We enjoyed breakfast then back to Preston we went, a pretty perfect and decent end to a 16-Lion weekend!

September had arrived and my 500th Red Lion was close, and as I headed to Great Brickhill (MK17 9AH) it occurred to me that a year from now I would be finished. I didn't want it over, but at some point this would end. To have come so far and to actually visualise the finish line was quite disturbing and mad at the same time. People had started to ask me 'What next? The Rose and Crown?'

The lodger was back in tow as we pulled up at this lovely, white–painted, brick front with a marquee outside and a garden area overlooking paddocks. The cool drink, fresh air and sunshine were just what we needed after being in the car for over three hours.

We then made the seven-mile dash to Leighton Buzzard (LU7 1EF), a traditional but well-kept pub with plenty of original features. The bar to the right was once the arch where horsemen would pass through to put the horses in the stables for the night, and the back had been extended to include toilets which were originally outside until as recently as 17 years ago. I remember painting my grandma's outside toilet, but 1997 seems pretty late these days!

Ginny was clearly a dog lover with a whole wall dedicated not to mirrors, but to photos of dogs – her own two chilling on the pub floor. She had run the pub for 20 years.

Noah, one of the gang at the bar, quizzed me on the Red Lions.

'Have you done Bedford?' he asked.

I told him flat there were no Reds in Bedford.

'Just testing,' he replied.

I left unsure if he was an expert or just a wind-up merchant.

Eight miles closer to my big 500th where I had booked a table at Studham, we found the beautiful village of Milton Bryan (MK17 9HS). As we entered, we chatted for ages to a man who offered to take our photo. He had once lived opposite The Red Lion in Plawsworth, County Durham.

Well travelled, he and his father had been in the forces and had lived in Mijas in Spain for 20 years at the same time I was in neighbouring Marbella. Small world again. We enjoyed the surroundings with half an Abbot's as the sun continued to shine.

The day had been going great until we arrived at Toddington to find the Raj restaurant where the Red Lion should have been *but* was also closed down; The Red Lion had probably been there for hundreds of years, yet the Indian restaurant hadn't managed to endure more than a few. This wrecked my plan of dining at Studham and celebrating my 500th.

Unsure what to do, I debated whether to fit Birchwood Green in to keep my 500th as Studham, but instead headed off to Houghton Regis (LU15 6JS), about three miles away, deciding we did not have enough time as it was already 5 pm. Again we sat in the quiet garden of this massive Crown Carvery which was already busy inside.

Next was my 498th, and after a long diversion due to the building of a new motorway junction, I only just spotted the Red Lion at Sundon (LU3 3PE) as the square, detached pub is actually painted green! We parked up, photos were done, and then I walked up the few steps and opened the door.

I was not prepared for what followed. I walked into a standing ovation: the whole pub was clapping, Pete asked what number they were, then what we would like to drink. We got to know everyone and all about the pub.

This Red Lion beat them all for multitasking. Yes, it had been a morgue, too, and yes, it had been a post office! Pete had been refurbishing for a year or so and it had been closed, but the volume of people in on my arrival clearly showed that it was back on its feet.

And some had been coming for years. Dai had been stopping by since he was 15. The school bus would pull up outside and he would come in for a pint, alongside his Coke, just in case the police called in. What a story, and a reminder that pubs hoarded local secrets and their own sets of laws.

This welcome beats all the other 497 hands down. Little did my lodger know what he was moving into when he came for the interview for the room and said those words 'I'll take it': in fact, his eyes had lit up when I showed him the Red Lion garage bar.

So, on to Studham (LU6 2QA) which was intended to be Red Lion Number 500 – a fairly sizeable landmark. Because Toddington was dead, coupled with a shortage of time, this was now 499. No less reason to celebrate in this beautiful village and lovely pub, and a great Red Lion is a great Red Lion.

They had reserved a little table for us where the bar meets the restaurant and I was struck immediately by the décor with quirky chairs, unusual artefacts and warm atmosphere. Gary introduced himself. He moved in around nine years ago with his wife who he sadly lost just over a year previously and was managing to carry on religiously with the support of staff and customers, still filling the Red Lion with fresh flowers as she used to. It gave my landmark some perspective.

500 was just a number.

The evening was spent chatting with Gary and other regulars and staff; the music was very chilled and the food amazing! Gary gives it his all, and clearly has the support of the community on every level.

So, the next day, Dagnall (HP4 1QT) and my Number 500 Red Lion. We pulled up at 11.45 knowing it opened at midday, but the doors were open so in we went. Ali, landlady of three years was still last-minute hoovering in anticipation of a fully booked Sunday.

The bar girl had moved into the village seven years ago and loved it. She had acquired all the local history, including the fact that one local horseman used to do the journey to and from Leighton Buzzard so frequently that the horse automatically knew the way, often pulling up with the horseman drunk or asleep! One evening, he was attacked by highwaymen and the horse brought him all the way back to the Red Lion where he died of his wounds. What a tale.

Sadly, just like in Red Lion 499, Ali had taken on the pub as landlady with her husband Martin, but *he* had passed away a year ago and this happened to be her first day back doing Sunday lunch. She wouldn't take payment for our coffee and wished me luck.

I wish her luck, too.

The Red Lion Quest gave me context. I had caught a glimpse of so many people's lives. Babies were born in Red Lions, people died in Red Lions, bodies had been stored in them, yet it is the community which holds everything together.

This one at Water End made me think of Waterfall in Stoke where there was no water in sight just the tiny pub. Here I expected similar. My apologies to Hemel Hempstead (HP1 3BD).

You are just brilliant. Arriving through a long, tree-lined, curved driveway, this is more of a restaurant than a pub and it oozes class, so large it realistically needs an overflow car park.

The kitchen is modern – with a large, open view and offering a great choice of antipasti, and the wood-burning oven pizzas' aromas are to die for. In the front garden we just sat people-watching, in plush, wicker sofas, checking out the interesting menu. Pork came from Lancashire, and only free-roaming hen eggs were used. This is the place to come for a very long, relaxing lunch with superb décor and quality food.

From here we made our way to Bozeat (NN29 7JR) through the beautiful village of Olney. It is clearly a popular place to visit, though I hadn't heard the name before. A thriving outdoor market was on, a band playing and the sun beaming down on people strolling round the village. A quick drink and the weekend ended here. 502 Lions were done.

DAY TRIP TO DROITWICH

It had been four weeks since my 500th. A trip to New York with Mum and a weekend in Latvia were to blame. On 18 October, I set off with my lodger to get two done. In just under two hours we went through the door on the right at Droitwich (WR9 8AT).

It is a Banks's pub and their sign is a golden lion, two Lions in one. We ordered drinks and chatted to the bar lad and the landlord. The man and lady next to him had run The Red Lion at Malvern between 1990 and 1993. I had been there with Mum and Helena the previous August.

Half an hour away, we struggled to find Redditch (B97 5NH) as Enfield Road, on which it stood, has been chopped in half with bollards. It was an uneventful Saturday afternoon: ten men quietly watched the football, and as I left the landlord appeared.

He knew of the Quest, and the resident cat of 14 years insisted on being in the photos! How could I refuse?

OXFORD AGAIN

By late-October 2014, it was back to Oxfordshire, and yes, that lodger was getting addicted. We set off at 3 pm after a long interview with John Gilmore on BBC Radio Lancashire. They liked to keep up to date with my progress every so often. Either that, or they were all asking under their breath 'Is she bonkers?' I enjoy going into the station. They are all super-friendly and I was too far in to question my sanity.

By the time we reached Old Marston (OX3 0PH) it was 7.30 pm after a sluggish trip down the M6. There are two small bars, lounge and dining room and a great exterior with a kids' play area. Cosy and full, it's a cute little pub.

We stayed 20 minutes, making for the historic town of Witney and its Red Lion. Confused by a diversion, we ended up asking a passer-by where it was. He duly jumped in the car to take us to the Red.

'But it isn't open,' he added as we pulled up. Scaffolding up, refurbishment all around, I discovered it *was* soon to reopen but as a Japanese restaurant.

Dead and not counted. I think the guy just wanted a lift up the street!

It was now my fourth Halloween on the Quest and 2014 was the hottest one on record at 20 degrees. We crept along the country lanes towards Aston, Bampton (OX18 2DL), as though it were a summer's night.

Bampton is a tiny village and, as is often the way now, there is only one pub. It is mad to think that years ago even hamlets supported more than one drinking house. Those days were gone and it was a joy to find this Red decorated for Halloween and a cosy, warm, relaxed atmosphere in a place that had only just reopened in July.

I have mentioned a lot of dead Lions, and a few needing TLC, but there were clearly as many undergoing cosmetic surgery and being rejuvenated. That is a good thing.

Stuart and his partner had worked hard here and we admired the lovely new dining room and open fire. His partner was upstairs with man flu but popped his head out of the window to say he had read about me in *Chat* magazine. It was always interesting to see what publications the landlords read!

Tired and hungry, we drove the seven miles to Faringdon (SN7 7HG) Red Lion, where I had booked to stay for the night.

The town was buzzing, almost everyone was out in Halloween dress in a town where there are ten pubs and three clubs! The pumpkins were rocking!

We walked through the door of the Red Lion only to be told 'we are closed'.

We stood there with our overnight bags. I had already called ahead to say it would be after 8 pm when we arrived so they knew we were staying.

'We don't want drunks in here,' the landlord mumbled.

'Ten pm is early to close on a Friday night,' I responded.

'It's a matter of supply and demand,' I was told.

Flabbergasted, I asked if we could check in. Sourly, the landlord told his wife to take us to the room without even asking our names. We were clearly the only guests.

Dumping our bags and dying to eat, we went straight back down and I couldn't resist asking again if we could have a drink.

'If you must,' he said. 'But be quick.'

We declined and went over the road to the Volunteer pub and had a great night chatting away with the locals, discovering that the town was rumoured to be inbred. It did strike me as an odd place.

I was told that the landlord at the Red had a reputation. It was full-on Basil Fawlty. I learned, too, he had only four more weeks in the pub. He made it obvious he couldn't wait to not be there.

Coincidentally, we ran into a couple from Kent in the takeaway who lived in Orpington from tomorrow's list and told me that their Red had closed. That was a handy piece of information and I regrettably had to cross it off.

And of course, as can sometimes happen, you find a different mood at a different end of the day, so when we woke the next day the landlord was vaguely pleasant and cooked us a pretty decent breakfast!

The pub was lovely, too, in daylight. It remains the only Red Lion where I have not left my card since having them printed. It was a sunny 1

November as we left behind this quirky town only to realise half an hour later that I had left my phone on charge in the room so had to backtrack to see Basil again: thankfully we still managed to meet the awaiting press in Overton (RG25 3HQ).

Overton is a long, cream-painted pub, probably a few cottages knocked through. They have a cute little outbuilding which was once a barn. Their chef-in-residence is from San Francisco. We walked into a group of women celebrating a birthday. The pub has a lot going for it, especially atmosphere. Reporter Paul did his photos, inside and out, and by the time he had finished all the women were involved and I was behind the bar! Whether you loved a Red Lion for its appearance or its history, the most important was surely atmosphere and the daily memories that left with you.

As we were leaving for Aldershot, Paul agreed that Faringdon of the previous night was slightly odd.

Aldershot (GU12 4UZ), however, is very much a different proposition – a military town I often hear mentioned but have never been to, much like Wootton Bassett or Leighton Buzzard.

The Red Lion is a large, Tudor brick building on the corner, rebuilt in 1920 after the original burnt down. So many Reds have gone up in flames!

We received a warm welcome as landlord Lee had tweeted me and came straight over to greet us. Then word spread down along the bar and the couple next to us joined in to say that they had just returned from the Isle of Wight and broke the sad news to me that the owner had passed away that February.

He was a truly lovely man.

This pub has tunnels leading from the cellar all the way down to the church, although they are now blocked off. That Red had been a halfway house taking prisoners to the Isle of Wight jail. The prisoners would be shackled up in the cellar while the officers drank in the pub. Justice was done differently in those days. One story goes that a German plane landed up on the green during the war and they locked up the pilot in the cellar, too. They forgot to collect him and unfortunately he died there and now haunts the Lion. This Lion in Aldershot served a gentle reminder. All around me the circle of life and death continued, and it was perhaps the greatest annotation to my story that people were adding to it, filling me in on places that I had yet to go to or long since left.

Next to Red Lion 510 at Redhill (RH1 1DP) dating back to 1600 and the second-oldest pub in the village – to The White Lion.

Even after so many Lions and so many miles, things still tickled me. This had been a blacksmith's but was then given to a teacher to pay off a debt and that teacher turned it into a Red Lion!

What kind of debt or deal was that?!

Natalie, at the helm, had messaged me to ask if I had been in previously. She had been there just three weeks. That was lovely that she was curious and did not want to have missed out on this Quest! She is originally from South Africa, so she and my lodger had a good old chat, as he is, too.

It is a great little pub and Natalie was all smiles. I loved it.

It was dark by the time we arrived at Bletchingley (RH1 4NU) at 5.20 pm – winter was on the horizon. The waitress recognised me somehow and proceeded to tell me about the artefacts. Ah, yes the artefacts… There was a shelf crammed with Toby jugs and a wall full of weapons. It seems that the owner was a bit of a collector! She told me that every day a new artefact arrived. I would have liked to meet him, but he was out. It is nicely done and certainly interesting, so much so that we stayed to dine on delicious bruschetta and seafood risotto as it steadily got busy for the evening.

We had a hotel booked at Northfleet, actually to revisit Terry at the Red Lion there. Mick Hayes, who lives in Norway, has known Terry for years and he comes over each November to play in his band at the Red. My first visit there was a weekday morning. Now I was going to see it as it is meant to be: a full-on music venue. Before that we checked out Sidcup Red Lion as it was not too far away.

We couldn't find it. No sign. We asked in another pub. It was now closed and had become a van hire office. How depressing. The rocking Red Lion, however, did not let us down. It was a brilliant night, and Mick Hayes has recently informed me via Facebook that there is a Red Lion opening in Norway and invited me over.

The next day we went through the Dartford Crossing and north of London to Knebworth (SG3 6JP). It is old-fashioned with a saloon door to the left and carvery to the right, already filling up for the £6.95 Sunday lunch. The bar girl was originally from this village and wanted to move back. The phone was ringing non-stop for table bookings, and I expected the saloon bar would be busy later for the football.

From Knebworth, we were lucky enough to find Weston (SG4 7DA), as it had only reopened nine weeks earlier after a huge makeover. This pub dated back to the 16th century and again had been a blacksmiths. What was that route that took a building from being a blacksmiths to a pub? Or was it just a building, a shell, four walls that just moved on over the years from one purpose to another?

It is lovely with open fires, and beams dating back to that era and on the hearth sat... a pumpkin with a lion cut out. The bar girl was really enthusiastic about my Quest, not quite believing that I had been to 512 Red Lions before this one, and making a fuss and ensuring my small Prosecco even sat in a mini-ice bucket.

Less than 20 minutes through the countryside and we arrived at Biggleswade (SG18 8ED), and as I pulled up I noticed how similar the pub looked to Aldershot – Tudor style with Red Lion in gold-coloured letters over the door. This is another Greene King pub. I have nearly done them all now. The landlord was a nice guy and put live bands on almost every night, just allowing a break on Tuesday for the quiz. The pub was due to close for a week for a mini-revamp, moving the bar to make more room for customers. It was home time now after ten Reds, three deads and a revisit!

TO THE SMOG!

The day after Bonfire Night it was back down towards London again, and Kings Langley (HP3 9TD).

I arrived at South Mimms Truck Park at 3 pm to pick up Braz who had already parked up for the night. That was not much of a life sleeping in motorway service stations, but fair play to him: he jumped at the opportunity get driven to new little places for a pint. At this large corner Red Lion it is easily the largest garden I have seen so far, almost the size of football pitch.

There were not many in but the barman asked if I had been to Water End, which I had recently. He explained that this was a summer pub focussing on the outside bar and BBQ, and attracting lots of boat people. Apparently coachloads of Wigan fans, around 1,000, stop off here when they are on the way to the capital, even though it is a big Arsenal-supporting pub!

But mostly I loved the fact that a couple at the bar had stopped off here for a drink two nights ago and hadn't moved on. Canal Red Lions were something special.

We left to find Watford – unsuccessfully. I have since checked and Watford is a dead Lion: apparently that was a football club pub and there was too much trouble in what was actually the Red and Yellow Lion.

We carried on to Bushey (WD23 3HN) right in the heart of historical highwayman country in leafy – surprisingly bushy – surroundings. The Red Lion would have been a significant safe haven from the roadside bandits. Today at 5.30 it was busy and lively, and food was looking good. We resisted and drove for 15 minutes, arriving at another large corner pub in the beautiful village of Radlett (WD7 7NP).

It has been a Red Lion since 1920, so relatively new. Young's bought the pub three years ago. It was busy doing food, the menu looked good, and already on 6 November they were taking Christmas bookings. This will be my fourth Christmas Red Lioning. That is a long journey!

From Radlett, Barnet (EN5 1AD) took an age to get to, but then 15-minute journeys did last 45 on the M25.

Barnet was typical London. It needed decorating, and football had just been on the TV! I arrived just at the start of Psychic Night. I hadn't seen that coming!!! I was aware that more and more pubs were having such evenings, though it was the first time I had seen this in a Red. It is tempting to conclude that it showed the need for pubs to change and put more on but the truth is, of course, that they were always evolving and many had doubled up with other uses in the past.

I am grateful to the landlady here who asked whether I had been to The Red Lion Carvery up the road. I didn't even know it existed. 518 Lions down and still new ones were coming out of the woodwork. That was both exciting and concerning!

I think the two Barnets (EN5 5UW) now take the title for the shortest distance between two Lions and, unlike many carveries, of which I am not really a fan, this is still quite personal.

We were pressed for time as I had been contacted by a follower, Peter Gill from Red Lion Stevenage, to say to get down there that evening. I didn't question why. I did as I was told. So manager Owen and Kayley made sure our food and drink orders were dealt with quickly... A small carvery with choice of four meats for Braz and a succulent prawn baguette for me! I couldn't fault it. The building, which had been a nightclub called The Dandelion until seven years before, is massive – hence it wasn't on my list. You didn't see many premises opening for the first time in the modern era as a Red Lion, so maybe it was a Lion long ago. Barnet now had two, and here quiz night was about to begin!

At last, our last Red for the night, Stevenage (SG1 3DW). This had that rare air of mystery about it!

Earlier in the day I had also been 'followed' by a big, hairy fellow and here he was.

There was a band on and he turned out to be the bandleader. The band's name? Jesus Hooligans! The place was absolutely crammed. It was an amazing night. Crazy, great, mental! Their instruments were huge barrels tipped on their sides beaten with tubes and chains and all very loud. Raw singing, yet professional and rehearsed. A fusion of punk, African and rock: just brilliant.

They finished off by handing out tubes and we all joined in with the banging. I had never seen anything like it. The manager, who was rushing around like mad, had been wondering when I was coming.

Just think Braz would have otherwise been tucked up in his cab missing out on all this fun.

The Chris Evans Breakfast Show kept me entertained on the drive home next morning, with Mick Fleetwood and Billy Idol in his studio – a much more sedate offering!

Eight days later, I made a visit back to one lone Lion in Glasgow. This was a revisit so I couldn't count it again, as I had done so in February 2013 when it was meant to be open but wasn't. Complicated rules, I know.

The reason for the long trip, for one lonely Lion was social media. I received a message from a Red Lion saying 'what about us?'

It didn't occur to me immediately that it was Glasgow (G51 1LQ). I replied to them that I had come and it was locked to which the landlady said that it must have been a Sunday as they only open at 12.30 then.

So, perhaps I had been there at a time when they *hadn't* meant to be open. That meant I had to return.

It is not a great area – a little tatty and scary. The Red Lion was originally the base of tenement flats and this is all that remains, but Nicola, landlady of 25 years, was very welcoming on Facebook.

Word was clearly spreading and they had obviously given up waiting on me – hence the contact – when one of the regulars also messaged me to say I should go to the candle party. I agreed without asking the question: 'What is the candle party?'

Halloween had passed so it could have been that. I couldn't see much beyond candles, music and dancing as the other explanation.

Denise, who came with me the first time, was up for it again on the spur of the moment. Accommodation was tough to find for an overnight due to a Scotland v Ireland football match. After leaving at 1.30 we finally pulled up on the Paisley Road just before 7 pm, parking on the pavement, four inches from the wall. I was afraid to leave the car further away.

So what would lie in store when we went in? Three men were drinking at the bar and said hello. Two were at the far end setting up a table of candles. It was that sort of candle party. Great, I love candles.

Nicola came over and introduced us to all her friends and we sat with them in a bay while Steve and his partner talked to us about the various scented candles! You could really make a night out of candles.

Every bit of the wall was covered in all things British and the Royal family, including Kate and William and The Tower with the ceramic poppies, which I had just been to see.

I had got the wrong impression of this pub. We were made very welcome in a friendly atmosphere. Never judge a book by its cover.

From Scotland, it was back to London 11 days later for Highgate (N6 4BE). In reality, it was late-November and I was going for Christmas drinks with 'Inapub', and then on to meet my friends Andre and Kevin in Soho but as you know, there is barely a place I have been without hunting a Red on the way.

At this time of year, it was getting dark by 3.15 as I walked up the tree-lined street to Highgate Village. What a classy place and excellent Greene King pub with lovely stained glass windows, wooden floors and a cracking log-burner. The food, under the stewardship of a chef from Central France, oozes quality, and if you want something a little more traditional, they now do takeaway fish and chips, too, plus a rarity certainly for English Red Lions: they have their own whisky menu.

Its beauty is also its location. One minute you are coming off the Tube in busy London, the next you are in here and could forget you weren't out in the sticks.

It also comes into that little but not huge category of having a little variation in its name. Highgate is The Red Lion and Sun.

The same was true the following morning. After an action-packed night wandering into the brilliant meat market at Farringdon, then meeting Andrée and Kevin for dinner, I took the Tube from Andrée's house at Putney to Acton (W3 9BP) and the... Red Lion and Pineapple!

It stands on the left corner of the High Street and is a Wetherspoons Red Lion, so to a degree you know what you are going to get. On the one hand, Jeremy Kyle was on the TV and mostly single men were dotted around (asking me to join them, though I declined until pestered beyond the point where I couldn't refuse anymore) and on the other, you cannot beat Wetherspoon value – fresh bagel and coffee coming in at £2.49.

'John' told me he had been drinking here since 1967 and explained the name of the pub to me. There had been two pubs attached to each other. They knocked through to make the pub one and that meant The Pineapple was where the restaurant is now.

Much of the history of Acton had been archived in photos around the walls. As I took it all in, the past met the future halfway as a group of young women barged in, downing cider and red wine at 10.45. They started early in Acton. These two opposite London Reds put me at Number 522.

I was back in the capital again a week later for the Dea Latis Beer Breakfast on 5 December. You could measure not only the duration of the Quest in terms of Christmases, but also the length of my relationship with the lovely Dea Latis ladies now. It seemed like yesterday when I was first invited to one of their functions.

I took advantage and booked an overnight Thursday in East Ham so that I could check out a cracking Red Lion at Leytonstone (E11 3AA).

As the cab drove me into the town, a large, white corner building had birds painted on it, the bridge had 'Leytonstone' written in twinkle lights, and the big Red Lion was on the right-hand side surrounded by scaffolding.

Building work was never very welcoming but inside was a warm Christmas atmosphere complimented by stone walls, wooden floors and very high ceilings, with old pillars propping it up. Interesting pictures and bookshelves lined the place. It had been 'Zulu Bar' until four years ago, and then derelict until it was time to be a Red Lion again in 2011!

Every one of the little tables and benches was occupied. Food was on continuous go from the kitchen. The band was warming up. It was friendly and bustling.

I found a little space at the end of the bar and ordered baked Brie and a Cusqueña beer which I love and first tried in Cusco, Peru. It is all natural and not widely available in the UK. Chatting to the bar staff, one of them laughed as he said his friend had met me in another Red Lion but couldn't remember which one. I had, of course, met many people in many Red Lions! He had 523 pubs to pick from.

On receipt of my card, the manager told me The Who had once played in the large ballroom upstairs. Some big names had certainly rocked out the Red Lions over the years.

Tonight, it was the turn of Crème De Chèvre – a fantastic ukulele band putting their own stamp on songs old and new. A great venue and a fun night.

I wasn't to know at this point that I wouldn't go near another Red Lion for eight weeks.

2015

My dad started being poorly towards the end of September and on 30 December we had managed to get him out of hospital and back home, where he died on New Year's Day. I have to be glad that he wasn't in pain and happy knowing he and my mum were still enjoying their Wednesday lunch outings up until November.

Also I know I am very lucky to have had both my parents in my life until now. It took me some time to get going again.

Dad had always been interested in what I was doing, though he had never technically joined me on the Quest, although one Father's Day early on Alan and I had taken him and the rest of our families to dinner at Mawdesley Red Lion, a memory I will treasure.

So into my next year of the Quest... Surely, the *last* year of the Quest.

You could never say definitely. There were still over a hundred to do, but I certainly began the year thinking 'this is it now'.

We were in the home straight.

And, as occasionally happened, competition had come along – well, more a 'mini-me' than competition.

I had been contacted by a Welshman who had been reading about me and decided to do a quest of all Welsh Red Lions/Llewod Coch... actually about 10% the size of my adventure.

We arranged to meet for his first and my 524th, leaving home at 9.30 for a seven-hour round trip with the lodger and Paula who had been on a bit of a Red Lion drought. We met Dylan from PubsCymru at Llanbedr, Crickhowell (NP8 1SR). He was underway!

This is a great Red Lion for coincidence. It had been built as a holding place for materials to build the 13th-century church in the village. Bought 12 years ago, the landlady only recently discovered that her ancestors owned the pub in the 18th century when it was a blacksmith's at the rear. Of course, that was always possible in a village where people often stayed all their life, but what was odd was that she didn't know as she was buying it.

As I was recording a little piece about the Quest with Dylan's niece, country walkers ambled in for lunch – it is a real ramblers' pub – and then we were distracted by the noise of Paula and Robert discovering a game called Bullring where a bullring is attached to a rope and then skilfully swung to hook it on a hook. It was probably of no interest to the locals, but a discovery to someone from Preston.

We parted from Dylan and headed for Llangorse, Brecon (LD3 7TY). He had yet to tell his wife of his mini-Quest!

This Red is a really long building with a brewery attached at the end, though no longer in use. It had once been Breconshire Brewery. The pub had been in the family on and off for some time. Upstairs, the landlady plus her mum and dad and her two kids all lived. The parents had owned it and ran it 14 years ago, then sold up only to return. I didn't ask why they had decided they wanted out but then wanted in, but now they had a new lease of life, planning to convert the brewery into three rooms for a B & B. The landscaped gardens at the back are beautiful, too. They were proud to announce their new wedding licence. We watched it all going on as we tucked into three hearty baguettes.

I had called ahead yesterday to Sennybridge (LD3 8PH), also at Brecon, to check opening hours. They only open at 6 pm but when I told Tim there of the Quest, he promised to open up early if I called when on my way. Which he kindly did.

He had only bought it four months previously quite cheaply, but having done a few jobs had already put it back on the market. As he lit the fire, four lads followed us in, so it wasn't as though there wasn't a demand.

Sennybridge is a small town but should be able to sustain a Red Lion as its Army training centre serves many countries around the world. Every March, the Dutch alone come and drink the place dry!

Tim had covered the pub from floor to ceiling with all his memorabilia which he takes with him every time he moves on. He is also one of those owners or landlords who has an endless supply of little phrases. He didn't stop talking once as we all listened in with a cup of tea, as one after another quirky lines came out.

'It's not what you take, it's what you make.'

But we were made really welcome and as we left his parting words were 'see you when you are older!'

ROYAL TUNBRIDGE WELLS

I was making slow progress in 2015. It was the end of February before I put together another long weekend down south.

Denise escaped from work early where my brother is her boss, and we hit the motorway by noon for a four-hour drive to Royal Tunbridge Wells. That means the M25 and that meant it actually took six and a half hours.

We needed our Beck's and Cava by the time we made Turners Hill (RH10 4NU)... a Red on Lion Lane.

Graham, the landlord, refused payment whilst doing everything himself, including selling eggs and game behind the bar. It was a big hunting area.

There had once been a White Hart in the village – the second most common pub name. Winston Churchill used to drink there.

Another nearby pub had been sold for £100,000 to a woman who wanted to redevelop it. Suddenly the laws changed and prevented her from doing so. Although it is unfortunate if she loses money, it is about time the laws changed. We agreed that Britain had lost too many pubs, destroying communities.

It was a great start to a long weekend with the brilliant Handcross, Haywards Heath (RH17 6BP), hot on its heels. The manager told us this was a pub that dated back to 1517, and much of its prominence was due to the London to Brighton route. He advised me to Google 'Slaugham Archives'. So I did.

Its most famous customer was probably Horatio Nelson. Nelson again? He got about! His younger sister Catherine is buried in the churchyard. Local folklore suggests that a highwayman Jack Riding was hanged outside the pub, which was also the location of the inquest into the deaths of ten people after a Vanguard bus crashed on Handcross Hill in 1906. It had hosted many boxing bouts, too. A former British heavyweight champ 'Bombardier' Billy Wells was the landlord of the pub during the 1930s. He is best remembered as the original man who banged the gong at the start of the J. Arthur Rank films.

The Slaugham Archives do not seem to refer to a specific incident, but more to a colourful past of which the pub seems to have been the centrepiece.

On the way to Lindfield (RH16 2HL) we passed at least four foxes on the way to this busy Ember Inn, a drinkers' pub with no food on and still 40 minutes from our hotel at Tunbridge Wells. As we stood at the busy bar, Denise spotted a bistro across the road called The Limes where we popped over for a delicious dinner, learning in the process that lime trees outside an establishment meant it was safe for smugglers!

We decided to leave Chelwood Gate until tomorrow and checked into our hotel just in time for a relax at the bar. The reception is a tall, cone-like ceiling typical of those used to hang the hops from.

The next morning at least one of those foxes was dead. As we passed through the charming village of Goudhurst, on the way to Biddenden (TN27 8AH), I realised that probably happened a fair bit round here. I was told Princess Anne had attended school here!

When we entered the Red Lion, Bob Hewitt the landlord of 25 years told us he wasn't open for another half an hour, so we popped next door to an amazing oldey worldy bakery with everything home-made.

Bob sat with us by the fire he had just finished lighting. He was ready to retire, and sadly a lot of knowledge will go with him, too. The houses go back to the 14th century when they were Dutch weavers' cottages. I sensed he was a bit disillusioned with the trade. This wasn't the first time I had seen this, of course, and I had seen some leave only to miss it and jump back in. For many, it was all they knew.

On we went to Romney Marsh (TN29 9UQ), which had been sleeping in my subconscious since a South African taxi driver told me in 2012 he knew Doris, the landlady. I needed him now as it was not easy to find – the normally brilliant sat nav sending us round in a circle. I am not even sure the roads were actually official. Eventually, we found the B2080 and then discovered the church and this amazing Red Lion with its toilets still a separate outbuilding. Stepping inside was literally going back in time, stepping into a haven of the past without being drab or dated.

The till was original with a farthing key and still in use, but they had a sheet of paper with today's prices written. You could spot Doris a mile off, holding court in the corner; her daughter Kate's partner Bob was barman, as Kate did the food.

In the back room a local showed me the game 'Toad in the Hole' of which there were only two left in the country. Take one square stool with a hole in the middle. Then throw brass coins from a marked line scoring three points if you get it in the hole and one if it lands on the stool. The first person to 21 wins!

The building dates back to 1540 and has been run by Doris's family for 104 years with only three licensees. Doris has clocked up 66 of those years, having come as a young lady to work in the Women's Land Army in 1947. She met her husband here and certificates of her release from the Army amongst many other old photos are dotted around the Aladdin's cave of a Red Lion. She used to grow vegetables and sell them in the back room as her husband worked in the pub which had once been called The Shepherd and Lamb. It was 1964 before taking the step of getting electricity! On the arduous way in, we had also passed The Black Lion in Appledore. That had been a Red until ten years ago.

I wonder why? From signwriting to business cards, that meant a lot of work.

This is possibly my best ever Red Lion, certainly in my Top 5, Denise didn't want to leave, she kept tapping me, 'Come and have a look at this'. Everyone should visit here! Apparently, Paul McCartney has signed the visitors' book.

Heading down the A259 towards Hastings we were greeted by a sign saying 'Welcome to 1066 Land'.

We arrived at Brede, Rye (TN31 6EJ), to chickens roaming freely and a sign '245¾ miles to Hull'. It turns out Gary the landlord is from there. There is a lot going on here in this 600-year-old building. Once a courthouse, there are tunnels from the cellars to the church house. It is real smugglers' country.

One guy at the bar had just come from the Red Lion Parliament Street and passed me its card, though I had already been three times. How many times had that happened? As soon as I explained what I was doing, people's reflex action was to tell me of other Lions they knew. I had come across it hundreds of times by now! Another said they had actually been discussing how many Red Lions there were when I walked in. I am sure that has been debated often, but I can honestly say I am probably the only person to know.

Across the Brede Valley, the view behind the church is spectacular and one steeped in history, as this is where the King would stand to survey his fleet of galleons in the river which was once half a mile wide but now only a few metres.

Paul McCartney had also been in here a few times, by all accounts living just a short distance away.

Travelling along the A28 coast road we found Hooe (TN33 9EW), passing the 'Welcome Stranger' pub on the way, and just eight miles from Pevensey where William the Conqueror landed in 1066.

Roger was standing in for his son Lea who had just recently taken over. It was due to close the following week for a refurb. It is a nice little pub with the usual hanging hops.

Red Lion Pevensey (BN24 5EG) stands on Lion Hill. At 3.30, we were barely out of the car when 'Alan', fuelled with cider, greeted us, jumping into all our photos. Drunk as he was, he was still very witty, and constant warnings from the bar girl to tone it down helped for a few seconds. I wouldn't like to think what state he would end up in. It was only 3.30 pm.

This was a community pub and he had downed more than his share of community spirit.

Red Lion Number 535 is the excellent Willingdon, Eastbourne (BN20 9HQ). At the foot of the South Downs in this beautiful village, for some reason this Red Lion finds its way into George Orwell's *Animal Farm* mentioned eight times, with the village being the inspiration for the story.

We decided to try Chelwood Gate (RH17 7DE). They *were* open but very quiet. Nicola, the landlady had only recently taken over, but also runs another pub, so I didn't get to meet her.

It is a good location so they should easily build business up again with five acres out the back and Ashdown Forest nearby, and a magnet for walkers with now dogs and children also welcome. A large, suspended old plough makes an interesting feature donated by a local man.

It has hosted interesting visitors in the past. Prime Minister Harold Macmillan and President John F Kennedy have both had a tipple here.

If this seemed barely open, the same could not be said for Wadhurst, which was dead and not counted.

I had read about Wadhurst in 2013 when the sign '100% helicopter proof' appeared on the board outside. Nine days earlier a helicopter had plunged into the Clutha pub in Glasgow, killing nine people.

The landlord at the time was unavailable for comment. Now, it seems, so was the whole pub.

Our last Red on a long day fell to Tunbridge Wells (TN4 8TE), the oldest brewery in Britain, Shepherd Neame, and the oldest Red Lion in Kent. First licensed in 1415, the pub was probably trading before that in its handy location for the London to Brighton road. Opposite the pub stand cottages where many clients would stop for the night. It is another Red Lion that has also doubled up as a mortuary.

Dave and Maggie hadn't been there long and it was still very quiet for a Saturday evening. I hope it picks up. Our drinks had already been paid for by the brewery which was a nice touch. Parking up at the hotel for the night, we ventured out and had the best Indian meal for a long time on the recommendation of our Bangladesh taxi man. Junkas is well worth a visit. Having lived in India for three months I had been spoiled as far as Indian dishes go!

The next morning we arrived at St Albans (AL3 4RX) just as they were opening. It is a 15th-century pub on Fishpool Street which is a lovely little place, so I was taken aback when the chatty bar girl filled me on its sordid past.

This lovely pub had once been forced to close as the street was a slum. The Red Lion had been a whorehouse. People used to cross over the road rather than walk past it.

And now, of course, it was a beautiful pub and its Sunday lunch was a sell-out. It makes you think, though, when you are standing there, what really went on in the past. Not only does it make you think, it's impossible not to.

You could tell it was old coaching territory, and now we know what they got up to! There were a lot of pubs on this street as there often were back then. Dave used to manage this Lion then left for a White Lion for a decade, only to return to buy this Red! And as we left, we turned out of the street to see a sign attached to the corner house saying 'Formerly the Black Lion Inn'. It is good to remind the present about the past. This one is a Lower Red Lion!

For some reason, the Red Lion at Wendover (HP22 6DU) was not on my list, but I had always known about it because Dolly the barmaid is famous, turning 100 in 2014! Fuller's Brewery gave her a proper birthday bash last year with their shire horses involved in the day. Wendover is a fantastic place, with many tourists calling in from their country walks. The pub has its original arch leading into the car park with pay and display machines – a clash of the eras! It is classy and casual with wooden beams and flagged floors. Oliver Cromwell once overnighted here and addressed his troops from the windows upstairs. My smoked salmon and egg sandwich was great – good, fresh ingredients – and Denise loved the place so much she plans on coming to stay with her husband.

A little further north and nearer to home, I had been waiting to catch Horley, Banbury (OX15 6BQ), for some time as, apart from Sundays, it only opens at 6 pm. The village is picturesque with thatched roofs aplenty, including the Red Lion which was rammed due to rugby on the TV.

I handed my card to the landlord, telling him he was Number 540.

'Oh yes, another gang is doing that,' he replied flippantly.

I convincingly replied that they weren't, and reminded him that I had rung once about the possibility of making this my last.

'Oh yes, it's you,' he remembered.

In contrast, one of the rugby fans who was from CAMRA introduced himself and asked if he could do an article for his regional CAMRA. I never expected a fuss but I didn't warm to pompous indifference either.

Later that month, the pub was awarded North Oxfordshire Branch Pub of the Year and one of the best 200 in the country.

We managed 14 Red Lions and Denise enjoyed coming south for a change, as her other trips had been Scotland and Newcastle.

BEDS AND HERTS

Friends were driving me on now. Helena suggested an overnight trip Red Lioning for my birthday, and so I chose Bedford where the closest cluster lies. I found a Holiday Inn Express for £47 and off we went just before 11 am. Due to a snail's pace drive around Luton, we arrived four and a half hours later.

Red Lion Number 541 was Breachwood Green, Hitchin (SG4 8NU). Although Greene King pub signs hung around outside, Jack the barman told me that the company had just sold 220 pubs. Dave and Dave – the two Daves – were now running the show here. Jack wasn't hanging around either – a teacher, he was about to leave for New Zealand for a few months. He offered me a shot for my birthday! Very kind but shots and daylight don't work for me. In fact, shots full stop don't work for me.

A nice little feature here was a shelf with a road sign saying Scotch Corner, which is the junction of the A1 and A66 that I had passed on the way up to the North-East Reds. By this sign was a good collection of whiskies! Hitchin had formerly had three pubs but now two were houses and only the Red Lion stood strong.

Preston's Red Lion was a first. That is not my home town Preston, but Preston, Hitchin (SG4 7UD). This was bought by the community in 1983 – the first in Britain and a great example of how to save a Lion's life. Proudly sitting on the green in this lovely village, it truly is at the heart of the community. I don't know much about the running of a community pub, but if it is all done properly and everyone gets on, surely there can't be a better social idea. As we entered through one of the two front doors – possibly a sign of two original houses – we saw pictures of the community adorning the walls.

In the garden, I saw my first-ever peahen. Like a white peacock but female. We couldn't resist buying two tickets for the massive Easter hamper. It helps the darts team, we like chocolate, and what better excuse for a revisit if we won? We didn't, of course!

Ray the landlord of six years said he had been waiting for me. The feeling was mutual as of course it shares the same name as my home town. The community had bought the pub from Whitbread after the death of a previous landlord and the brewery's intention to turn it into a steakhouse. Now all these years later, it was still flourishing and they all had a stake.

I reflected on what a great wonderful concept this was as we wound our way along the rural roads to the delightful little haven of Great Offley (SG5 3DZ). This little retreat has accommodation and good food. The L-shaped building has a lion on the flat roof and a lion fountain feature at the door. It always makes it more liony when Lions have lion features!

A couple of characters run this pub. Louise, who was coming up to 13 years here this August, served us a glass of bubbles for my birthday. Then in popped her husband in the midst of his London Marathon training. He had run the race in 2014 but injured his knee and walked half of it, but everyone here remembers it for his posters around the pub in which he misspelt 'landlord': he had omitted the second 'l', so now he was known as Landord!

We said goodbye and made our way to Wilstead (MK45 3HN), as my ex-husband called me to say there was a Red Lion featured in the remake of *Poldark*.

'I bet you haven't done that one, Cath,' he said.

I Googled it and discovered it was only a stage set! Nonetheless, an interesting new category of untouchable fictional Red Lions!

We arrived at Wilstead at my favourite time. Saturday at 5 pm was most definitely Red Lion O'Clock. It might be something to do with people gathering for football scores and I was happy to see Preston had won with a game in hand. There are a lot of walkers in this dog-friendly pub, too.

Chris and Alyson had been expecting me since my last trip to Bedford and today was the day. It is one of just two remaining pubs in the village which had seen eight others fall by the wayside. It had once been The Bell, then Three Compasses, but a Red Lion since 1856 with the first recorded licensee Charles Tow, who served from 1876 to 1894.

Last Red of the night was the Sizzling Red Lion at Elstow (MK42 9XP).

That is a brand name rather than any sort of description. It is the only pub/restaurant around so it attracts a mix of all ages. Ed, the manager of six years, was about to leave that Thursday. I had caught him just in time. He had been with the company for 16 years but was moving to a career in auditing for a better social life.

I am sure running a Red Lion or any pub takes its toll.

My Red Lion list is printed on 23 sheets with 32 Red Lions on each one (apart from the last sheet with 26 on). I highlight them in yellow when I have visited and in pink if they are dead, and a few of my sheets just needed one more doing before they were complete. It was now time for a couple out on a limb, then I would get that satisfying feeling putting another sheet into the completed section. The first was Melton Mowbray (LE14 4HS). This brilliant little pub stands at the heart of its village – the route in is nothing but fields. At the end of the crammed car park, a new first – The Red Lion vegetable patch.

Attention to detail is what makes this Lion stand out. Stone floors, open fire and an old, small bar do not depict a dated look at all. They work a treat and everything from the soap in the Ladies to flowers dotted around, to using their own home-grown veg, tells you no element is too small to care about.

The bar girl was intrigued by the Quest and brought over a Red Lion glass for me to take home. That garage bar of mine was filling up nicely.

I left thinking how lovely to have a local like this.

The next Lion all by itself was Bottesford (NG13 0EE) in Nottingham, and that rare chance to stand in a bar which resembles someone's front room. I had called last year and spoken to the landlord's brother who had been running it then. All part of brotherly banter, I am sure, but the current landlord ensures me his Sunday lunches are better than his sibling's! A couple of locals chirped in, telling me Pie Night was a winner, too!

I was not entirely sure that the landlord himself will be there too much longer. The asking price for taking over the lease seemed high, with £20,000 alone wanted for fixtures and fittings. It is in a great location but needs support and renovation.

After a great weekend stepping into seven excellent Red Lions, it was back to my local for a few birthday cocktails! Another year older – and still on the Quest!

BRIGHTON'S BEST

The next weekend with Robert the lodger, it was down to the South Coast once more. Clear motorways made a pleasant change and we reached Reading (RG1 2QL) by mid-afternoon. Though looking a bit grim on the approach, the inside was pleasant, the bar girl was alone watching *Jeremy Kyle* but she said it would be busy with drinkers later. This was not the first time that show has been on in a Red Lion! We drove the eight miles to Mortimer West End to find it only opens at 5.30 pm. I would need to return here as I didn't want to waste an hour hanging around.

Bracknell took ages to get to and then we walked past it several times before realising it was a Red Lion no more and now called The Stonehouse. We popped in for a drink anyway but it was an ex-Lion and not counted. We reached the Royal Oak, Hawkhurst, where we were staying both nights with three attempted Lions. As the song goes, two out of three ain't bad, but one out of three is terrible!

The next morning, down on the coast we found Hove Red Lion tucked away down a little street to be told by workmen that it was no longer, with the inside gutted and soon to be 'The Better Half'. Oh dear, I hope the pattern changes soon.

So a relief to find Shoreham-by-Sea (BN43 5TE). We were delighted to find this lovely, 15th-century coaching inn a few miles down the coast.

It is a long pub with the far end once being a petrol pump and the main building starting out as a morgue. This was becoming all too familiar. Two solid, three-legged tables in the lounge area, where drinks were now resting, were the original tables used to sit the coffins on! I can't imagine the IKEA furniture of today sturdily surviving for hundreds of years. Church pews also make up the seating. We arrived a fortnight away from their massive festival showcasing 58 real ales and 50 ciders.

I left with a Red Lion pint pot souvenir and some good advice to switch the order of my next two Red Lions.

So, 12 minutes later through rural country roads we found two buildings joined together to make Pulborough (RH20 3DD), with the one on the right looking like it was originally the barn. Spacious with wooden tables, stone floors and interesting pictures, it is a stylish and natural pub/restaurant. We sat at a cute wooden table watching as the place got very busy with lunchers.

On the way to Arundel (BN18 9AG), the magical castle appears in the distance. Arundel is a fantastic historic market town and port and the 200-year-old Red Lion is one of its busiest pubs in the heart of the hustle and bustle. International ships left from here, sailing the five-mile river journey to the sea. The Red was a hive of activity inside, full to the brim with people eating, drinking, chatting or watching the rugby. I bet it was the last pint in town before setting sail many years ago. From here, great stories were born.

It's a town and a Red Lion not to be missed. As we were leaving, I spotted the huge 3D Lion standing out on the chimney breast.

We had planned to meet an anonymous blogger later whom I had met three years ago while at Blewbury with Paula. Oakhanger is the only Red Lion on today's list that shuts between 3 and 6 pm so I ended up rearranging all the pubs because of this, as I couldn't miss it.

Sussex is a lovely part of the world. We passed through Chichester and on into Hampshire and the 12th-century Red Lion at Horndean (PO8 0DT), now part of the Table Table chain. Number 552 was a quick expresso and then into another gorgeous village.

Chalton (PO8 0BG), thatched and detached and on the green, is said to be the oldest pub in Hampshire and, as sometimes happened, we walked straight into a drinking session where the blokes in question find everything hilarious. It had moved on now from quizzing me about the Quest to asking me about the book.

I was still working on the title at this stage. Their offering? '553 Shades of Red Lion'. Apart from being a rubbish title, there were still other Lions to go. Of course, one of the guys began muttering that he was going to be in the book now.

It's a great pub, though, easily in my Top 50 with wooden and tiled floors, and shelves lined with books throughout many rooms. I can vouch for the delicious food. Fuller's high standards never let you down.

Next stop: Petersfield (GU31 4AE) and a Wetherspoons, who always keep the décor in line with local history. The oldest side of the pub on Heath Road was known as 'The Tap' and dating back to the 16th century but originally recorded as just 'The Lion'. The section fronting onto College Street was described as 'The Red Lion' in 1734 and then modernised in 1760, with today's façades dating from then. Wetherspoons refurbished it in 2010, some 300 years later. Three centuries and nobody had touched it!

The penultimate planned Red of the day was the beautiful Fernhurst (GU27 3HY). It was busy, and taking an age to get served, mainly due to a large group all paying individual food bills. A very boring, pompous man (who had no idea about me or my Quest) talked at us about anything and everything, making me keen to leave. As we were edging away, his final comment was 'I don't suppose you know this, my dear, but 'Red Lion' is the most common name for a pub, and if you were to go to Oakhanger you would also find one there!'

The pub is a very cosy location on the doorstep of the South Downs National Park facing onto the green; inside, low beams and some lovely wooden furniture. It is perfect for walkers.

By 7 pm, it was time to meet Shane, my follower, who wanted to get together at the very same Oakhanger (GU35 9GQ). Dark, barely lit, tiny lanes, sharp bends and diversions didn't make it easy-going. Gail and Nik were in charge for the last 11 years and the pub had once been called The Rising Sun. Shane and Sue were waiting for us at the bar.

Shane updated me on his news, as you would an old friend. He had split from his wife and got custody of the dog which I had met at Blewbury two years before! He had now met Sue, moved house and was underway on his very own pub Quest! He has declared to visit every Green Man pub in Britain and thinks there are 123. I had been in one near Preston about 30 years before, but was pretty sure it had closed.

It was flattering to be imitated, but equally I am not sure if there was much point!

After deciding to make this the last one of the night, I realised we would actually be passing Godalming (GU7 1HF), so decided to squeeze in this and its neighbouring one.

One local filled us in on the history. Godalming had been the main stopping-off place between the Royal Fleet at Portsmouth and The

Crown in London. It was exactly halfway and that bought trade and stories from principally the wool or tanning trade. The pub is haunted, was once a courthouse and has the honour of being the town with the first electric street lighting in the UK. However did they stagger home before that happened? This would have been great to end the night, but we needed food and the next Red Lion stopped taking orders at 9.15.

With one minute to spare we rounded the night off at Shamley Green (GU5 0UA), another pub... on the green. We burst through the door to that smell... delicious, fresh-cooked food. Sometimes on these outings we didn't always get the chance to eat when we were hungry. Either the Red Lion didn't do food when we were, or we were pushing to get to another one before it closed. Warm goat's cheese and pine nut salad, lobster bisque and Red Lion burger hit the spot. Divine. With friendly staff, delicious food and cute little Red Lion teapots on the window sills (the pub had originally been tearooms), it ranks highly.

This was our tenth Lion of the day with one also dead, and we still had that two-hour journey back to Hawkhurst where we were overnighting.

I needed more days like this if I was to finish by this summer. We began the long journey up the motorways, Robert rarely finding the right one. Men drivers! It had been a brilliant day – easily one of the best for continuously good locations. Only in Oxford with Paula had I done more in a day, notching up 11 on that occasion, but today I definitely clocked up the most mileage.

Only at midnight did we arrive back at The Royal Oak.

In the morning I declared we could incorporate three or so more in the direction of home. The tricky bit is working out which ones opened, given it was a Sunday, and that normally meant midday. Plus, it was Mother's Day 2015 and my daughter was preparing a meal for 6 pm, so that was the cut-off point.

So, to begin we picked the first of two Eghams on Village Road (TW20 8UE). Sitting on a comfy sofa facing the fire, we watched the girls tying up balloons and making the place look lovely for the big day, which was a sell-out.

The second Egham on the High Street (TW20 9EW) bears a plaque above a bricked-up hatch on the side wall saying 'AD 1521', but also has just undergone a £350,000 refurbishment. I have seen the pub trade at various stages through the recession. It was good to see it coming out the other side, having been closed between January 2013 and March 2014. The previous landlord had left suddenly and now Sean was in temporary charge, though he was actually a reporter and film-maker!

There is so much to do around Egham from Thorpe Park to Windsor Castle to Eton, Legoland and Ascot. I would imagine this pub picks up both local and passing trade. It is perfect, really, being so near everything yet maintaining its rural identity. One local, Tony, explained to me that in the old days as the coach and horses turned into the Red Lion stables, the luggage would be taken off through the hatch and appear in the rooms before the guests had dismounted and checked in.

Tony had lived here for 30 years and had witnessed the Red Lion ghost having come in at 11.30 one morning at a time when the bar had been in a different place. It was just Tony, getting warm by the fire and the waiter cleaning cutlery. From nowhere, a fork flew across the room, landing on the stone floor. The two of them saw it. There remains no explanation!

Red Lion 561 was Windsor (SL4 4QF), in touching distance of the castle. And what a surprise. This is Gita's Red Lion Indian Restaurant. She bought it with her husband last year when it had been a Chinese Red Lion.

Their lunch menu was English, the evening was Indian. I was delighted. The chef was originally from Goa. They were experimenting to find the right balance. The inside has a warm, family feel to it. Gita's son and family were all gathered along with many other families just enthusiastically coming through the doors. This stands as a landmark Lion because it reflects changing cultures and palettes. In the same way all these ghosts and coaching horses pointed the way to Britain's former past, this, too, marked the same. The only difference was that this is contemporary culture evolving in our own lives in real time.

On that note, Robert has now done as many as 52 Red Lions, a great way for a South African to get to know Britain!

ROSS-ON-WYE

Six days later, I had really begun to rediscover my momentum. I knew the clock was ticking and there were at least 80 more Lions to do and already the end of March was upon us. Good old Paula suggested an overnight trip, as our friend Joanne wanted to experience the Quest. Plotting a route was becoming harder and harder with so few Lions left and such random opening hours. Evesham (WR11 4RE) was not even on my list.

I had only just learned of its opening via Facebook. As we entered 'The Historic Riverside Market town of Evesham' or, as the locals say, 'Aysem', this couldn't have been a more picturesque first Red for Joanne. This was a Red Lion from 1720 then closed as a pub in 1910, going on to be a house of ill repute, an electrical wholesalers, a religious bookshop, then a shoe shop! Thanks to Gerald Harvey who in 2014 took on the lease, bringing it back to its original purpose and birth name.

The banter began as soon as we walked in, with two merry chaps at the bar telling me I was bedroom material! Honestly, I must have heard it all now. I sat with Gerald as he told me he never drank until he took on Cannon Royall Brewery near Holt seven years previously. His wife was a CAMRA member and he would be the one drinking the tea. How things change: he now brews and sells real ales in his small bar.

Bedroom Material Man apparently comes in every day and drinks 12 pints of real ale followed by triple vodkas and then goes home – except on a Sunday, as his bus does not run! I imagine everyone was his bedroom material.

Gerald gave us the full tour. The Quest opened up many doors for me, including cellar doors that I would never have normally got to experience. These used to house the local convicts from the sheriff's court who were left to die before being buried in the churchyard. We were a barbaric lot once – down the short walkway along from the Red Lion stands a magnificent abbey we were urged to see before we left.

Joanne had experienced a typical introduction to the Quest.

We were well out in the sticks when at 4.30 we found Bredwardine closed, so we meandered ten minutes further into the countryside to Madley (HR2 9PH). This is a trick pub – gorgeously picturesque on the outside, but madness with bonkers locals on the in!

Everyone was chatting to us; a dog was barking, through which a baby slept; they didn't believe who we were, thinking we might be the Hotel Inspectors off the telly; and we must try the 6% cider! I think the comical paranoia as to our identity was merely a reflection that not many outsiders come in. Paula duly obliged on the cider, only to be told that it gets you wasted. One woman said that she needed to go back on to Strongbow now to pace herself! Another said it makes you shit the bed. Honestly? We clearly had novelty value – except to the landlord who had no interest in us or the Quest and was borderline rude, as if to question what on earth we were doing in his pub!

By 5 pm, needing to escape, I had called Bredwardine to learn they opened at 6.30 despite being a hotel! I mentioned the Quest and asked if we could pop by only to be told 'No, you cannot.'

Fair enough.

There was a long old drive to our third Lion in the medieval Tudor town of Pembridge (HR6 9DZ). You could see this in all the buildings – crooked and bowing outwards. We had arrived to a packed pub, all eyes on the screen: England had just got another try, bringing the score to 41-25 in the 55th minute. More rugby! Paula had no interest in the slightest. Joanne was still getting to grips with the Quest so, on we headed to Peterstow (HR9 6LH) in the darkness.

Dave and Kath run a very busy pub, able to cater for around 130 people in one go, with such delights as crab thermidor.

Kath introduced herself and knew about me, prompting another couple at the bar to randomly come out with the fact that there are four pubs called 'As You Like It' in the UK. The conversation of the Quest always added to everyone's knowledge, as people made comparison adventures in their own mind. She had named her own business after that Shakespeare play.

After a night in the King's Head, Ross-on-Wye, which I have to say is highly recommended, Paula and Joanne were in no rush to get home so I gave Ampney St Peter a go. It is strange to measure again that passage of time, but it was 2011 when I was in the area last. It only opens random hours, so we rolled up at 11.45 for hopefully a midday opening.

All was quiet. I called and could hear the phone going off inside. I could also hear zero response. The void was broken by a lady pulling up in a red MG who told me that the landlord had sadly passed away in the December after suffering a stroke. Sadly missed, he was by all accounts some character. Regrettably, the pub would not be opening anytime soon.

How sad it was that I had seen death in Red Lions on a far too regular basis, even though the statistic remained a very low one. I am sorry to write that this literally is a dead Lion. A peep through the window was a peep into the past: tiny rooms filled with character and history.

Contemplating, we made the 50-minute drive in the opposite direction to Preston, aiming for Axford, Marlborough (SN8 2HA). This pub reminded me that once in the past you had a career for life, now through economic circumstances, such as redundancies or the intolerance of modern life, many people found themselves finding second or third careers. Running a pub was not easy and there were no guarantees, but there were still plenty wanting to take it on. John at Marlborough had been in for seven months, having abandoned banking.

I worried, though, as the pub was quiet. He told me some days it wasn't and appeared disappointed we were not eating, as only one other table was occupied.

Just inside the door of the restaurant is a fish tank with fish and a shipwreck in it. If you can spot the hidden treasure you win a free meal. I couldn't see it. Two soda waters and half a lager cost £6. I didn't say anything but that is expensive. I wasn't entirely sure that a man whose career had been about margins had struck the right note here. There is a lot of scope, too, with a lovely patio dining area for a warmer day.

Paula and Joanne were keen to fit in one more so Red Lion, Mortimer West End (RG7 2HU), again it was. Just nine days earlier this is the one Robert and I had arrived at too early.

It had reopened under new ownership last August and was now full-on Italian and doing brilliantly, busy despite being down a remote country lane. It was interesting that an Italian had kept the Red Lion element and, like Gita's Indian Red Lion in Windsor, reflected modern-day culture changes. I suppose what they were doing was taking a known local premises and then putting their spin on it. We were amused at the couple's assumption on the next table that we were the Cheshire Housewives from the TV! Preston does not sound like Alderley Edge! We couldn't have been more content sitting in the sunshine in this glorious setting with a mozzarella salad, chips and a Peroni to end a gallivanting weekend. But no, Paula and Joanne said, just one more!

So our seventh of the weekend took us over a little toll bridge at lovely Whitchurch, through Hungerford and into Britwell Salome, Watlington (OX49 5LG), a delightful Red to really end the weekend. Where these Red Lions getting better and better? Maybe I had saved the best few to last.

This pub is not on my list – principally due to mischief. It *had* been a Red but someone changed the name to The Goose for several years! Now it is back to its real name, and Ayley and Andrew, a Michelin-starred chef, have built up a booming business. If I am honest, there were not many other Michelins in the Red Lion kitchens of this Quest.

There is also a tiny, cute shop selling local pottery. I had long come to accept that Red Lions also had many other functions that bore no synergy to the business of ale!

It was great to meet Ayley – she had been following me on Twitter. This happened often now. When I walked in the pub it was a throwback to one of my early Reds. Deer skulls and antlers greeted me, loaned to the pub by a friend who had shot them!

The pub has lots of awards for food. They lease it from a local farmer who owns the Red Lion Farm and the Red Lion Shop! They were all doing a roaring trade!

With no more untamed Lions in this patch, we made for home.

THERE'S A CERTAIN
DUTCH TRING ABOUT IT

The clues are all there. As I was sighting the end of the UK Lions, I was lining up the overseas ones. Late-April 2015, Amsterdam made my tenth abroad. That future Quest was just bubbling nicely and potentially could mean another decade on planes, trains and automobiles.

Braz the trucker informed me he was to be parked up at Eddie Stobart's truck stop again! He is clueless timewise partly due to his character – add to that driving conditions – so, not relying on him at all, I made for Marsworth (HP23 4LU) in gale-force conditions, driving rain and accidents left, right and centre.

I passed a pub called 'The Bleeding Wolf' and was relieved to pull up and warm up in front of the log-burner and a friendly atmosphere. At a little wooden table I made a few notes. There was a good choice of real ales and a good beer garden for better days. The sun was out as I left for the truck stop on now my fourth visit here and then on to Raunds (NN9 6DL). This pub gets the nomination for Dippy Barmaid of the Year.

I quizzed her about the photo on the wall – where was it? She had been here six years and had never even noticed it! Clueless, she confessed to me that she thought Torquay was in Canada! You could clearly get some good banter and have a few laughs, but don't ever plan your world tour here!

We ended the day at Rothwell (NN14 6BW) which thankfully had just reopened after a big refurbishment. We walked into 'Open Mic Night' and some Irish music. Hayley the bar manager followed me on Facebook and bought me a drink; the chef once lived above Yardley Hastings RL. The hotel has 11 rooms and the stables at the back are function rooms. It's a good, lively atmosphere and we left after watching a couple more bands. Back at the truck stop just 20 minutes on from here all was silent; drivers from all over Europe start out as early as 2 am, making my 6 am start seem like a lie-in. Traffic is good then, and I was home in no time.

Four days later the surge was swelling and along with Paula, Joanne and Sharon we were Ipswich-bound. Paula had notched up more than a hundred Lions now.

We decided that Easter Saturday would have less traffic than Good Friday, and would have preferred to stop at Cheveley, but it only opens at 6 pm so we popped Finchingfield into the sat nav. Suddenly, two miles too soon, Joanne spotted a Red Lion I had not counted on: Great Sampford (CB10 2RL). It was always good to have fresh eyes on the lookout beyond the predetermined route.

The 'problem' with this pub was that it had been closed due to a very big fire of which I was shown photos. I had it down as a dead Lion but was grateful to discover it has reopened. So now, so close to the end of the Quest, I began to check for reopenings. And this pub needed to be open. It was the only thing in this small hamlet – the kind of place where we found locals had gone out shopping only to stop at the pub and never even make the shops.

On the old wall hung a picture of Walter and Alice Hitchens who had been landlords between 1878 and 1886, also running the bakery from here.

The landlords were the great storytellers and the never-ending constant of the Red Lion story.

Reluctant to leave, we pulled up a few minutes further along, at the beautiful village of Finchingfield (CM7 4NN) up Church Hill and past the village green, taking in the white windmill. Those landmarks set the scene. The landlady is a Facebook friend and came straight over with a 'I Got Roaring At The Red Lion Finchingfield' T-shirt – the latest in a long line of random Lion merchandise, though ironically I had been roaring in very few of them.

In for just a year, they are doing well with live bands and open mic night, too, plus we stood on the step where you could almost touch the competitors as the Tour de France passes right by, an annual bonus. That must have been some sensation standing there with a pint watching the world's great cyclists fly by.

We left Sharon dashing for her train at Margaretting, then stopped briefly at its Red Lion (CM4 0EQ). She left us at this point but missed nothing. This Lion was open but empty.

Springfield Road, Chelmsford (CM1 7RA), was the total opposite, wandering into a private party for someone's 18th. This is a very food-orientated Lion.

Like many of the Red Lions, the ceilings are very low. One wall of the pub was filled with clocks of all shapes and sizes – unusual without being tacky and also, by a mile, with the best selection of lions I had seen. One was made from thin pieces of wood, some were from pot, and a large mesh one sat near the toilets. You couldn't move for lions and clocks.

Next stop was Billericay (CM12 9AJ) – a place I liked the sound of but for some reason I had always thought was in Ireland (almost as dippy as Torquay being in Canada). It is actually close to where *The Only Way Is Essex* is set, a show I have never seen. This is a packed Essex bar on the main street: we sat in the vibrant lounge with a drink and chips surrounded by the 'shat ap' Essex accent. Time was ticking so we needed to move on.

We found Witham (CM8 2AF) friendly but a little strange. In 1925 it had somehow come second in 'Best Bar Parlour in the United Kingdom'. As we entered at 6 pm they were preparing for another person's 18th while a few men played the noisy bandits and loud music blasted out: it looked like it would get messy later on!

Ten miles away and up to Marks Tey (CO6 1LT), a *Dirty Dancing* CD played in the background, food smelled good, and they had Red Lion place mats. Still new little touches were surfacing this late in the Quest!

It was enjoyable driving around these parts, with narrow lanes and open fields it was relaxing, very different from the M6 and M25. I entered Honey Tye, Leavenheath, next in the sat nav and came across The Lion, all on its own, nothing else was here. I nipped in to ask whether this was actually a Red Lion, as this didn't even seem to be a village or anything. I was told *this* was originally the Red Lion but had now been just the Lion for some time. I crossed it off: not counted.

Our eighth Lion of the day on top of our nearly five-hour journey was a hidden Red Lion at Belchamp Otten (CO10 7BQ).

Night had fallen and the road had become a track. The full moon was our only guiding light. My dipped beam had also failed. What a setting, then, and slightly frustrating when the sat nav took us to someone's farm. Now, normally she is very good, but we were in bleak wilderness;

I began to doubt whether there was even a pub here, let alone a Red Lion. Finally, in the distance, shone the welcoming lights! And it was open. In we step into an oldey worldy den, much to the surprise of the local men bemused by the Quest. Hard to find, but a little treat when you do! They do food here and live music, but today was just a friendly drinking crowd. We reached our hotel at Clare just in time for dinner at the Bell Inn: I wonder if it was always a Bell Inn or maybe at some time in its past it was a Red Lion.

Waking up to a lovely day, I couldn't wait to get back on the road after a quick run. At some point we were to meet up with my brother who left Preston at 7 am to join the trail. At midday, Thorrington (CO7 8JN), a barn-like building, we arrived to catch large groups strolling in for family Easter Sunday lunch. The lack of an outside sign was not affecting business: it was probably going to be a full house on yet another beautiful day.

The next was at St. Osyth (CO16 8PA) five minutes away but right on the coast, so I couldn't resist popping down to the sea wall to take in some fresh air as we were almost overrun with caravanners.

St. Osyth is a long, Tudor-style, old-fashioned pub, and very popular. The *Ipswich Journal* seems to place it at around 1754, as it had hosted a cricket match they reported on. It had also been a post office.

Today, a very simple touch overlooked by so many pubs greeted us. The bar was laid out with bowls of gherkins, cheese and crisps. It didn't take a lot of doing and doesn't cost a lot of money: by the time you have nibbled your way through one bowl, the need for another drink is looming. At the bar, we learned that a Lion down the road had just reopened a month before. I was relieved not to miss it, so far away from home as I was. Brother David was close now so we arranged to meet him there.

And as we arrived at Kirby-le-Soken (CO13 0EE) my brother walked in at the same time: he loves rural English villages, so this was perfect for his first stop! They had done a great refurb. Charles and his parents were now running it once again, having been here in the 80s and had been warned I was in the Red Lion trek. That was a long time ago and the world had changed a lot. It obviously was a huge part of their lives.

The food was excellent, based on fresh product. I am sure it won't be closing again.

Now next came Manningtree (CO11 1BG), a gorgeous village on a slopey street with a Red Lion bike outside chained to the wall. That's a new one. I believe it is for the Peddling Publican Tom, who regularly raised money for Great Ormond Street after life-saving treatment to his sister Beth when she was 15. Pubs are great places to build charities around, as I have seen over and over, and obviously everyone here knew Tom's story.

Tom has got this 1605 pub running like clockwork with a Red Lion clothing shop and a barrel drop delivered to your door within five miles. There's a lot going on and in a professional way. We resisted the good choice of real ales and sat with tea, coffees and mini-chocolate eggs. It is Easter! A group of locals asking where we were going next warned me that Bildeston may not be open, then efficiently text a friend who confirmed the worse. It had been the local for the notorious Kray twins and there had been a recent stabbing in the village. I will need to recheck before my final one.

I called Great Bricett which is a vegetarian restaurant with a good reputation, but it closes after Sunday lunch until Tuesday. I have a long journey back just for that one! Here we were in one of those pubs where you were completely at ease and could while away an afternoon.

And so it went on. Our next stop was past an amazing old church at East Bergholt (CO7 6TB). All was quiet: the pub was closed!

I peered through the window. All was not lost. Rick the landlord spotted me, opening up spontaneously. Someone had been posting him newspaper clippings of articles about the Quest.

He had been there 15 years and the pub was known as 'the pub with the big dog', a Leonberger which we didn't get to meet, though, was surely hard to hide! The old church of Virgin Mary is unusual in that its bells are on the floor outside in a bell cage. They are manually pushed every Sunday because when the church was being built they ran out of money, so they never got put up. It is the heaviest five-bell peal in the country!

Not wanting to intrude on Rick's free time – of which there is little as a landlord – we headed for Bramford Road, Ipswich (IP4 4AY). It is a long road and the Red stood looking dubiously on the left. It isn't a particularly nice building, brick and basic. A blackboard announced 'Jane and Claire Welcome All'.

Walking through the door it felt like that scene in *Dirty Dancing* when she walks through the door of the club with a watermelon in her arms, or *Phoenix Nights* again. At not even 5 pm karaoke was in full swing, and drinking was well underway. Flashing lights flashed away. As I looked towards the DJ box at the end of the room, the DJ came out holding a four-month-old baby.

I think you get the picture. The folk were friendly but mad, and in a world of their own.

It was a relief to get to Martlesham (IP12 4RN) just 15 minutes up the road and a world of difference in character. As we drove into the car park I noticed the huge Lion head towering over the front of the building, and Rob Lusher, the manager, greeted us at the entrance.

He has been here seven years. The pub is a Chef & Brewer but does not feel part of a chain. In fact, it is timber-framed and Grade II listed, and located in the ancient riverside market town of Woodbridge and had been a coaching inn, this time on the London to Yarmouth Turnpike Road.

It is mainly a restaurant and was already busy. We were seated in the smart bar area where Rob joined us briefly without taking his eye off the ball. He handed me a book entitled *The Lion of Sole Bay*, explaining that the Lion head on the building was a figurehead from an old Dutch boat sunk in the Battle of Solebay in 1672, a large naval battle of 75 ships in the Third Anglo-Dutch War.

The story he handed me is fiction written by a local lady called Julia Jones, who has adapted that battle into a modern adventure story.

Nearby, the Sutton Hoo burial mounds on a landowner's property had been excavated in 1939 to reveal the burial ship of an Anglo-Saxon king complete with a body, armour, jewellery and ornaments, and it had been sitting there all that time.

A thriving Victorian brewery once stood here, too. If every landlord or owner was as communicative as Rob, I would have learned a lot more.

Perhaps they needed a little plaque here so Rob didn't have to tell the story every time. Poor Rob was just going for a two-hour break before returning for a stocktake.

Our eighth and final Red of the day was just nine minutes beyond at Thoroughfare, Woodbridge (IP12 1AL). We were now in a busy touristy area with lots of campsites around. Davey and Ryan had bought the Punch Taverns pub not even a year before, and this had also once been a morgue and a bakery. They filled me in on a tiny pub in Bury St Edmunds nearby that measures only 15 ft by 7 ft, so small that they barred one customer for being too big and taking up the space of two men. Pubs are the centre points where interesting, important and trivial information changes hands. I love it. As brother Dave took my photo at the front, ten men who were drinking outside the British Legion across the road decided it would look better if they were in it. It did actually and was all good fun.

I really felt I had to crack Great Wakering (SS3 0EF) on this visit. This was out on a limb, and whilst I knew I would have to come back some of the way, I didn't want to be this far south-east again.

On a sunny Easter Monday, it was a slow trudge through Southend-on-Sea alongside noisy motorbikes and scooters. Great Wakering was recovering from a busy weekend and there was not much going on, but Graham, landlord of 14 years, lit the special Red Lion fire grate just for the photo. Paula and I had a quick Coke, and I called Dave who was miles behind and told him to miss this and divert straight for the next Red as that was another 40 minutes on as well.

Latchingdon (CM3 6JR) is first recorded in 1839 under the landlady Elizabeth Taylor and various times as been the Lion Inn, the Latchingdon Lion, the Red Lion Public House and the Lion Hotel. I suppose new landlords like to put their mark on the name and this is good because they kept 'Lion', the most important part. Here we met up with Sharon and her cousins for her to come back up north with us. We chatted over coffee then made a move home: Preston was a long way off.

We had conquered 18 Lions on this long weekend.

COUNTDOWN TO THE BIG 600

It was now 10 April 2015 and Paula and I simply decided we had to get Castle Caereinion, Welshpool (SY21 9AL), ticked off in all its isolated glory.

The funny thing is that I have passed here the most but never when it was open. Indeed, as we pulled into this very sleepy farm village, the shop over the road was called 'Not' Open All Hours, so you get the picture.

The village's only pub proudly announces:

'Open most days around 7 pm.

Occasionally as early as 5 pm.

Sometimes as early as 12 midday.

We close around 11 pm.

Sometimes as late as 3 am.

Sometimes we aren't here at all.

But lately we have been here a lot.'

And that is how it was – a beautifully laid-back hub of the community living by its own rules but full when we arrived under the leadership of Joan for the last 16 years who cooks, lives above, has a few B & B rooms, and is also a farmer.

She mentioned the eggs at the bar but implied not to tell anyone as if the Health and Safety Police had a problem with it! Her pride and joy is the poolroom which is a large, smart area with fitted benches and shelves of trophies.

The whole bar chatted along with us and were lovely. Places like this should never close down... This was Paula's 133rd Red Lion.

A fortnight later I was back down south at Chesham (HP5 1ET), beginning with a live interview on BBC Radio Berkshire and a dash to pick up Amanda who so far had just seen one Red Lion in Porthmadog and fancied a weekend. Chesham is the only one in this area I had yet to do. I had kept running out of time whenever I was near. I arrived to find an unexceptional large brick building, not an old one. We stayed for just a quick soft drink.

Disappointment followed at Hayes. I had been close in 2011 when I visited Greenford and had I known what was to become of it, I would have done it then. It was now boarded up, seemingly permanently closed. Another dead Lion, not counted.

On we drove through the Asian community to Southall (UB1 3DN). I found it hard to believe there was going to be a Red Lion at the end of this road but, sure enough, there it was.

Parking was a nightmare, squeezing through a gap in the street market to pull up at the back. I could see it was very old with half the letters of the Red Lion signage missing. There was a solitary Asian man at the bar. The bar girl told me *all* the regulars were on holiday. Blimey.

It was in a sorry state but about to have a facelift and be transformed into The Red Lion Shots Bar and Grill! They had to keep the Red Lion bit as it is a listed building. The new owners of four years were really going to do it this time! This should be a revisit in six months to see the transformation, if there was one!

I then became quite confused as we went towards Ruislip, Hillingdon (UB83 QP), thinking I had done this one before because Greenford in 2011 was on Ruislip Road. *This* was Royal Lane Ruislip. I wouldn't forget a name like that and my good memory actually confused me today.

This Fuller's pub was the opposite of Southall. Up to now, Amanda's Red Lion pubs were quite uneventful, but the odds were it was likely to change. Fuller's consistently proved their excellence.

I learned that King Charles I, once disguised as a servant, stopped here for refreshment in 1646. Can you imagine that happening now? Can you really see our Prince Charles of today standing at the counter dressed as a servant ordering a gin and tonic!!

It is a lovely, smart bar with excellent accommodation, but the building takes a curious form. Parking at the side, we entered the hotel part, walking a long way through the building before reaching the bar. Leaving by a different door on the way out, we had to go right round the front back to the car park. It was only then that I realised that, although the building was one long, detached building, the centre was actually a funeral director's with its own door! The Red Lion was on either side.

Presumably these were three different buildings once. What a unique structure.

It should have only taken 40 minutes to get to Enfield (EN3 5PP) from here, but Saturday teatime on the M25 was the usual hell. A friend of mine had been in regularly and told me it was a dump.

It wasn't. It has a lot of sport on and live music, and every Sunday is an 'Irish Sunday' which, as far as I could ascertain, meant Irish singers in keeping with its staff! The league football games were just finishing which meant tension with Preston on the brink of promotion, but they always seem to get beaten in the play-offs. For some reason I was confident we would win at the final at Wembley. Watch this space!

We couldn't stay too long here as we had arranged to be at Harlow around 7 pm for a 'special' welcome which I have no idea what it was but left me very intrigued.

FROM IRELAND TO IRAN AND ITALY.

At Stanstead Abbotts (SG12 8AA) we found that what was once a monastery is now a beautiful Red Lion with its own branded Italian Amico di Amici within. It had been called Coco de Mer until the Red Lion returned! The landlord, Massoud, was Iranian and had patiently been awaiting my visit. What a splendid mix of culture in a place steeped in history – an authentic British pub where the barrels of ale are still out front in the bar area, a throwback to the old days when it was brewed down at The Maltings and taken down to the famous Waltham Abbey along the river. How magical would that be to see your beer coming in by boat! It has to be revisited so that I can stay longer and sample the pizza.

So on to Harlow (CM17 9AH). Well over a year ago, I had received an email from a Ray Potter asking me to contact them when I was coming as they wanted to do a little something. I was curious and had been close many times but I gave them notice a couple of days ago and today was the day. It never left my mind as it was such a nice gesture, and coincidentally it was Ray Potter who had contacted me and the Red was on Potter Street!

Again I had been told it was rough but that never bothered me. From that early Lion in Bootle over four years ago, I went with no preconception except that I expected variety.

I was excited as we got out of the taxi and, of course, I entered to the warmest reception, greeted by landlord Noel and his lovely wife, easily spotting Ray from his Facebook picture with his jolly face and white beard.

And then it happened. Out came the cake!

'Welcome to Red Lion Harlow', it announced.

The cake had been made specially by Nicky Johns who had just won a cake-making competition so my luck was in. Nicky told me she had moved here four years ago and the Red Lion had taken her into their fold. The pub once had been rough but these people were the salt of the earth and, even though I had seen the best and worst of community on the Quest, this was the first time I sensed family. Plus it's not every day someone makes you a cake.

So when reporters routinely ask which are my favourites and I respond with a pub like this, they would initially not understand. You can't write the recipe down for it. It just has a heart.

When it was time to leave, our taxi was booked and had already been paid for. In what can sometimes be a bad world, the kindness of strangers still had the power to touch.

Back at our hotel, we cut the cake, glowing. It tasted even better than it looked.

The next day began at Shephall Green, Stevenage (SG2 9XR), now a Hungry Horse and another ex-Greene King pub. Hungry Horse are always good on price and families were coming in for a good breakfast. Our coffee and toast set us up for the trip home. Unfortunately, I left my sunglasses here and called to see if they had them. Their promise to mail them didn't materialise: it was a busy place, and they probably just didn't get round to it.

At 597 Red Lions I had barely lost a thing. That wasn't too bad.

Three to go before the magic 600, with my friend Sammy even jetting in from Australia. How had we even got here from just over four years ago and a chance drink in Hawkshead?

Heading home, at Warmington, Peterborough (PE8 6TZ), was another lone Lion where all around had been visited. A slight diversion on the way back to Preston saw us pulling into an almost full car park to the sight of a large marquee in the garden. We ran into the chef/owner on the way in who said it had been erected the day before and was staying up for the summer. Weddings at Red Lions had been few and far between but there were going to be plenty here. It gave you confidence in the catering and their ability to run a pub, and the food looked fantastic in a packed family environment. We found two quirky little seats either side of the open fire.

The rooms were decorated with beautiful candelabras and cabinets and chairs more like elegant house furniture than a pub. It gave it a unique atmosphere – the ability to be 'at home' inside and to cater impressively out.

And a bonus – I was staring at a large print of a Lion when one of the waiters thoughtfully pointed out John Hyland, its artist sitting in the beer garden! He had done 75 limited editions, so I ordered Number 12.

A Red Lion all by itself, well worth diverting for and a Lion in a league of its own. This was Number 598, leaving only one more to do before Gatwick Airport's Red which had been booked for 21 May.

RETURN TO WORRALL ROAD

The lion arrived a few days later and now hangs impressively in a wooden frame in my house. I have so many memories. There was still time to make a few more.

It was 8 May 2015 and somebody had to be Red Lion 599. Hello again, Worrall Road, Bristol (B28 2UE). My brother, who lives there and runs a relocating company, confidently notified me that it had reopened since my first visit in April 2013, and that reminded me of the problem. It was time to reassess the definitive list once more, checking whether any previous dead Lions had come back to life. My Australian visitors had taken off to Cornwall for a few days actually on their own mini-Red Lion trail so I drove to my brothers to catch up with him and the kids. Then my sister-in-law Jess drove us into Clifton.

Barman Clive was having a smoke when we pulled up in a nice part of town just off Whiteladies Road near Blackboy Hill! The merchants used to live on Whiteladies Road. The ladies of the manor would walk down on The Downs. Blackboy Hill goes back to the slave days.

I shall remember Bristol for its pirate jokes. It was not the first time I had stumbled across a male environment that felt the best way to converse was to impress me with jokes I had heard a hundred times before!

'What is a pirate's favourite shop?' I was asked.

'Aaaargos,' came the predictable reply.

And once the jokes forum ended, Red Lion talk began, with one local asking if I had been to Garston, Liverpool. Sometimes people had done this as it had been their local ones; others did it to test me.

I knew there wasn't one. A quick Google confirmed it had been destroyed in 2009. Red Lion talk quickly moved to football as the Brentford v Middlesbrough play-off game was on the TV. They laughed because Bristol automatically went into promotion and Preston were struggling in the play-offs. I confidently told them we would win at Wembley. I wouldn't be showing my face in there again if we didn't! Then suddenly in walked Sammy and Gary, my Australian friends, on their way back from Cornwall. They were buzzing after an adventurous cruise around the West Country discovering special Red Lion places I had recommended, such as Clovelly and Newquay. The locals looked at me as if to say who else will be dropping in?

Now I would wait 13 days before the milestone 600th so in the interim why not squeeze in a trip to Turkey, as this Quest was nearing its conclusion, that overseas one was really taking root.

Then it was upon us.

Sammy, Gary and brother Dave joined me.

I posted on my Facebook that I was beside myself with excitement and I meant it. Along with all my Red Lion accomplices I had come a long way and all the emotions were swirling. You couldn't not think about all the events on the way and the twists and turns of life, alongside which the Quest had been the only constant.

So here we go. Number 600 is Gatwick Airport (RH6 0PJ), North Terminal, Airside Departure Lounge. It is an extraordinary one. I would normally have to be flying out somewhere to be here but down to the participation and helpfulness of the managers at the Red Lion, Wetherspoons and Gatwick Airport (especially Laura Seymour) they made it all happen on my behalf!

We had stayed the night in the Premier Inn at Gatwick arriving at the South Terminal at 9.30 for a great breakfast in The Beehive, and a meeting with Laura and Barry from Wetherspoons and Gill, their photographer. They wouldn't allow us to pay for anything.

One at a time we all went into the office to complete our ID forms – madness, really, if you think how busy they are and how much paperwork is involved behind the scenes in an airport. Once that was done we made our way to the ID Centre where we waited in turn for badges with photo ID. The process took an hour but security is number one priority and it was all very interesting.

From here we took the shuttle to the North Terminal. We weren't flying but all the usual airport scanning ensued! I could have just got on a plane at that moment, too, except for the fact that I was bursting with joy and excitement when I turned the corner to see the largest-ever illuminated Red Lion sign at the end and the open-fronted pub overflowing with holidaymakers each with their own excitement about their individual destination. I had reached mine.

So many people were coming and going with drinks and food, and staff rushed around as Gill was taking photos along with Sammy and Dave, officially or otherwise. It was a juggling act. We took some on the steps on the side and others avoiding rushing prams and children. You know the scene. You know what Brits in a pub minutes before their flight looks like.

Why was this Number 600? It had been in my head for a long time, then Laura, the Manager of Gatwick Red Lion, contacted me with this very suggestion. Perfect!

In short, this is the busiest Wetherspoons in the country, open 20 hours a day and selling 11,000 pints a week, 2000 of which are real ale.

I posed with half of the latter but have no idea which it was as it was madness all around as I was trying to consume a brief history of Wetherspoons. In 1979 Tim Martin opened his first in North London. The JD Wetherspoon name came from one of Martin's teachers in New Zealand who could not control his class and told Belfast-born Tim he would not succeed in business… or so the story goes!

It was one massively cheery hour then we all made our way back to a more peaceful North Terminal where we were treated to a bottle of bubbles. By 2.30, we had taken up five hours of Laura's time and she herself was running a staff of 124. Not wanting to leave, and wanting to saviour the moment for as long as it would linger, we had lunch and reflected on the day, and it was 4 pm before we picked up the car from the hotel, getting home only at 11 pm.

What a day for so many reasons from the fascinating way an airport churned customers professionally whilst also remaining a border patrol, and then there was the milestone. I was happy I had picked the right place to spend my 600th Red Lion.

The funny thing is… we were pretty much back there three days later to watch Preston North End in the play-offs at Wembley. Unbelievably we won and gained promotion. I just knew!!

THE HOME STRAIGHT

The highs of Wembley and Gatwick left me buzzing but focussed. 13 days later, it was time to go again and a bit like playing in a World Cup final and then having a kick-about at the village green!

Poor old 601 would never get the status that 600 had earned. So very close to Gatwick is Slinfold (RH13 7RR). I was back off to Sussex and The Red Lyon. Why the change of spelling?! Maybe it knew it was 601 and would struggle to stand out.

Four and a half hours on from an early start, I met a cider producer Stephen at this 14th-century pub in a lovely village. That was a first. Apart from the odd Lion where a brewery had been on-site or down the road, I had rarely met many 'manufacturers' outside of official functions. He had been following me on Twitter.

It was a reminder of the friendships I had made on the way and the level of curiosity I had attracted. Stephen was on his way to the Southampton Beer Festival and was coming along for the ride. I checked into my hotel at Cuckfield, then was on my way to a cluster of five around Fareham 60 miles away.

'Weirdo' were the words of Ian, landlord at Cosham (PO6 3EE). His bar girl of 16 years advised him to be careful as I was writing a book. We chatted and posed for photos for *his* Facebook page. In a world where very few Red Lions were the same, this reminded me of Kidlington, part of the same group, also large with a pizza oven and busy.

At Fareham (PO17 6EF) on the South Coast the maritime theme dominates the Lion story. The Golden Lion had been for the officers, and this Red Lion was the beer house, licensed only for beer and cider and with a floor of just sawdust.

The village still had a naval base for HMS *Dryad* and would be overrun by sailors and wrens. It was known as the D-Day Village. The operation had been partly planned from here with Churchill and Montgomery frequenting the place, making it known as the village that went to war.

It was very powerful stuff when you think the Normandy Invasion that changed the face of the 20th century had stemmed from here.

Passing the estuary, Portchester (PO16 9UZ) is a town precinct pub that is nicer than it initially appears. It was still sunny as we left my 604th. So that took us to Stubbington Green (PO14 2JY). As we sat enjoying the sun I was highlighting the ones we had been in when I became confused about Fareham, which for some reason was not on my list. It has happened less than a dozen times, a pleasant opposite to finding one closed down, but still worrying for me. It would have been a mistake to miss this 17th-century coaching inn with a 'stable function suite' at the back. Stephen was still with me as we reached Fareham (PO16 0PB), only stopping here briefly with the Southampton Beer Festival still an hour away. These Lions ensured a lot of driving and I wasn't really heading that way as I had done Southampton's three Red Lions in 2012 en route to the Isle of Wight, which seems a very long time ago!

Next morning on my way home it was via Bromley (BR1 3LG) to find another Greene King pub. Of the approximate figure of 35 Greene King Red Lions, one of them is dead, now a Japanese restaurant in Witney. I have a big question mark against Kelso, Scottish Borders, and two still to visit in Dorset. I still had a huge amount of miles to do.

At Bromley, I was the only person in the pub. It was always difficult to work out if that was normal or not. Chris and Shevon, 20-year landlords, were on holiday so I was served by a relief worker who knew his stuff. As he made my coffee he happily chatted about the pub's history. It opened in 1731, selling groceries and haberdashery!

In 1813 it became Lion from Lyon and had once been the only building here in the fields, giving an open view across to Crystal Palace in the distance. When Queen Victoria opened it in 1854, the pub followed suit, changing its name to Crystal Palace! In 1869, it became the Royal Oak and the groceries ended. Many years ago the first theatre in Bromley was erected in wood and canvas next to the Red Lion and cost 3d admission. The green wall tiles remain some of this Red Lion's traditional features.

Backtracking through Croydon, passing a pub called the Bricklayers Arms, I reached Wallington (SM6 7AX) and a tatty Red near the bridge but proof that warmth costs nothing. I met the landlady who told me that every May a group of lads have a 'Jolly Boys' Outings' visiting… Red Lions. This May had been Magaluf. She was straightaway on the phone telling them I was here.

Despite its appearance, this pub can't be touched due to its listed status. The previous owners lost it to gambling and the area behind it is the site of the original and world-famous Battersea Dogs & Cats Home.

Ten minutes onwards came Ye Olde Red Lion Cheam (SM3 8QB) and a busy place for lunch in a lovely little town. One chap pointed out the well to me. I nearly missed it, even though it is 60 feet deep, covered with a grid, and dates back to 1550. Built in timber and with a bow front, this is one of the oldest inns in Sutton. Despite alterations in the 1920s, much of the original structure remains and wells remain lovely features. This is the first one in the garden. Setting off home in the belting sun, I could almost guarantee that Birmingham would bring clouds and, by the time I reached Preston, rain. Today was no exception!

I had to wait another three weeks before the drive to Dorset and Lions 610 onwards. I collected Amanda again and headed to the bottom of England. Today was blissfully traffic-free. That almost never happened. I appreciate that cars are faster than horses, but all those travellers stopping at coaching inns in the 1800s never had this problem! Britain was clogged up with motorway improvements, a never-ending problem.

I needed to do nine Lions. It really was the last chance saloon for Dorset. This was the point of no return. Yet, I would have to come again if any failed me.

Beforehand, I discovered that the Red Lion Cerne Abbas had become the 'Giant Inn' so that made eight. We could faintly hear the music in the distance as we skirted by Glastonbury, then our travels took us through Crewkerne, a beautiful but sad village where all the houses seemed to be for sale and the shops for let. People were leaving en masse. At Beaminster (DT8 3AX) we met a barrier and a policeman telling us the square at Beaminster was cut off for a local festival. It was festival time of year!

It is a very rural thing and on a summer's day looked wonderful with the bunting up and down the street and the stage assembled. That meant the Red was empty. All the customers were in the beer garden lapping up the sun. It was how it was always meant to be.

This is a Palmers pub, a local brewery based in Bridport close to where filming for the *Broadchurch* series was done, and I was just in time to catch Pauline the landlady before her imminent retirement. She will be saying goodbye to the only beer garden in town, a pub football team and a skittle alley. Wasn't it strange that, with all the distractions in the modern world, the skittle alley survived?

By the time Sturminster Marshall (BH21 4BU) opened at 6.30 there were already nine people forming a queue outside. There was something still wonderfully magical about having opening hours in a rural community. Of course, it had proved frustrating for me at times, and you would go bust in London, but in the sticks it was quaint, and this is a lovely village dotted with farms. The pub is traditional in a modern way, oozing class and offering proper food and an alternative wheat-free menu. The landlady is originally from Preston and her dad had seen me in the *LEP* and wondered when I would turn up! Perhaps bored or naturally artistic, the landlady had covered a large lion in beer labels to great effect. On a darker night, you would do well to avoid stumbling into the cows known to graze in the old churchyard opposite.

The days were at their longest now which drove us on to Winfrith Newburgh (DT2 8LE) and a bustling pub with camping and glamping out the back. Indeed, four Polish lads were setting up their tent for a mere £10! The barman who served us told us that he had come to help his son out who had been running the place for seven months, only for him to be delegated to a tent, too, as all the rooms were full! Out the back the accommodation looked like something out of *George Clarke's Amazing Spaces* on Channel 4, with 'shepherd huts'. These are hard to describe but perhaps think of the corrugated iron by the side of a road where workmen would erect a little hut. Now think of it as clean, compact, with lighting and a bed, and in a field! Dead cute, and unusual.

The son told us he had been offered the Hungry Horse Red Lion at Hamworthy, but declined as it was rough. We were due there the next day.

Before that we had to endure 28 men on a stag party at Wareham (BH20 4AB) taking over our photos. They were only in their tenth hour of drinking! The stag gave the game away somewhat in a fetching little pink scarf and small fascinator. They were all farmers and all sloshed – but well behaved, insisting I write all their names down. Some now follow me on Facebook; others will have woken up disbelieving, I am sure. They tried to convince me to go to the Red Lion in Weymouth where they were heading for the evening. There isn't one, I confidently declared. Not on my list. It was a fun half-hour.

Rock-solid sober, we took the only road in and out of Swanage – the A351. Passing along the lovely promenade, to say the town was heaving was an understatement. Literally hundreds of people were standing out in the streets, 95% of them in fancy dress. What had we stumbled into? I had never seen so many pirates, togas and hippies.

On further inspection, it emerged that this was the annual rowing weekend when teams come from all over the South-West on the Friday, row on the Saturday, and party in fancy dress that evening. It was hysterical. Add to that a huge number of holidaymakers and Armed Forces Weekend! And I should stress *rowing* as in oars, and not *rowing* as in having a domestic. I didn't see one ounce of aggravation. One oarsman, Matt Bailey, came up with a title for the book. 614 Lions in and I still couldn't decide on it!

We were overnighting at Swanage (BH19 2NP), and took the airy, disabled room with a stable door! There were just five rooms at the Red in a separate building from the pub.

The next morning the Irish chef told us a familiar story over breakfast. He had been there ten years and had no idea how he ended up here. Pub work was often thus!

We had arrived in festival season for sure. Never mind the rowers, jazz, blues and folk were all coming to town. At £55 a night, this Red is well worth a stopover, and with 50 or so ciders on the go at any one time. I am not sure I have ever seen more.

And so to Hamworthy, Poole (BH15 4JQ), and that Hungry Horse pub, packed by 10 am and serving breakfast. It *has* had a recent makeover.

The member of staff writing up the blackboards asked me if I had been to Tottenham Red Lion. He knew well that I hadn't as the landlady had burnt it down. The story goes that she had been told to leave and her parting words indicated that if she couldn't run it, nobody could. It was now a McDonald's.

Next… to Amanda's cousin living in Poole for a flying visit. She hadn't even met her cousin's husband. We like to keep up with the families on the Red Lion journey.

I cannot recommend the coastal village of Milford on Sea (SO41 0QD) enough. Obviously the name of the town is a clue, but it is one of those pubs that is afforded natural light on its exterior by its location.

It was not always the way, though. Built 300 years ago, it had started out across the road! The landowner decided it spoiled his view and rebuilt it!

That was a lot of effort just for a view and that effort continues today through the work of Jan and Stuart who bought it two years ago, serving a more mature and civil clientele. There are three other pubs and a wine bar in this small town, but they told me their only problem is getting staff. There is a lot of money in the area and people don't necessarily need to work.

Just a quarter of an hour away lies Boldre (SO41 8NE) dubbed 'the quintessential New Forest pub close to the bustling Georgian town of Lymington'. The car park was huge. The pub was large with three separate rooms. We couldn't get a table!

We were guided through a game of musical chairs until those who had reserved the tables arrived and then we moved on to the next one, eventually ending up in the stable room decorated with horse wallpaper and full of framed pictures of the same. It didn't need pointing out that this was fox hunting territory.

The manageress was apologetic that she couldn't get us a table, but our coffee and cheeseboard tasted great at every table! The phone did not stop ringing for bookings. The waitress could not believe that we were now down to our last 25 Red Lions. Or so I thought.

I don't know if it makes a pub feel happier to be nearer the end rather than the beginning. I certainly knew how I felt…

HAPPY 4 JULY!

What better way to celebrate American Independence Day… than with a trip to, er, Scotland!

I collected Braz mid-morning to drive the three hours to Kelso (TD5 7DP) which had been troubling me. I had known about it for some time, though it had seemed closed with no sign of life, then about a month ago it popped up on Facebook. Now was not the time to just start springing into life!

So off we went, hopping on one of the better scenic drives into a very historic old town with an abbey and Floors Castle. The bizarre thing is that we were literally going for one drink and then heading home. I know, but what choice did I have at this stage?!

In a street behind the square is the stone Red Lion. Inside, Braz began staring at the ceiling. Joanne, the landlady, still to notch up her first year, told us it was the hull of a boat. The bell on the wall was from a ship named Stuart that sank, and the floor was done by an Italian POW from Springwood Camp. The pub itself was built in 1826 then remodelled in 1905. What secrets did that boat above our heads hold? It was built into the room as a feature and I am sure the seamen could not have foreseen this being preserved in a Scottish pub.

That was not the only mystery in front of me. About to head home, I suddenly heard the inevitable.

'Have you been to Earlston Road?' I learned it was 11 miles away, but it was closed when I last checked.

'Oh, and don't forget Chirnside Red Lion…'

That was 22 miles away.

Thank goodness they spoke up. One Red Lion became three.

So we made for Coldstream (as in the Guards) along a 'Guards Road' towards the East Coast and Berwick again. If only I had known when I had done Berwick's two. Really with Chirnside (TD11 3UF) being Lion

278

619, I perhaps should have been asking earlier in the Quest if 'there aren't any more around here while I am in the vicinity', instead of waiting on a chance comment.

Landlord Tony greeted me with complimentaries. He knew of my mission and threw a mild challenge my way. The most common name for a pub in Scotland is…? The Black Bull. Tony also told me they had been the subject of a Channel 4 documentary in 2009. The programme had a brilliantly creative title.

It was called *The Red Lion*.

It was *definitely* festival time of year! After more breathtaking scenery we drove back inland to the decorated streets and last rites of this year's celebrations at Earlston (TD4 5DB).

This Red is spot on for launching scenic tours through Scotland or the Borders, though it wasn't here at all for a year before Richard bought this five-room hotel in April 2013. He didn't need to be persuaded of its potential. The brass tap at the end of the bar is a nod and a wink to his first pint he had here as an 18-year-old: I was too polite to ask how many years ago.

He filled me in on some of the bizarre licensing laws in Scotland that I had no idea about. He was legally allowed to serve a pint to a hotel guest at 9 am but not give them breakfast, for example. It is the ideal breakfast for some.

Now Braz had heard a play on Radio 4 about *The Common Ridings*. I was clueless. Richard filled us in, telling us that all the Borders towns would do a horse ride of the perimeter of the town to check everything was in order and that land and animals were intact. This was a huge annual ceremony where the horsemen, charged with keeping order, would drink rum (!) and milk and take snuff every morning before they began. It was traditional for all the towns except Earlston to do the Festival of the Common Ridings, involving around 400 horses and two of his own bar girls.

Two years ago, Earlston decided to have its own festival. And why not! What a fascinating area and two surprise Lions with lovely characters, great stories and unique features.

I made the three-hour trip home and then, of course pulled into my nearest Red Lion at Longton for their Longton Live festival.

There were just a few Lions left to meet. 620 were put to bed!

Top 5 live Music:

Longton
Little Sutton
Northfleet
Leytonstone
Stevenage

BACK TO WALES

My aim to finish the Quest by September 2015 was looking trickier than I had envisaged. New ones were popping up, closed ones were reopening, and they were all a long way away.

So, it was back to Wales on 11 July 2015 and a second attempt at Bredwardine (HR3 6BU). With Braz for company, I needed to play by the rules of the Welsh – in other words, avoid afternoon closures. I phoned New Radnor (LD8 2TN) on the way to check and theirs was a 3 pm closure. We made it here by 2.20 into the tiny hamlet on the banks of the River Wye. It was well worth a second visit and one of the great Lions for walking and golfing, but also as one from which to go fishing. It is almost un-Red Lion, much more a hotel, though the pub does have a notable room named 'The Courtroom'. The judge used to sit here to make his rulings.

The bar is frequented by local fishermen, as well as visiting ones, and they love to tell their stories and show off their fish. One had caught a 43.5-lb salmon in 1987 which came up to his chin.

I think if you lived here you had no need to travel, as proven by landlord Mike who left Chorley just six miles from my home some 33 years ago almost never to return.

One man mentioned the Red at Weobley, but I knew that had closed years ago. Another said he had been on a date there so I asked how it had gone.

'Well, he never took me out again,' he replied.

So it was an epic 'fail', I said.

Yes in fact his name was 'Phil'.

I could have stayed all afternoon but the sat nav said 27 minutes to New Radnor (LD8 2TN) which closes at 3 pm. Worryingly, the fuel light was also on. The car had been down to its last few miles over the last four years but this was the first time a mad dash meant we were on the verge of running out.

There weren't exactly many houses round here, let alone petrol stations. The pub's own website describes it as one of Britain's best kept secrets. Now was not the time to go into hiding! We were past the point of cutting it fine when Braz spotted a garage open but I refused to stop, knowing that I had to get in the Red this afternoon. It was now or never and never was not an option.

He was concerned about being stranded. That was the least of my priorities. Stressed and sweating, we pulled up at 3.05.

The door was locked.

A note said: 'If locked, ring the bell.'

I rang the bell.

Nothing. I called (for the third time today). The landlord answered from the other side of the door.

'Could I please come in for a drink. I am on this Quest and I have driven for four hours,' I pleaded.

No.

Braz and I looked at each other. That was just mean. I decided to alter my rules. I will have a drink: go back to the car for my bottle of water, and have a drink *outside*. My photos have a closed door behind me. I was gutted. And not alone in the process.

A lovely group of four Londoners also pulled up for a late lunch only for the same rejection. Naturally they quizzed me about various London Lions and I passed with flying colours. But there were six disappointed people here and presumably more in the past and since. Coincidentally, I learned the next day that my brother had passed by here on his weekend away at 4.15 pm to find the same. It was only a small hotel and I didn't expect favours, but FIVE minutes, please. In return the landlord probably lost out on £100 combined.

It really was Britain's best secret because none of us got to see it.

Dejected and in need of fuel, I remembered my last trip to Wales when I had been told to call ahead for Sennybridge which then opened up an hour early, with the landlord lighting up a fire and with five other locals profiting from his kindness. Attitude can make or break a pub.

All was not lost. At least we had not just come for one pub to no avail. Bredwardine had been wonderful and I regretted having to dash for this and Llanbister, Llandrindod Wells (LD1 6NT), awaited.

I had 11 miles left in the tank. It was not the time to go the wrong way. Thankfully, a helpful man on a mower put me at ease, saying there was fuel six miles ahead. The gauge had better be right and I really couldn't afford to miss it! This is as close as I have come to ever running the engine dry.

Refuelled, of course the drive became more enjoyable again. Then I became confused arriving to find The Lion Hotel. The sign was red but it was the Lion. That explains why it was not on my list when the mini-Red Lion Quest (Wales) man told me about it. We desperately needed to chill and eat and were relieved to meet Janet. She and her husband, who have been here for 20 years, lived behind the hotel. It has a relaxed, easygoing feel about it with one character as involved as everyone else in conversation. My first Red Lion parrot! How much fun could Red Lions have with parrots at the bar!!

But it was nagging me. I didn't know whether to include it as it was a Lion and I had included some straight Lions, though not all of them. I decided in favour when they told me it had been a Red Lion but then was knocked down and became The Lion for local hunters. Add to that they let us in, they let us drink, and even food was allowed!!!

But more stress as I left. Two ladies asked me if I had been to the Red Lion Weymouth.

'Oh yes,' I replied. 'But it's not exactly Weymouth, it's Winfrith Newburgh. I was there a couple of weeks ago.'

They weren't so sure. I began to question myself. Google would be judge and jury. They were right. There was a Red Lion on Hope Square and I hadn't known about. Oh Weymouth... I could have joined that stag party after all!!! I began to panic. As I got closer, I got further. I had been telling people for a month there were only 20 left.

The goalposts kept moving. I was never going to make it.

LIST GETS SHORTER,
LIST GETS LONGER

I was torn with making plans for my final Red Lion, yet discovering new ones. Like all these landlords did every night, I had to call time at some point. That moment kept getting longer as the push to the finish line only meant others were coming out of the woodwork and the pieces of the geographical jigsaw were all over the floor in no particular order.

The closest at over two hours away meant 19 July and Riddings (DE55 4EX) – Derbyshire's remaining Red Lion was slipped in after Andrée's neighbours' 70th party in Hope Valley. So, right to the last, personal moments were Red Lion excuses.

Thankfully, a slow, beautiful drive through the Peak District makes it worthwhile to see this Red back on its feet with Tim and Deana, bought five years ago and bringing it back from the dead.

Tim's attention to detail and the care the pub now had shone forth when he was mortified at his hanging basket man letting him down! Some plants were still round the back pot-bound! You could tell they were on the move – installing a kitchen for the future. He and the pub were recovering from someone's 50th party the night before: we chatted over a Coke then I made tracks.

Six days later and it was the long trek back to Kent. I say it again – for the last time!

With Brian driving my brother Dave and his Russian girlfriend (who lives in Germany), we made for Faversham, and Marina had only just flown in. Welcome to the Quest. Well, the UK Quest: she came with us to one in Germany!

Then, after nearly five hours on the road, confusion reigned. I wasn't the first and I won't be the last mistaking Gillingham, Kent with Gillingham, Dorset. We drove around the wrong Gillingham, asking for the Red Lion – to blank faces. I knew I had spoken to the pub to ask for opening times, so I gave them another call to be told I was in the wrong county! This final leg was proving tricky, and not without discomfort – as I approached Badlesmere Lees (ME13 0NX). We were delayed for an hour on the M2 by an overturned caravan with the poor kids sitting on the grass verge by the side of the road. This was not a good start to their holiday.

It had now become nearly eight hours in the car. Marina was starving. She could easily have struggled to see the sense of it all, but luckily we found a beautiful Red Lion over 500 years old with a lovely garden area and random strawberries and tomatoes casually growing. And just like a handful of Reds before, you could camp out the back – in the paddocks!

In theory, the next four Lions were within 15 minutes of each other. So, next came Fernhill (ME13 9JR), dating back to 1364 with the numbers boldly announcing so at the front, overlooking another cracking village green again, with Kent's traditional hops hanging everywhere. Picture-perfect.

Inside, you could see from the floors how the design of the pub had changed, with the uneven stone floor clearly joining a more modern, smoother end, whilst the bare brick walls and wooden pillars retained that old character of yesteryear.

The crooked stairs got me thinking straightaway. What little secret was up there? Just as I was about to ask, the bar girl invited me up – to the Champagne Bar. Oh yes!

'Drink champagne and dance on the tables', announced the sign. It was party time upstairs and all around bottles and demijohns of champagne lined the bar. There was even one stool made in the shape of a champagne cork!

I noted, too, their pride. Their cooking looks awesome. They even go to the trouble to include some of their recipes on the website, which is almost giving the game away or exuding great confidence, depending on your viewpoint. It's a great pub.

At Dunkirk (ME13 9LL) we found an official Red Lion Caravan Park. These were few and far between, if not almost unique. Inside, it was all a bit haphazard, or perhaps casual. The lady who served me was covered in paint – and ironing! The odd child would just randomly wander in from the car park. It was all very friendly and relaxed, but still a little odd.

A plaque outside highlights the Battle of Bossenden Wood in 1838, describing rebel rising in the wood! It had been the era of the Tolpuddle Martyrs when working conditions were worsening and rural unrest was widespread. Under the leadership of a madman, Sir William Courtenay, they fought with militia from Canterbury. Courtenay was later killed and his body was laid out to rest in the Red Lion. And you can see it in the picture on the plaque.

Onwards to the world-famous Canterbury (CT4 5LB) and past its cathedral into Bridge (CT4 5LB). This was Red Lion 628 and my first French landlord. I hadn't even considered there might be such a thing. Rene Renault from Rennes – yes, really! – had been here six years! I think he had placed his expertise from across the channel dans la cuisine, whilst retaining the traditional Kent hop looks dans le bar.

Interestingly, especially as I was really looking forward to it, some locals here began to flag up Stodmarsh (CT3 4BA) where the notorious ex-landlord is said to have drunk 15 pints every day.

So, a quarter of an hour down the sat nav road that was in fact the road to nowhere and a never-ending track, and we were lost momentarily before spotting an arty sign announcing we were in Stodmarsh. A few houses, a lot of fields and a Red Lion pub – this was it! And absolutely marvellous.

Carol and Richard had taken over 20 months before from a 15-pint man!

And we were staying the night with the newish owners, so kind and attentive in the little detail, like the fresh roses in the corner of the room, and they excelled themselves in the kitchen, too, with a feast of prawns, scallops and belly pork steak without us breaking the bank. Chef Darren is officially the Best Steak Chef in Kent. These were two villagers with no previous experience and yet the evidence in the pub gives you no clues. Richard, who still works in the City, speaks highly of the previous owner Robert Whigham, who was clearly a right old character.

The next morning had to be a brisk walk to check out the fantastic tranquillity of Stodmarsh, then delicious breakfast. Marina had a flight to catch, my brother had a game of squash booked at 5 pm, and I was flying to Jamaica the next day and… two Lions at Wisbech loomed.

Watching the clock, we made for Cheveley (CB8 9RH) instead.

We found an immaculate pub. Again, it had been closed for a considerable time. Red Lions didn't just close for a week. Often they were gone for years. And if you think potentially how much money can go through those tills, then you can understand both the level of loss for being shut, and the years of neglect that caused such a long period of inactivity.

Originally an old beer house in 1860, it is actually now mainly a food place. When I introduced Marina to Deane at the helm, coincidence prevailed again. It seems he had been a caterer for a large American oil tanker company in Moscow and Kazakhstan. Some people genuinely had incredibly interesting lives.

We were 630 Red Lions down, and real life now intervened. Surely we were nearly done.

LONDON'S LAST?

It was now 14 August. Jamaica was of course, credible. On my mind, though, the book, the end of the Quest, and whatever else might come my way.

Almost immediately, I was back on it at Feltham (TW13 4AB). Leaving the house in torrential rain, my plan was Ipswich and a visit to my friend Carol at Shooters Hill. The drive was horrendous with accidents aplenty, so I rerouted to London, arriving shockingly late to a landlord of three weeks whose original intention had been to stand in for three days only to find the previous landlord never returned.

A nice chap, he was up to speed on the Quest, having read about Gatwick as the 600th in the *Wetherspoon* magazine. I had never seen it. He told me the pub was hectic. I understood that as rowdy and left fearing the worst over my potential Congestion Charge.

Isleworth (TW7 6QJ) was a big one in a beautiful area. They have a little stage with a curtain saying, 'Welcome to the Red Lion Music Room'. It is quite unique and a nod and a wink to all the live music that sometimes a London pub can thrive on. The beer garden was also thriving, and inside, general relaxed chatter was the background. The owner has another pub splitting his time, and must be constantly on the go with looming jazz nights and Twickenham round the corner.

Thames Ditton (KT7 0SF) looked dull – not helped by the rain – though inside it is a shabby chic restaurant/coffee shop with deliberate odd pieces of tatty sofas, wooden floors and beautiful wallpaper with swans. An assortment of old doors make up the front of the bar just like I had in my own garage bar at home!

Back towards London next and Shepperton (TW17 9HX) and naturally, if you know London, a fantastic location on the bridge over the river, completely newly refurbished, too, in a smart but casual, classy way. It is on the go all day long, but staff never waver in their goodwill. The fish and chips are a must.

By the time I had reached my friend Carol's that evening, I had been on the road ten hours. There was going to be plenty more of this in the next few weeks. Literally touching base over a Prosecco, no rest for the wicked as we walked round to Shooters Hill (SE18 3RN) and a karaoke session in full swing. That was something I keep away from! There have been moments, but it didn't seem the phenomenon it once was. Carol told me the pub was possibly up for sale. Still, right at the death, the Red Lions' futures were still under a cloud.

The following morning it took two hours to reach Chelmondiston (IP9 1DX), but it's worth the wait in a beautiful part of the country on the yacht-filled Stour Estuary.

I had been close by at Easter only to find it didn't open on a Monday. Thank goodness I came back. You can tell by talking to Amanda, the owner, just what it means to her. Bought four years ago, it took two to do up, creating their wooden bar and granite top, but also their website had given me insight. They make no bones about what they are proud of and seemed to have thought of everything – from the need for space to home-made bread etc. The menu is right up my street, too. If you are passing by and you like scallops, sardines, skate wing… you are in the right place. A place I will be back to.

Great Bricett (IP7 7DD) was also closed on Mondays so we were back there, too, and in the middle of August can there be a better place to visit with more windy lanes lined with tractors on the go and bales of hay everywhere you look?

Interestingly and perfect for me, it has won numerous awards as a vegetarian restaurant. Its phone never stops ringing either! Curiously, as I sat at the bar, I was bemused by the number of people given carrier bags of food. Initially, I thought it was a doggy meal from lunch, but it turns out they offer a ready meal service with a selection of African, Indian and Thai frozen meals. I duly ordered three for £10. I hadn't seen this in a Red before.

Then came a problem – of a good nature. Five miles away stood Bildeston (IP7 7EX). It had been closed at Easter, the one where someone rang a friend about it from Manningtree. Now, it was definitely open. The Red Lion rumour mill came up trumps again but, just as I thought I was finishing, I was also still adding!

So Bildeston was nearly done up and you could still smell the paint after its closure in December 2014.

Now here was a funny thing. The landlords are Christopher Smith and... er, Christopher Smith! It's a father-and-son operation. I met the latter who was out the back in the beer garden just mingling with the customers. That was rare, too. So many landlords stayed behind their territory of the bar.

Still, at this stage, interest in the Quest was high with word spreading like Chinese whispers that I was in, encouraging the locals to come in and share Lion tales. I could have stayed all day but at Red Lion 639 with 15 (or more) to do, I had to leave this welcoming Grade II listed building and its 11th-century church. Next day, new stop – Scotland.

IT'S A LONG WAY TO TILLICOULTRY

I was on the road by 10 am, having only just made it back from London at 7 the previous evening. Thankfully, Robert was driving, enabling me to get my notes in order as we set off for Tillicoultry (FK13 6DU), which is a lovely town and again afforded me a fun and friendly Scottish welcome.

Clear skies made for excellent views from the foot of the Ochil Hills. Behind those hills lie Blackford and Auchterarder, reachable by a lovely, relaxing walk.

The pub, though, was busy and rowdy! Notable clientele include the one chap who came out the back to see me with his two women. He hadn't made it to bed the previous night and was still drunk in his bright orange sunglasses!

The pub, too, was almost in no man's land. Arthur and his business partner (the butcher) are in the process of taking on the lease. They plan on making home-made sausage rolls and selling butchers' packs from behind the bar. We chatted in the sun surrounded by green hills as his enthusiasm made me think he would be making steady changes for the better.

We weren't done yet. What can I say of Motherwell (ML1 4JS)? One hour away just out of town at the end of a dead end road. It did not look great from the outside. On entering it looks like it had a makeover just yesterday, with beautifully covered seats and lovely lights, and generally classy. The landlady told me that her husband bought the pub 26 years ago without much consulting and he had never pulled a pint. He passed away four years ago and she continues with the full support of many members of her family and is well respected.

So many Red Lions down, it is almost impossible to award new categories, but Agnes should know that this is the most spotless Red Lion of all of them!

And Prestwick (KA9 1AJ) has the honour of completing the list for Scotland.

Please – no more! I would have happily visited more Lions in this great part of the world, but right now it was all about getting it done by 5 September 2015.

I reckoned I had 13 left in the UK and now was not the time to learn I had missed one in the Shetland Islands or Outer Hebrides. Don't forget the ghost of Weymouth still loomed large.

THE CLOCK WAS TICKING

Now it was 22 August 2015. All roads led to Norwich and High Street, March (PE15 9JA). This time the lodger also brought his daughter for a trip to the seaside. They were expecting me after reading an article, but they must have wondered if they had been forgotten! I was slightly amused by the pub we passed on the way named as 'The Men of March'. Were ladies not welcome? That was an unusual name and probably a quest of one! Landlady Jen and locals were keen to add to mine, asking if I knew of Southwold and Wisbech (PE13 1JR). Southwold was to be my furthest east the next day. Wisbech was next…

Mmm… 'North Brink' turned into a track and then into a sandbank. No sign of a Red Lion. I was well versed by now in those last difficult metres in finding a Lion, and it always gave extra pleasure when we finally got there, but any kind of delay now was going to add to the self-created pressure that 5 September had created.

Worryingly, too, it was 2.20 and that could mean closure. So I called to learn I had passed it. How could that be? It was right at the beginning of 'North Brink' and yes… it was now closed. I daren't play the Quest card and beg her to open just for me.

Well, OK, I did dare. I had no choice. She was still closed. Disaster.

We had to pass it anyway and the back the door was still open. That was all I needed, especially at this stage, snapping away with the camera.

It was almost as though my words in our phone conversation had had a delayed reaction because the landlady then appeared, realising what I was doing. Next thing – we were welcomed inside and having a drink! Thank goodness.

I was thinking I would have to get up before I went to bed next week and 'nip' back! And it's a good pub, too, run by the landlady and her daughter. The former had retired from the trade altogether, only to miss it and return; the daughter is now the brains behind the catering. Awards on the wall tell the story – plus it is a great location overlooking the river. I did not want to overstay my welcome so we headed for Hockwold (IP26 4NE), an hour's drive away through fields of pumpkins with the August sun getting greater as we encroached on the village green.

Lion Number 645. I had been telling people for a year there were around 620. At the same time, I was on the pressure of a book deadline. I think I have to come to terms now that there may be future editions and further updates. I can only do what I know to be open now.

There is little else in this tiny village, almost hamlet, so from a cultural viewpoint I was pleased to learn that this was back from the dead four years ago after a long time closed. It is now a fantastic, long, detached pub with typical flint walls bursting with colour from the plentiful hanging baskets. I felt obliged to try the Red Lion Ale – there have been a few on my journey.

I just had two more to fit in today and next was Swaffham (PE37 7AQ).

The funny thing is that when we arrived it was as though time had stood still. The bunting still remained from the Medieval Festival which had been celebrated for 800 years! Wow! The marketplace was busy, with people sitting outside this and other pubs and wandering round, but the market had already packed up for the day.

'I've heard of Crazy Cath,' said Robert the landlord when I arrived.

Was I that mad or just perceived so by the Red Lion family? It didn't matter. I was way past too far in. He had spent a year doing it all up and redesigning the eight en suite rooms. I had really struggled to find accommodation in the area and all along here was a Red Lion room I could have stayed in. The Greyhound Pub next door had played host to a Stephen Fry film, too.

Oddly, many years ago this Red used to breed rabbits and send them to London. I have no idea why. One Emma Dickenson had been the longest-serving landlady here and was awarded a silver plaque from other British landlords, and Robert here is one of the most enthusiastic landlords and very proud of the pub's history. He has researched all the old photos of the marketplace, the pub and the church back to the 1800s which hang around the pub, one so large it fills a wall and shows in detail the celebrating crowd.

We departed with a souvenir glass and baseball cap, of all things.

The next Lion looked a bit scruffy at Dereham (NR19 2DJ). Inside, with the landlords on holiday, one drinker was testing Chelsea, the bar girl, to see what he could get away with before she barred him. She wasn't fazed at all and took it all in her stride asking me to confirm HOW MANY Red Lions I had been in??? As I repeated 647, it even sounded bizarre to me!

Now I had got really excited about Southwold (IP18 6ET), which one of the locals at March had visited as a kid. I don't know why – possibly because it was my last seaside one – or the furthest east.

Along the choppy North Sea right at the end beyond the beach huts and the pier stands the Red Lion on South Green, one of Southwold's nine greens. In the town's great fire of 1659, much of the area was destroyed and the Red was one of the few survivors. Many areas were not rebuilt on because of the marsh conditions, making it a brilliant nature reserve. It is a fantastic pub to sit outside at and reminisce of beach holidays of yesteryear. It is massive, leading back to more dining areas, and by the time we left an hour later it was full to capacity. We had just got our lunch order in before the mad rush. Three brilliantly fresh sandwiches and my favourite East Coast Blonde beer from Adnams Brewery from literally five minutes away. We strolled back to the car picking up an ice cream on the way and pricing up the beach huts at £20 a day sure that this will be somewhere I will come again. That makes 648 Red Lions: what was going to be the final figure?

WEYMOUTH TO WALES

This had now become the nightmare scenario. Already it was Wednesday the 26 August 2015 and all the remaining Lions were scattered everywhere. Bringing the gym session forwards to 6 am, I left the house alone by 8.00. First port of call was Gillingham, Dorset (SP8 4AA). That is the correct, Gillingham. I made it by 1 pm which is some feat – passing on the way so many places I had already called in at, like Wincanton and the lovely Babcary. I came face-to-face with a lion on the way in, an excellent painting of a sympathetic beast appearing to walk through a door! The back part of the old coach house here was demolished in World War II as a German fighter jet crashed into it.

Another hour away stood the elusive Weymouth (DT4 8TR). I was finally here after it had been toying with me for some time, as you know. With the sea to my left, as I drove slowly into town it looked a picture as the last of the season's holidaymakers lapped up the sun.

I crossed over the bridge to find the Red Lion tucked away on a lovely square near a few other pubs. Weymouth – you are Red Lion Number 650! This pub is one of five in a group known as The Cheshire Cat Company. The other four are in…Cheshire!

This one is notable for its rum. I particularly loved the cheeky lion's face on the hanging sign. Inside, they seemed to like the fact that they came in near the end of the Quest. I was told that many of the pubs around here are not open in the winter, or perhaps just at the weekends. In this part of the world, trade really did depend on the weather. Did I really have to leave this sunny holiday spot? It was mid-afternoon. I was on the road again, heading for my brother's at Clevedon ahead of my last mega day in Wales!

Now it was 27 August 2015 and Stow Hill, Newport (NP20 1JH), was calling. I really could not decide the best way to tackle these last five Welsh Lions. The Newport trio are only 40 minutes or so from my brother's, but Newbridge only opens at half-4. The usual Welsh dilemma of random opening hours!

So it began at Stow Hill. I was only the second customer of the day, but the day was still young. Brian, the landlord since 1999, was bombarding me with Quest quizzes! He and the other guy loved it; they informed me that the parking wardens were very hot so I didn't hang around, too, plus this was going to be an extremely long few hours for me.

I thought I would go to Caerleon (NP18 1AR), then quickly head up the M4 to catch Llandybie before its 3 pm close. How badly do I wish I could have stayed here longer!

'Oh, it's you,' said the bar girl, pointing to a full-page article of me from *Waitrose Weekend* stuck on a pillar. I was happy to sign and date it for her as I had never even seen this piece before. It really is a lovely pub on a quiet street with excellent themed food evenings from curry to pie. Even in the middle of the afternoon, it seemed as though everyone was in there. The couple next to me at the bar kept taking a little sip of wine which then seemed to make them think of another question to ask me. There was not much Lion stuff I didn't know by now.

I did it all wrong: in hindsight I should have chilled here for lunch then made for Llandybie for their 5 pm reopen.

Stressed, I hit the M4 for Llandybie (SA18 3JA), and by 2.45 I realised I would not arrive until 3.10, so I called to see if it would still be OK after their 3 pm closure. On this occasion all was fine, though I had been burnt in Wales before of course.

As I arrived, everyone else was leaving. Apologetically, I rushed in, the bar girl telling me to take my time and recognising my accent from the phone call; thankfully, another couple turned up, too, so they weren't just staying open for me. The owner lives on the Isle of Wight, so his grandson Huw and girlfriend now run this large pub which dates back to 1780. Little did I know that I had arrived on the first anniversary of the pub reopening. Nice little moments like that which I had been unaware of always made the Quest special. If I had arrived the day after, I would have wandered into the Real Ale Festival as well!

I couldn't linger. I had to retrace my route back down the M4 to Newbridge (NP11 4CH). I was annoyed at myself for such bad planning! After Newbridge, I still had a two-hour journey to Aberaeron, followed by my own over three hours to Preston.

I walked in to five men standing neatly lined up at the bar, nodding in acknowledgement, and asking what I was doing here. It was one of those pubs where I well and truly stood out. I gulped down a lime and soda knowing I had a trek ahead. With just two Red Lions left to visit, I was way past the point of questioning what I was doing.

Indeed, as I drove to Ffos-y-ffin (SA46 0HA) through the Brecon Beacons, I almost went into flashback – I silently travelled through a beautiful sunset with the air and peaks of the valleys and mountains causing me to relive so many of the miles and people I had already visited. It really was coming to an end. Genuinely emotional, I have seen the finish line from a long way out, but now I was literally in the home straight, it suddenly hit me. It was so nearly over: for four and a half years it had taken up and been such a huge part of my life.

Inevitably perhaps, my penultimate Lion met with anticlimax. You couldn't ever know what state you would find a Lion in, except on a couple of special occasions like Mum's 80th, Gatwick and my last one.

I had put a plan together. On 27 August 2015, Lion 655 hosted just one customer other than myself. That was a Welshman with such a strong accent I had to keep saying pardon. He was maybe slurring a bit, too!

The only thread of conversation I managed to follow was that *The Archers* today had been terrible. I had never heard any of its 70-year run on Radio 4 and I didn't find out why so. The landlady and landlord have been here for 24 years. That is a lot of Archers.

I bought some crisps and a soda water and told them what I was doing, though they weren't really interested. Just as I was leaving, I explained to the landlady that I had finally run out of my Red Lion cards and would they like to know what number they were.

She simply replied 'No'!

The man at the bar spoke again but I just couldn't grasp what he said. It did give you a snapshot of what was important to people round here.

They were pleasant, but I think *The Archers* had got to them. I imagine they debated it heavily every night. Each to their own.

It was time to go, heading towards the coast and watching the late-August sun go down, arriving home at 11.45, tired and feeling odd. My AA map marking all the Red Lion pubs was in shreds. I had just one Lion left to tame.

THE END OF THE ROAD

I couldn't quite believe this day had come. And I was drained before it had begun. The previous day, the razor-sharp Christian O'Connell had invited me back onto his Breakfast Show on Absolute Radio, insisting I should be called Red Lion Rita! He said he liked the title of the book, though, which was a great comfort as that was very much a work in progress.

By the time you read this, this detail will be long in the memory, but we had already changed the title once when it became clear that the original '640 pubs' was now, in effect more, and as a note of caution we decided to leave it at '650 plus', given that I would be a fool to think this thing was really over!

I knew more would appear and others would reopen. That title could be changing from now until the end of time.

And so today began early at 6 am with interviews at the ever-supportive BBC Radio Lancashire and a 'link in' to BBC Radio Oxfordshire.

Finally, by mid-morning, Amanda, Helena and I hit the M6 with those ahead of us already telling me that there were queues, roadworks and all the usual. I simply replied: 'This is what it is always like Red Lioning!'

That said, we arrived at 'The Cottage' B & B in Standlake with literally 20 minutes to freshen up.

Approaching Northmoor, a familiar trait rang true. This was not going to be entirely straightforward to find. How did I know? From a couple of miles out in the neighbouring village, little Red Lion signs advertising an ale festival began to appear at the foot of the road junctions. Experience taught me that meant this pub might not be sat nav-friendly.

That has its advantages, too, of course… Hard to find is often easy to love, and I can't speak highly enough of this gorgeous little village. And it was true: the natural bend of the road took you away from the village, but a cunning right led you down a single lane track passing incredible houses like those seen on *Grand Designs* and then, there it was, right in front of me, discreetly off the road. My final Red Lion. It did the occasion justice.

My friends had done me proud, too – a grand total of 16 of us, including some first-timers, were in the convoy that would find its way to the beautiful Oxfordshire village of Northmoor (OX29 5SX). Without planning, I suddenly realised I was at the heart of Prime Minister David Cameron's constituency.

What were the chances of him wandering in to send the Quest into the sunset? Actually, better than you might think. One of the first things I was told on arrival was that he *did* come in from time to time.

I was running on adrenaline now, so it would be wrong to say I wiped a tear from my eye, but inside I was emotional. I know it's daft, but it represents more than the end of the Quest. It is not passion for the pubs, though I had certainly gone through the mill in my relationship with them in the last five years. Yes, it was a bizarre hobby and perhaps an eccentric thing to do, but I think arriving at the end signifies all that has happened in getting there – from the crazy people and gorgeous pubs, to the people who had come and gone in my life, and, most importantly, those who were still there.

Let's face it, when you end anything which takes up this amount of time, reaching a conclusion is exhausting mentally!

But of course I was happy. I was ecstatic, and it meant the world that so many friends were coming for the ride. That was true friendship. They knew what it meant to me, whatever they thought personally. Kevin and Andrée came from Putney for a few hours and then were to drive back. Sheila, Gareth, Christine and Trevor could only get a hotel five miles away and battled traffic to get here. Brother Dave drove down with Marina, Braz and South African lodger Robert who told everyone who would listen that he was proud of me and it had been a brilliant way for him to see the country – and some of these overlapping circles of friendship were meeting for the first time, or the first time in a long time. It really did feel special and I am hugely grateful to have so many kind, caring, supportive friends.

But, like a good wedding, it was going to be ages before I got to sit down and chat to them! The press were snapping almost before I had got out of the car. My friends didn't mind – the locals and the staff were more than welcoming our family into theirs. Remind me to tell you about Grenville…

Thankfully, I was wise to the whole media thing now, so I came armed with several outfits! Look at me – the girl from Preston, mastering the art of the rapid costume change.

The funny thing is, I brought a blue top which I had never worn, but which I had seen Samantha Cameron wearing on television! This became the defining image of the mammoth, 90-minute photo session. When I was done, I was then called back out for more to ad-lib a promotional video for this book which, six takes and three Proseccos later, I just about nailed.

I had barely even stepped in the Red Lion at this point, which meant I was the only one who hadn't met Grenville.

First I was greeted with a specially made beer glass marking the occasion, then I was presented with flowers. I have hardly met sweeter landlords than Lisa and Ian – so kind, polite and sincere. Then, when I finally made it to the bar, I saw the pump clip of the specially named ale dedicated to my Quest from the ever-supportive Hooky Brewery.

Lisa and Ian, however, were not owners of the Red Lion. Everybody was. This became a community pub just over a year ago after lying empty.

Frankly, I can't think of a better example of such a thing or a more appropriate place and set of 'landlords' to have this relatively new concept.

It was, of course, right at the end an ideal – the dream model. When you think of all the deads and those who had gone decades without a refurb and the theme of this book that the pub is the heart of the community, then it made perfect sense for the community to take the pub to its heart.

It felt so right, wonderfully so. At the Quest's end, the pub was back where it belonged.

Grenville was telling everyone how it happened.

Greene King had put it up for sale. The villagers feared they would lose their local which had stood beyond the churchyard since the 1700s.

Whilst new money has come into this tiny pocket of the Oxfordshire countryside, the spirit of yesteryear saved the pub, with over 70 people buying shares in the raising of £300,000.

As far as I could see, that meant it could stand tall forever and a day. It also implied that there would always be someone in it! You have to look after your interests.

What is remarkable about that figure – as Grenville was explaining – was that in 1853 there were 253 people who lived in the village. That was the same number as now. Somewhere between a third and a quarter of the community had bought in, and if you remove children from those numbers, the figure probably represented most of Northmoor.

It spoke volumes and you felt it in the pub, too. All the produce was locally sourced or grown in their very own Red Lion garden, and when we came to eat, that was obvious in its perfection. Equally, courgettes were four for a pound at the bar!

A stroll around the village confirmed I was in a unique place. The agenda for the parish council meeting made me smile. The first few items consisted of: Apologies for absence; Declarations of interest; Minutes of the previous meeting; Reports from councillors; Finance (grass cutting to be approved); Planning applications; Correspondence (an offer for salt for the roads for the winter); Any Other Business.

I finally was in an episode of *The Vicar of Dibley!* I imagine that meeting probably lasted hours. It was cute and quaint and to be envied, given all the bureaucracy of today's world.

Also displayed was a poster for 'Men's Breakfast'. What was this medieval cult?! Ah, every second Saturday of the month at The Red Lion itself, men could meet for a Full English and 'hear interesting speakers' at 08.30 in the morning! It was a chance for them to get together and discuss men things. Or if you like, the pub just opened early!

And so to Grenville…

Well, I came across him because of the trophies. I am sure we would have met anyway. I should say that the pub's interior feels like a cosy, warm home – the dining area just like you would want it at yours, and the outside housing smokers in a little unit called El Fumador. The little signs around the place give character – 'Duck or Grouse' at the entrance, finally acknowledged after several had banged their heads stooping to get in.

And yes, on the side, stood tall a trophy marked 'Village Idiot of the Year'. There was only one name on it.

'I'm Grenville Reeves, the only elected village idiot in the country.'
It was time for Grenville.

He had held the title since 2012 when pub banter turned into a title
and he was crowned King.

'I drink too much,' he explained.

He was born and bred in Northmoor, explaining how he had lived
there forever and that his wife was an angel and that he had been her
number one priority until they had a child, only to have more children
and grandchildren and chickens, and now he was somewhere behind
the chickens and the grandchildren and the children in the priority
list.

'I'm strong in the arm and thick in the head,' he told everyone!
Though he was clearly smart, just warm, rural and from a different era.
I loved it.

'How did you become Village Idiot of the Year?' I asked.

He explained the whole scenario. People voting for him had to place
a pound coin in a cup and that would decide the winner.

His rival was heavily supported by one individual who went for the
jugular by placing a £20 note in his. The problem was that the title was
decided on the weight of the money, rather than the financial value, so
the generously backed candidate didn't claim the title but the smarter
Grenville ironically did.

There is a certain charm about a pub that will be passing on a story
like that until the end of time.

And I think it's fitting to end all that I've seen on a character in a
community pub. I *had* seen it all. The circle of life had come round
the whole way. I had breathed in history, acknowledged the present pub
climate, and could very much see a future.

I had met so many people and my personal story had rolled on
another five years.

To meet an official village idiot in a pub owned by that community
was a perfect place to call time for the last time. It represented all the
incredible people I had met along the way and it showed me a model of
how the pub could survive and thrive in the future.

I thank you, Northmoor, for coming into my life. I am happy that
you were the last stop on The Quest. My thanks, too, go to everything
and everyone which produced a weekend I will never forget.

At dinner, I stood up and delivered a poem. It was put together in a rush and is certainly not an award-winner, but they were my words and they described how I felt:

When I began this Quest they all thought I was mad
They just didn't know what fun can be had
Each one is different, no two the same
The highs and the lows, it's an interesting game –
I've seen Red Lions with brass bells
And those with bad smells
Smart helpful staff
Locals up for a laugh
Breweries at the back
Red wines in a rack
A brilliant cask ale
A pub up for sale
I have sat on church pews
Seen estuary views
CAMRA pubs of the year
Cask Marque-approved beer
Wacky live bands
A drunk's slurry demands
We have sampled great food
Seen a landlord who is rude
Red Lions less deserving
Yet carry on serving
A perfect thatched roof
Staff cold and aloof
Friends came back for more
To enjoy and explore
The worse and the best
Of this Red Lion Quest
All this I have seen
In every Red Lion I have been
So thanks all for being here
Raise your glasses for a cheer!!

And we were done. I was both empty and full. This had been a defining passage of my life without it necessarily meaning anything at all. It had been fun, borderline obsession. But, as the barman of the pub drove us back to our B & B after the Red Lion Northmoor had closed for the night, I was touched by the kindness that this whole Quest had untapped.

Mapping a route in and out of strangers' lives was a wonderful experience. It left me with no choice. We were not done at all.

Four and a half years on with 90,000 miles on the clock at a cost of Heaven only knows what, I had visited what I believed to be the definitive list of 656 Red Lions in the UK.

That only left one plan of action... Now where are those overseas Red Lions?